First Ladies of Arkansas

First Ladies of Arkansas

Women of Their Times

Anne McMath

August House / Little Rock

P U B L I S H E R S

Printed in the United States of America

10 9 8 7 6 5 4 3 2 1

LIBRARY OF CONGRESS CATALOGING-IN-PUBLICATION DATA

McMath, Anne, 1920-
First ladies of Arkansas: Women of their times / Anne
McMath. — 1st ed.
p.   cm.
Includes index.
ISBN 0-87483-091-5 (alk. paper): $24.95
1. Arkansas—Governors—Wives—Biography.
I. Title.

F410.M18   1989
976.7'0092'2—dc20
[B]

89-14887
CIP

First Edition, 1989

Cover design by Wendell E. Hall
Production artwork by Ira Hocut
Typography by Lettergraphics, Memphis, Tennessee
Design direction by Ted Parkhurst
Project direction by Hope Coulter

This book is printed on archival-quality paper which meets the
guidelines for performance and durability of the Committee on
Production Guidelines for Book Longevity of the Council on
Library Resources.

AUGUST HOUSE, INC.   PUBLISHERS   LITTLE ROCK

This book is dedicated to my husband. It was his idea that I write it, and he has patiently listened to every word over and over as I talked my way through the composition of this manuscript. Without his constant encouragement and inspiration, I would never have finished this project.

Contents

*For terms of office that lacked a First Lady, the governor himself is briefly discussed.

Acknowledgments

RESEARCHING THE LIVES of these ladies has proved to be both an adventure and a challenge. Usually there is a relative who has assumed the role of family historian and when this person could be located the task was made much easier and more exciting. Scrapbooks, old letters, pictures, and family memorabilia are a valuable source of information about the lives of these ladies.

The staffs of the Arkansas History Commission, the Little Rock Public Library, the Special Collections Department of the University of Arkansas libraries, the Southwest Arkansas Regional Archives, and the Old State House were most helpful in making available to me materials in their files. Jill Waddell of the Old State House shared questionnaires filled out by the First Ladies or members of their immediate families and short biographies she had compiled about these women. These were a tremendous help, since ill health prevented some of the living First Ladies from answering my questionnaire.

My husband joined in the research by writing to out-of-state friends, asking them to provide me with photocopies of articles from their newspaper files and libraries. He hired a private detective to locate a descendant of Governor Miller. William Read Miller III provided me with a copy of his grandmother's memoirs—a fascinating story that deserves a book of its own.

During the last few months of this project, the expert research of newspapers and libraries by Anne Farris was instrumental in speeding up the project and allowed me to finish the manuscript almost on time.

In preparing for this project I read many books of both Southern and Arkansas history. I will not list them because I have not quoted from them. Many of them are repetitious and borrow from each other in wording and conclusions. The oldest books that I found and those with original material were John Hallum's *Biographical and Pictorial History of Arkansas* (1887); Josiah Shinn's *Pioneers and Makers of Arkansas* (1908); William F. Pope's *Early Days in Arkansas* (1895); William Speer's *The Encyclopedia of the New West* (1878); and volumes 1 and 2 of *Arkansas and Its People,* published by the American Historical Society and edited by David Thompson. Quotes from them or any other books are identified in the text.

I have talked with the following people, most of whom are descendants of my subjects, some of whom are historians, and some of whom are friends who were helpful in locating descendants: Bernice Cole, William J. Smith, June Westphal, Mavis Plunkett, Mrs. Cecil Pederson, Linda Trapp, Joe House, H.A.T. "Ted" Bailey, Mary Medearis, Mary Jane Wilkes, Jo Claire English, Jill Waddell, William Read Miller III, Ellen Shipley, Jim Dunnaway, Lillian Wills, William F. Rector, Jr., Carrie Remmel Dickinson, Mamie Treadway, Marvin Corbett, Price Roark, Powell Berryman, Jane Bell, Mary Minta Sigman, Dawn Dockins, Mary Frances Perry, and James Pilkington. I had a personal interview with Betty Bumpers and telephone interviews with Lucille Laney and Alta Faubus.

Foreword

IN JULY 1985 Selma Wooley called and invited me to talk to the Centennial Chapter of the Daughters of the American Revolution on the subject of former First Ladies of Arkansas. I accepted for two reasons: one, I wouldn't have to give the talk until November, and two, I knew that Sid and I had a book in our library entitled *First Ladies of Arkansas* by Mrs. Peggy Jacoway. I thought I could thumb through this book, pick up a few facts and a story or two, and have my twenty-minute talk. Little did I know what I was in for! I found myself reading and rereading Mrs. Jacoway's book. I was unfamiliar with most of the historical events to which she referred, so I was soon buried in a crash course on Arkansas history—something I had never had time for before. I did not grow up in Arkansas and had lived here only a few months before I became totally involved in making Arkansas history, not studying it.

As far as I have been able to determine, Mrs. Jacoway's book is the only definitive work on Arkansas First Ladies. Her final chapter is about Mrs. Homer Adkins, First Lady from 1941 to 1945. My husband began urging me to write a new history of these women, pointing out that all who have served since Mrs. Adkins are still living and that their story should be told as well. I resisted. I knew it needed to be done, but I did not want to put forth the effort required. At a meeting honoring all former governors, my husband in his talk praised the First Ladies of the past and stated that someone should write their story. I was surprised that he would use this forum to goad me into this enormous task, and I was stunned by the enthusiastic applause from the audience. This made me feel that such a work was

truly needed and would be well received.

For the next two years I continued to study Arkansas history and to research the lives of these ladies. Not only was I having fun learning, but these women had begun to fascinate me. They had become real people and not just names on a page.

Every afternoon when my husband came home from the office he had to listen to what I had learned that day. Finally he convinced me I should write it all down, and that is how this book came about. I have recorded the history of each of these ladies as factually as possible, based on the information available to me. It is a simple telling of what I have learned about these women and of the times in which they lived. I have not attempted to compete with the historical experts, but I hope that this book is easy to read and will stimulate the reader to study Arkansas history further.

I have taken no liberties with the truth of history here. For instance, slavery was very much a part of life in Arkansas before the Civil War. Ignoring it here would not erase the fact that it existed. If I omitted it, I would not be truthful about the way things were at that time. We cannot learn from the past if we do not know its truth.

This country was settled by people seeking freedom, but it took a revolution for them to gain the freedom they sought. These revolutionaries wrote a passionate declaration of natural rights: "We hold these truths to be self-evident, that all men are created equal, that they are endowed by their Creator with certain inalienable rights . . . ." Thus our forefathers expressed the noblest of purposes and set forth in no uncertain terms the cause of human rights in this great dream that is America. The realization of this dream was delayed by ignorance and cruelty. It took another war to release a segment of our society from bondage. Not until 1868 were all men granted the right to vote. It was 1920 before women were given this privilege, a symbol of freedom. Today we witness the continuing struggle for women to obtain full participation in a free society.

It is a long road that we travel to our goal of freedom and equality, but it is a goal, an avowed goal, and we are on our way to one day accepting ourselves according to the American dream—a land of free and equal citizens.

Arkansas history can be approached from many different viewpoints, but none is more instructive than the study of our political history. The characteristics of the men who shaped and controlled public affairs in this state also shaped and controlled our state institutions and councils. For example, it would not have been in character for Governor James Conway, a guileless, trusting farmer, to question the motives of his friends and supporters who proposed the creation of the Real Estate Bank and the State Bank. These people of ulterior motive robbed Arkansas and threw it deep into debt for generations to come. They boarded the ship of state and took command from the captain.

Or take Robert Crittenden, who was often acting governor—a man of strong character and personal ambition. He was of genteel and aristocratic manner, handsome in a cold, aloof way, meticulous and fashionable in dress, of superior intellect, an exceptional lawyer and an eloquent speaker. At the time he was scheming and ruthless in pursuing an objective, loyal to his friends only as long as they were of use to him, and more than a little power-hungry. He had studied law and politics in the office of his brother John Crittenden, the kingpin of Kentucky politics, and had learned well the lessons of manipulative maneuvers. Crittenden was appointed first territorial secretary and had things well in hand—his hand—by the time the first governor arrived in the state. Crittenden, with his forceful personality and superior mind, out-

foxed Governor Miller at every turn. Miller tried to take charge, but soon lost interest in the office, leaving Crittenden with a free hand. It is fair to conclude that Crittenden, the wily politician, dominated early public affairs in Arkansas not only during Governor Miller's term but for years to come.

However, this book is not about governors of the past; their stories have been told many times by serious historians and writers, while too little has been written or even recorded about the women who worked side by side with them to help build this state. Documented history of the ones who served in the early years is sparse, for in those days women were relegated to a domestic role, yet their stories are tales of lives well spent while braving a fierce and savage frontier. If there had not been women with a pioneer spirit, courageous enough to withstand hardships, then the settlement of Arkansas as a state would not have begun as early as it did. For the men who brought their families with them were the ones who stayed here to settle and build. These pioneer women contributed to the history of this state as surely as the men—and the wife of the governor was just as susceptible to diseases, floods, and Indians as were her contemporaries!

In studying the lives of the wives of the Arkansas governors we see how the nineteenth-century governor's wife survived frontier conditions and a civil war, fought for the right to vote, and emerged from a cocoon of housewifery to community leadership.

The twentieth-century governor's wife changed with the changing times. She became a better-educated person who in responding to the challenges of the times showed the same pluck and determination as her predecessors. She entered the all-male world of politics by actively campaigning for and with her husband, eventually acquiring a public and political image of her own as her role expanded. At the time of the writing of this book, the late 1980s, our First Lady has a full-time career of her own. She is as typical of the era in which she lives as all the others have been.

Introduction

ONCE THE EXCITEMENT of politics has been tasted it is hard ever again to resist it. Yet when filing date approaches, anyone who has held office spends a while pondering whether or not he should run again. Should he pass on his power to someone else or try to hold on to it? The bustle of the political parade forming is almost irresistible—the challenge of planning strategy, the crowds, travel, late nights and early risings, the chance to be a leader and shape the lives of people, to put your own ideas into being, draws like a magnet.

Politicians believe that any political problem can be solved with a good idea—theirs— the courage to implement it, and plenty of money and good will from their supporters. Each candidate is confident he can provide the leadership to pull all of this together.

A campaign is a somewhat frustrating experience. Candidates are spirited from person to person, town to town, without ever seeing, saying, or doing all that they want to or should say or do.

The wives of these men march in the political parade—they hear the drums, live in the glare of the lights, receive adulation and criticism, glory in their men's success, experience their frustrations, and ache and hurt over their defeats. In short, they see it all, feel it all, and share it all.

The Changing Role of "First Lady"

In the early days of our state, women were homebodies—including the women who bore the title of "Wife of the Governor." The governor's wife didn't take an active part in the life of her community. She didn't campaign or even attend his inauguration. She stayed home, as did all other women of her time, cooking, cleaning, and caring for her children. She was content to live in the shadow of her prominent husband. As times changed and women in general became more active in their communities, so did the governor's wife. She first advanced from her realm of domesticity through her church. By the late 1800s she had begun to attend college and to have a teaching or nursing career. She became interested in self-improvement and joined a culture club. She studied music and art and gave classes in these subjects. When social welfare work was organized, and women became active on behalf of underprivileged children, prisons, and schools, so did our First Lady. She began to participate in her husband's campaigns, attending public functions with him—even his inauguration!

In the beginning neither the wife of the president nor of the governor was called "First Lady." Use of the term came about gradually; history is not clear exactly when. Martha Washington was referred to as "Lady Washington," "Presidentress," and "Mrs. President." Mrs. Jefferson Davis was referred to as "First Lady of the Confederacy." Lucy Hayes was acclaimed as "First Lady of the Land" after she accompanied her husband on the first presidential trip from coast to coast.

Gradually the wives of the presidents began to have a popularity of their own, and more and more public attention was given them. The New Deal and World War II drew attention to Washington, D.C., and picture magazines brought the nation's power and color into our homes on a weekly basis. Eleanor Roosevelt and Mamie Eisenhower became as familiar to us as our neighbors. Before Mamie became First Lady of the

Land she was known as the "General's Lady," and all America knew her recipe for fudge, her enjoyment of card-playing, and her determination to keep her bangs! As these women received more attention from the press, use of the term "First Lady" became more common. Not everyone liked it. Jackie Kennedy at first refused to allow her staff to use it, but later, when she learned its power, decided she liked it.

Since we have a republican form of government, "First Lady" fits our purpose as well as any, although some presidents' wives have been called "queen"—"Queen Jackie"; Mary Todd Lincoln, who was called "Republican Queen"; and James Buchanan's niece, who served as his official hostess and was referred to as our "Democratic Queen."

On the national level the role of First Lady has become a prominent part of the presidency and has expanded continuously since Edith Roosevelt, the wife of President Theodore Roosevelt. She was the first to hire a staff to help her run the White House and handle the press, correspondence, and entertaining. Her husband considered the presidency a "bully pulpit." With his use of the office as a forum and Edith's efficient running of the mansion to entertain large numbers of voters, they drew the nation's attention to themselves and set the stage for the increased awareness of the First Family. Until this time, the wives of presidents had often hidden behind a plea of ill health or grief and had for the most part remained in the background. Dolley Madison had certainly been an exception.

Since Edith Roosevelt, each lady has served as she saw her place in time. Lou Hoover made radio broadcasts from the White House; Eleanor Roosevelt, the "Flying First Lady," was her husband's eyes and ears; Betty Ford talked about subjects considered taboo and took public stands opposing her husband's views; Rosalynn Carter attended cabinet meetings and set herself up as her husband's alter ego; Edith Wilson so shielded the world from President Wilson when he

had a stroke that she was accused of running the government—she did not hand over the reins of government to the vice president; Nancy Reagan did not call on the vice president either, but instead left her husband's bedside to represent him in receiving important guests of government. When President Eisenhower was in the hospital, Mamie did call Vice President and Mrs. Nixon to attend an important dinner with her, but she did not seat the vice president in the president's chair. She sat alone at the head of the table in her throne-like chair.

The role of vice president has changed little since the first one—John Adams, vice president under George Washington, thought the job the most insignificant office ever dreamed up. Woodrow Wilson's vice president described it as being in a cataleptic state, saying that he couldn't speak or move even though he was conscious of everything. When President Eisenhower was asked what his vice president did, he asked for a week's time to think of something. Yet, in contrast, the role of presidential First Lady has evolved into one of considerable power.

In Arkansas the role of First Lady has changed dramatically since the Governor's Mansion was built. Having the mansion has made a public figure of our First Lady and has given her the responsibility of running a state institution. She has no constitutional authority, is not elected or appointed, yet she has a full-time job for which she does not get paid. One might say she doesn't even volunteer for the job—it is hers simply because the man she married got himself elected governor. Each woman fills the role in her own way. In the following chapters we will learn something about the style of each one.

Forty-one men have been elected governor of Arkansas, and there have been thirty-six First Ladies. In the early years the governors often resigned before their terms were over, thus allowing an acting governor to take office—sometimes for a few days or weeks, and on two occasions for almost an entire term. Only those who were elected in a regularly held election will be given space in this book.

The number of First Ladies is not the same as the number of governors because two men were bachelors and three were widowers when they held the office.

Of these thirty-six First Ladies, two became brides and First Ladies in the same year; another had her fiftieth wedding anniversary while in office; two eloped on horseback to marry their future governors; some had no children, one had twelve; and according to my research there have been only three children born to a First Family while in office—Ernestine Flora Rector, Bruce McMath, and Chelsea Clinton. The most common first name has been that of Anne (four); we have had three Marys, three Margarets, two Mabels, two Marthas, and one Cinderella! Cinderella Drew, Ina Davis, Mabel Parnell, Alta Faubus, and Hillary Clinton all served more than four years. Nine Arkansas governors went on to the United States Senate. Twenty-nine of the forty-one were lawyers; there were one Baptist minister, one physician, one pharmacist, and one newspaperman; and six held the military rank of general. There were several planters and businessmen, and two brothers—James and Elias Conway, the first and fifth governors.

Early Years in Arkansas

The most influential families in the early settlement of Arkansas were the Conway, Rector, and Sevier families. Any discussion of early Arkansas history must begin with them. In the early 1700s the governor of Virginia sent agents to Siegen, a rich iron-producing and manufacturing district of Germany, seeking skilled workmen to come to America and open the iron mines of Virginia. Forty persons—twelve or thirteen families—agreed to come. They came as freemen and settled a free colony on the Rappahannock River in 1714. From this handful of Germans have come many promi-

nent Americans. One of these original German settlers was John Jacob Richter (Rector, in modern language), a member of an old family of the German Empire. Among his descendants were five Arkansas governors—James Sevier Conway, Elias Nelson Conway, Henry Massie Rector, Thomas James Churchill, and William Meade Fishback—and a surveyor general of Arkansas, William Rector.

The Conway family traces its ancestry to Edward I of England and the Conway Castle on the Conway River in north Wales. Because of the British laws restricting the right of inheritance of property and title to the eldest son, Thomas Conway, noble scion of the House of Conway, immigrated to America and settled in Virginia about 1740. Many other noble-born Britishers who immigrated because of the laws of entail also settled in Virginia, giving rise to the name "First Families of Virginia" for these people. Henry Conway was the only son of Thomas Conway, the immigrant. Henry was a general in the Revolutionary War; his daughter Nellie was the mother of President James Madison; and his son Moncure was brother-in-law to President George Washington.

The Seviers were Huguenots in their native land of France. Like thousands of others, they fled their country to escape the widespread persecution that existed under Louis XIV. Many of these people settled in Virginia. In their native country the name was Xavier but somewhere along the way it became anglicized to Sevier.

When the Revolutionary War broke out, the Conways, Rectors, and Seviers of Virginia decided that for safety's sake they should move their families and property out of Virginia. The wives, children, and slaves moved over the mountains into the western part of North Carolina. The men remained behind to fight, joining their families after the war was over. These families became leading citizens in their new community. John Sevier, a distinguished revolutionary soldier and a hero of Kings Mountain, was the leader in forming the area where they now lived into the new state of Franklin. He was elected governor of this new state and Henry Conway was named president of its senate. When this area later became the State of Tennessee, Sevier was elected its first governor and served six terms. His friend Henry Conway decided not to continue in politics, but turned his attention to farming.

Henry's son Thomas married Ann Rector. Her brothers William and Elias were the first of the three families to leave Tennessee. They were land surveyors whose work took them farther and farther west until finally they were based in St. Louis. Ann wrote to her brothers and asked if there were any job openings in St. Louis for her husband and grown sons.

Elias Rector immediately advised her to persuade her family to come west. Ann's oldest sons, James S. and Henry M. Conway, were the first to join their Rector uncles in St. Louis. The rest of the family moved singly and in pairs until finally they all lived there. In addition to his surveying work, Elias Rector had become postmaster of St. Louis. He made Ann's son James his assistant in the post office and her son Henry his assistant in surveying.

William Rector was promoted to surveyor general and given the commission to survey Illinois, Missouri, and Arkansas. He had sixty-two deputy surveyors, four of whom were his brothers and four his nephews. The position of surveyor general was a powerful one, for surveyors even more than land speculators knew where the best lands were. These men all became wealthy by simply knowing which land to buy, or sometimes taking a choice parcel as a commission.

As surveyor general, William Rector made the first governmental survey of Arkansas and brought with him his nephews, William Rector and Henry W., James S., and Frederick R. Conway. This was the beginning of the influence of these families in this state. In Arkansas the Seviers, Conways, and Rectors, closely bound by ties of blood, were

even more closely bound by the commonalities of independence, power, and wealth, and in political affairs they acted as one. They established a political dynasty that reigned supreme over this state until the Civil War, when one of its own members, Henry M. Rector, son of Colonel Elias Rector, cut it to its knees. It was never to rise again.

This political machine has been called various names by different writers. In this book it will be called simply "the Family." In the beginning it was only the Rectors, then it became known as the Rector-Conway faction, and later, Rector-Conway-Sevier. With the rise of Sevier, the Rector influence diminished and the Conway influence increased. The Sevier influence gave rise to the Conway-Sevier-Johnson dynasty, which lasted thirty years. Seldom has one family dominated the politics of a state for so long. At the end of this chapter is a statement of terms of service and offices held by members of this political machine. This statement, which includes the offices held by five of Thomas and Ann Conway's sons, is taken from one compiled by John Hallum and published in his book *Biographical and Pictorial History of Arkansas* (1889).

Ann Rector Conway, the mother of our first and fifth governors, had ten children. Of the three daughters all that has come to light is that they made good marriages, for it was the custom of early recorders of history to refer to women only as "the mother of" or "the wife of." Much has been written about the seven sons and their achievements. They were: Henry W., James S., Frederick R., John R., William, Thomas A., and Elias N. Conway. John R. Conway became an eminent physician and Thomas A. Conway died at the age of twenty-two.

Primarily because of these illustrious sons, Ann Rector Conway has been given much attention by the early historians. However, she became a personage in her own right—a highly respected, much revered woman. She was a leader in her church (First Methodist Church, Little Rock), but like all other women of her time she stayed in a well-defined role of domesticity—and of survival. For it must be remembered that these women, along with their husbands and families, braved a wild frontier and shared in the taming of it.

The philosophical differences between these pioneer women and women of today are not years but ages apart. However, in breaking down the barriers of the male worlds of business and politics, women of today have displayed the same bravery and determination as frontier women did in conquering the wilds and establishing a civilization. The First Ladies well reflect the changes that have taken place.

Terms of Service and Various Offices Held by the Powerful Family Connection of Conway-Rector-Sevier

Governor

John Pope, 1829–1835	6 years
William S. Fulton, 1835–1836	1 year
James S. Conway, 1836–1840	4 years
Elias N. Conway, 1852–1860	8 years
Henry M. Rector,[1] 1860–1862	2 years
Thomas J. Churchill, 1881–1883	2 years
	23 years

Secretary of the Territory

William S. Fulton, 1829–1836	6 years

Clerk of Territorial House of Representatives

Ambrose H. Sevier, 1821–1823	2 years

Territorial Legislature

Ambrose H. Sevier,[2] 1823–1829	6 years

Territorial Auditor

Elias N. Conway, 1835–1836	1 year

Surveyor–General of the Territory

James S. Conway, 1825–1836	11 years

Receiver of Public Moneys

Henry W. Conway, 1820–1823	3 years

Territorial Court Judge

Benjamin Johnson, 1821–1836	15 years

Federal Court Judge

Benjamin Johnson, 1836–1849	13 years

State Circuit Court Judge

George Conway, 1844–1848	4 years
William Conway, 1840–1843	3 years

State Supreme Court Judge

William Conway, 1846–1848	2 years

State Auditor

Elias N. Conway, 1836–1849	13 years

State Treasurer

Thomas Churchill, 1874–1881	6 years

Prosecuting Attorney

Robert W. Johnson, 1840–1842	2 years

State Attorney General

Robert W. Johnson,[3] 1840–1842	2 years

United States House of Representatives

Henry W. Conway,[4] 1823–1827	4 years
Ambrose H. Sevier, 1827–1836	8 years
Robert W. Johnson, 1847–1853	6 years

United States Senate

Ambrose H. Sevier,[5] 1836–1848	12 years
William S. Fulton,[6] 1836–1844	8 years
Robert W. Johnson, 1855–1861	6 years

Confederate House of Representatives

Robert W. Johnson, 1862–1862	1 year

Confederate Senate

Robert W. Johnson, 1862–1865	3 years

U.S. Marshal

Elias Rector	20 years

Indian Agent

Elias Rector	10 years

Aggregate	190 years

[1] Elected for four years, served only two.
[2] Was elected speaker in 1827.
[3] Resigned this to accept a seat in Congress.
[4] Was elected to a third term, but killed in a duel with Robert Crittenden in fall of 1827.
[5] Resigned in 1848 to negotiate treaty with Mexico, and died December 1848.
[6] Died August 1844, before expiration of office.

First Ladies of Arkansas

First Lady	Was Born	Inaugurated	Age
Conway, Mary Jane	——	September 13, 1836	–
Yell (deceased)	——	——	–
Drew, Cinderella	——	around 1815	–
Roane, John (bachelor)	——	——	–
Conway, Elias (bachelor)	——	——	–
Rector, Flora	March 1839	December 15, 1860	21
Flanagin, Martha	April 3, 1830	November 14, 1826	32
Murphy, Angelina	——		–
(Daughter Malilla Berry)		January 20, 1864	–
Clayton, Adeline	January 26, 1843	July 2, 1868	25
Baxter, Harriet	early in 1830	January 6, 1873	43
Garland, Virginia	March 28, 1835	November 12, 1874	39
Miller, Susan	June 20, 1829	January 11, 1877	47
Churchill, Anne	March 12, 1830	January 13, 1881	50
Berry, Elizabeth	September 29, 1848	January 13, 1883	34
Hughes, Ann	November 30, 1836	January 17, 1885	48
Eagle, Mary	February 4, 1854	January 1889	34
Fishback (deceased)	——	——	–
Clarke, Sallie	January 28, 1856	January 18, 1895	38
Jones, Margaret	February 11, 1845	January 18, 1897	51
Davis, Ina	October 6, 1862	January 18, 1901	38
Little, Elizabeth Jane	April 3, 1861	January 18, 1907	46
Donaghey, Louvenia	1862	1909	46/47
Robinson, Ewilda	April 24, 1876	January 16, 1913	36
Hays, Ida	August 24, 1873	August 1913	39/40
Brough, Anne	April 17, 1880	January 10, 1917	36
McRae, Amelia Ann	October 6, 1856	January 21, 1921	64
Terral, Eula	July 24, 1899	January 13, 1927	25
Martineau, Mabel	December 25, 1870	January 13, 1928	56
Parnell, Mabel	1885	March 14, 1928	43
Futrell, Terra Ann	January 10, 1933	——	–
Bailey, Margaret	February 21, 1892	January 12, 1937	44
Adkins, Estelle	July 13, 1889	January 14, 1941	51
Laney, Lucille	March 10, 1906	January 1945	38
McMath, Anne	December 20, 1920	January 1949	28
Cherry, Margaret	August 21, 1912	January 1953	40
Faubus, Alta	August 31, 1912	January 1955	42
Rockefeller, Jeannette	July 12, 1918	January 1967	48
Bumpers, Betty	January 11, 1925	January 1971	46
Pryor, Barbara	May 5, 1938	January 1975	36
Clinton, Hillary	October 26, 1947	January 1979	31
White, Gay	March 7, 1947	January 1981	33
Clinton, Hillary	October 26, 1947	January 9, 1979	32

Governors of Arkansas

Governors under French Rule
When Arkansas Was Part of the Territory of Louisiana

Marquis de Sanville	1699–1701
Bienville	1701–1712
Lamothe Cadillac	1712–1716
De L'Epinay	1717–1718
Bienville	1718–1724
Boisbrant (ad interim)	1724–1726
Perier	1726–1734
Bienville	1734–1743
Marquis de Vaureuil	1743–1753
Baron de Kelerec	1753–1763
D'Abbadie	1763–1765
M. Aubry	1765–1768

Governors under Spanish Rule
When Arkansas Was Part of the Territory of Louisiana

Antonia de Ulloa	1767–1768
Alexander O'Reilly	1769–1770
Luis de Unzaga	1770–1777
Bernado D. Galvez	1777–1784
Estevan Miro	1784–1791
Fransisco de Luis Hortu	
Baron von Carondelet	1791–1797
Gayoso de Lemos	1797–1799
Sebastian de Caso Calvoy O'Farrell	1799–1801
Juan Manuel de Salsedo	1801–1803

Governors Appointed by the President of the United States
to Serve Arkansas during Territorial Days

James Miller	1819–1825
George Izard	1825–1829
John Pope	1829–1835
William Fulton	1835–1836

Governors of the State of Arkansas

	YEAR ELECTED	TERM
James Conway	1836	1836–1840
Archibald Yell[1]	1840	1840–1844
Samuel Adams	Acting	

Thomas Drew [2]	1844	1844–1849
John Williamson	Acting	
Richard C. Byrd	Acting	
John Roane	1849	
Richard C. Byrd	Acting (1849)	
John R. Hampton	Acting (1851)	
Elias N. Conway	1852	1852–1856
Elias N. Conway	1856	1856–1860
Henry M. Rector	1860	1860–1862
Thomas Fletcher	Acting	
Harris Flanagin	1862	1862–1864
Isaac Murphy	1864	1864–1868
Powell Clayton [3]	1868	1868–1871
Ozra Hadley	Acting	1871–1873
Elisha Baxter	1872	1873–1874
Augustus Garland	1874	1874–1877
William Miller	1876	1877–1879
William Miller	1878	1879–1881
Thomas Churchill	1880	1881–1883
James Berry	1882	1883–1885
Ben Embry	Acting	
Simon Hughes	1884	1885–1887
Simon Hughes	1886	1887–1889
James Eagle	1888	1889–1891
James Eagle	1890	1891–1893
William Fishback	1892	1893–1895
James Clark	1894	1895–1897
Daniel Jones	1896	1897–1899
Daniel Jones	1898	1899–1901
Jeff Davis	1900	1901–1903
Jeff Davis	1902	1903–1905
Jeff Davis	1904	1905–1907
John Little [4]	1906	Jan.–Feb. 11, 1907
John Moore	Acting	4 months
X.O. Pindall	Acting	about 18 months
George Donaghey	1908	1909–1911
George Donaghey	1910	1911–1913
Joe T. Robinson [5]	1912	Jan.–March 10, 1913
William K. Oldham	Acting	3 days
Marion Futrell	Acting	about 4 months
George Hays	1913	
Special Election		
George Hays	1914	1915–1917
Charles Brough	1916	1917–1919
Charles Brough	1918	1919–1921
Thomas McRae	1920	1921–1923
Thomas McRae	1922	1923–1925
Tom Terral	1924	1925–1927
John Martineau [6]	1926	Jan, 1927–Mar. 4, 1928
Harvey Parnell	Succeeded	Finished Term
Harvey Parnell	1928	1929–1931
Harvey Parnell	1930	1931–1933
Marion Futrell	1932	1933–1935
Marion Futrell	1934	1935–1937
Carl Bailey	1936	1937–1939
Carl Bailey	1938	1939–1941

Homer Adkins	1940	1941–1943
Homer Adkins	1942	1943–1945
Ben Laney	1944	1945–1947
Ben Laney	1946	1947–1949
Sid McMath	1948	1949–1951
Sid McMath	1950	1951–1953
Francis Cherry	1952	1953–1955
Orval Faubus	1954	1955–1957
Orval Faubus	1956	1957–1959
Orval Faubus	1958	1959–1961
Orval Faubus	1960	1961–1963
Orval Faubus	1962	1963–1965
Orval Faubus	1964	1965–1967
Winthrop Rockefeller	1966	1967–1969
Winthrop Rockefeller	1968	1969–1971
Dale Bumpers	1970	1971–1973
Dale Bumpers	1972	1973–1975
David Pryor	1974	1975–1977
David Pryor	1976	1977–1979
Bill Clinton	1978	1979–1981
Frank White	1980	1981–1983
Bill Clinton	1982	1983–1985
Bill Clinton	1984	1985–1987
Bill Clinton	1986	1987–1991

[1]Governor Yell resigned on April 29, 1844, to run for Congress. He was succeeded by Samuel Adams, president of the senate, who served until the inauguration of Governor Drew on November 5, 1844.

[2]Governor Drew resigned January 10, 1849. He was succeeded by Richard C. Byrd, president of the senate, who served until March 14, 1849, when John S. Roane was inaugurated.

[3]Governor Clayton resigned March 17, 1871, to take his seat in the United States Senate. He was succeeded by Ozra A. Hadley, who served until January 6, 1873, the date of Governor Elisha Baxter's inauguration.

[4]Due to ill health, Governor John S. Little left office on February 11, 1907, and John Isaac Moore, senate president, became acting governor. When Little did not return to office by the time of the legislature's adjournment on May 14, 1907, the newly elected president of the senate, Xenophon Overton Pindall, became acting governor and served for the remainder of Little's term.

[5]Governor Robinson resigned March 10, 1913, to become a United States senator. He was succeeded by W.K. Oldham, president of the senate. Three days later when the legislature adjourned, Oldham was succeeded by J.M. Futrell, who served until July 23, 1913, when George W. Hays, elected in special election, was inaugurated.

[6]Governor Martineau resigned March 4, 1928, to accept an appointment as U.S. District Judge of the Eastern District of Arkansas. Harvey Parnell, the state's first elected lieutenant governor, succeeded him as governor.

Wives of the Territorial Governors of Arkansas
1819–1836

RUTH FLINT MILLER
1819-1824

ON THE DAY after Christmas in 1819, Brigadier General James Miller stepped ashore at Arkansas Post to begin his term as the first governor of the new Territory of Arkansas. He immediately encountered entrenched political opposition from the other members of the new government who had arrived at the capital in July.

In March of that year President James Monroe had signed the act passed by Congress that created the territory. The governing body of the territory was composed of a governor, a secretary, and three judges. President Monroe appointed General James Miller of New Hampshire as governor, Robert Crittenden from Kentucky as secretary, and Andrew Scott from Missouri Territory, Charles Jouett from Michigan Territory, and Robert P. Letcher from Kentucky as judges.

Secretary Crittenden, a bold, ambitious man, planned to be the dominant figure in Arkansas politics by whatever means it took, fair or foul—he had learned both back home in Kentucky. Ordinary discretion dictated he wait for the governor to arrive, but instead he preempted Governor Miller by calling the legislature into session on July 28. They met for seven days, established two circuit courts, decided the laws of the Territory of Arkansas would be essentially the same as those of Missouri, and levied taxes in the amount of $4,816.87$^1/_2$—the sum needed to operate the government for eighteen months!

By the time the governor arrived, in his specially outfitted keelboat emblazoned with "ARKANSAS" in big gold letters and his own flag flying beneath the Stars and Stripes, Crittenden had already won over a large following of frontiersmen by dispensing political favors and making key appointments. He meant to do battle with Miller and to win. He had begun by taking actions that could have and should have awaited the governor—even though the secretary was the senior official in the governor's absence. Being secretary of the territory was not demanding and left Crittenden plenty of time for nursing prejudices and indulging in politics. He was a master at both.

Miller failed in his every effort to replace lawlessness with law-abiding civilization, and on December 31, 1824, he resigned as governor while at home on a visit with his family in New Hampshire. Apparently he just couldn't face returning to Arkansas. Many of Governor Miller's biographers say that he was totally unsuited to frontier life. History seems to bear this out.

There is no record of Mrs. Miller's ever having come to Arkansas. Upon Governor Miller's arrival, the *Arkansas Gazette* reported that he had an entourage of twenty gentlemen and one lady—"We cannot forbear to mention, for the gratification of our female friends, the arrival of one lady in the company, the wife of Captain Spencer, late of the U.S. Army." All indications are that Mrs. Miller stayed home and looked after their seven children—five of their own and two of his from a former marriage. She can't be blamed. Moving a family of seven children from New Hampshire to Arkansas would be an undertaking even today, but travel conditions in those days made it unthinkable.

Ruth Flint Miller was no pioneer woman. The idea of moving to the wilds of Arkansas was probably repugnant to her. There was a sprinkling of educated people among early Arkansas settlers, but there was also the usual rough element of adventurers, outcasts, fugitives, Indian traders, and Indians. The governor's wife would have wanted no part of this mishmash. Her family had lived in New England for about two hundred years. They were civic-minded, well-educated people of high social standing—American patriots who were leading citizens of New Hampshire. Her husband was both a successful lawyer and soldier (Nathaniel Hawthorne called him "New England's most distinguished soldier"). Altogether, New England provided a proper and secure setting to bring up the Miller children, and Ruth chose to stay in the secure and supportive environment of family and friends.

In Ruth Miller's time it was not the accepted thing for women to have identities of their own. They shared their spouse's work behind the scenes and received little public recognition. Unless a woman ran afoul of the laws of the land or church, she appeared in the record books only at birth, marriage, and death. We know little of Ruth Flint Miller other than that she was born in 1780, the daughter of Ephraim and Catherine Flint. She married James Miller on April 10, 1806, and died in 1830.

Ruth Flint Miller must have been made of stern stuff. She obviously carried her responsibilities well while the general was away at war, and then again while he served as gov-ernor of the Arkansas Territory; otherwise he would not have put up with the loneliness and Crittenden as long as he did.

Governor Miller's resignation left the post open, and Robert Crittenden wanted to be governor. He had served as acting governor before Miller's arrival and during Miller's long absences when he made trips back home to New England. When Miller resigned, in fact, he had been in New Hampshire eighteen months. Crittenden had probably served as governor as many months as Miller.

In 1822 Crittenden had gone back to Kentucky to marry Anne Morris. As wife of the secretary, who was second in command of the territory, Anne had served for two years as the territory's official hostess in Mrs. Miller's absence. Anne and Robert Crittenden felt they were the logical ones to receive the appointment.

But the time was not right for Crittenden. The new president, John Quincy Adams, gave the gubernatorial post to his friend, Major General George Izard of Philadelphia and South Carolina. Crittenden—alas—was reappointed secretary.

ELIZABETH CARTER FARLEY BANISTER SHIPPEN IZARD
1825-1828

GEORGE IZARD HAD hoped for an appointment in the diplomatic service, but the charge he received was far more foreign and in the opposite direction from that. He accepted an appointment as governor of the Territory of Arkansas and came west to the wild frontier.

Crittenden was not of a mind to relinquish the reins of government gracefully. To slight the new governor, when he was due to arrive both Crittenden and the acting secretary went to Kentucky for a long visit. Crittenden left some matters behind for Izard's attention, thinking that they would keep Izard busy until he returned, and took other government business with him. But Crittenden had not reckoned with the systematic efficiency of Izard's military mind. Izard wasted no time in setting about the business of government. He soon discovered that Crittenden had run the government in a slipshod manner, even leaving things undone. One government check in the amount of $3,000 had never reached its destination. Another one, for $10,500, should have been cashed and disbursed to the Indians. When Izard attempted to cash it, there wasn't that much money in Little Rock. He had to wait until money could be brought in from either Memphis or New Orleans. The record is not quite clear as to which city furnished the funds, and some historians hint that the courier never got back with all the money, but spent part of it himself. Izard had no tolerance for incompetence or neglect of duty. There was a cold welcome waiting for Mr. Crittenden on his return. The episode was a bad beginning to a relationship that only got worse.

Governor Izard did not bring his lovely wife, Elizabeth, to Arkansas. She remained in their home in Philadelphia, a city where she had deep roots, family, and friends. She had lived there for many years, owned property, had a busy social calendar, and was accustomed to living in the most advanced form of civilization that the country then had to offer. She had buried two husbands and two sons and was in her fifties. Frontier life had no appeal for her. In those days it was not unusual for men to be away from home at war or on a business venture for two or three years. Women simply did not pack up and go with their husbands.

Elizabeth came from a family of generations of wealthy landowners in Virginia. She was born in a mansion and never knew any life other than manorial. She was born about 1769 at Westover, the home of her grandparents, Colonel and Mrs. William Byrd III. Westover is one of America's foremost examples of an eighteenth-century Georgian house. Nothing was spared by Colonel Byrd in constructing it. Some claimed that he had the finest seat in Virginia. It cannot be disputed that Elizabeth Carter Farley Izard was "to the manor born."

Her early years were spent at Westover, Carter's Grove, and Shirley Plantations. All three were stately mansions, important today both from an architectural and a historical standpoint. Her second marriage added Farley in Pennsylvania and Stratford Hall in Virginia to her life. Farley was the country seat of the Shippen family, and Stratford Hall was the family home of her husband's mother. Stratford Hall was the birthplace of Richard Henry Lee and Francis Lightfoot Lee, both signers of the Declaration of Independence, but is most famous as the birthplace of General Robert E. Lee. Elizabeth's third marriage added another Westover, the family seat of the Izard family of South Carolina. She lived all of her life surrounded by fine objects in splendid homes, and a high degree of civility.

Elizabeth Izard was the fourth generation of Elizabeths in her family. Her great-grandmother, Elizabeth Hill, married John Carter. Their daughter, Elizabeth Hill Carter, married Colonel William Byrd, III. Their daughter, Elizabeth Hill Byrd, married James Parke Farley, and their daughter, Elizabeth Carter Farley, married George Izard.

Elizabeth Izard's father, James Parke Farley, was the son of Colonel Francis Farley of Antigua, West Indies. His family had long received choice appointments in this British colonial possession, and in addition to their West Indies holdings the Farley family had acquired large land interests in colonial America. A sale recorded in 1735 of 26,000 acres of land in North Carolina names the buyer as a Farley ancestor. The Farleys became prominent, influential, loyal citizens of this country. James attended William and Mary College and fought in the American Revolution.

As early as 1612 the early settlers along the James River in Virginia had established a fast-growing agricultural economy based on the production of tobacco. Ships loaded with hogsheads of tobacco sailed down the James River and on to England, often returning by way of the West Indies, a flourishing slave-trading center. Here they added slaves to a cargo of spices, books, wines, fine fabrics, and beautiful furniture for the Virginia plantation owner. These plantations in the highly fertile coastal region produced an abundant crop that was much in demand, and their owners soon became rich and powerful, forming a new affluent society all along the eastern seaboard from New England to Georgia. They spent their money with the same vigor they had used in making it. They built mansions in the fashionable Georgian style. These classical homes, bold in size, seem to

exemplify the ambition and pride of the men who lived in them and who founded important mercantile and political dynasties.

The planter class of Virginia became its aristocracy. During the golden years from about 1770 to 1820, Virginia produced more political and historical giants than any other region of America at any other time—people who not only made their mark in Virginia during colonial times but influenced the rest of the country as well.

Elizabeth Izard was their descendant, and her husbands were of the same pattern.

Her first marriage was to John Banister, Jr., a descendant of Reverend John Banister, a missionary in Virginia from the Church of England and of a grandmother who was a direct descendant of Pocahontas. John and Elizabeth lived in Battersea, Virginia. He died after they had been married only a few years. This union produced no children.

Her second marriage was to Thomas Lee Shippen of Philadelphia. The Shippens were prominent in social, professional, and political circles, and Elizabeth quickly assumed her rightful place in our nation's first capital. Although this marriage caused her to move to Philadelphia, she did not have to break ties with her home state of Virginia. Her husband was the grandson and namesake of Colonel Thomas Lee, a governor of Virginia and master of Stratford Hall. Visits to this family home allowed her to keep in contact with her Virginia family and friends. There were two sons born to Elizabeth and Thomas Shippen. One died in childhood, and the other, William Shippen, survived to adulthood.

Elizabeth's third marriage was to George Izard, of the prominent South Carolina family. As Mrs. Izard, Elizabeth divided her time between Philadelphia and South Carolina, as did her mother-in-law, Mrs. Ralph Izard. A published account of social life in Philadelphia describes Mrs. Ralph Izard's salon and card parties as among the most elegant and attractive of society.

There were three sons born to Elizabeth

and George Izard. James Ralph Farley Izard and George Izard both died young and unmarried. A third son, James Farley Izard, a graduate of the United States Military Academy, was killed in action in the Seminole War; he is buried on the battlefield at Camp Izard in Florida. Therefore there were no heirs, and eventually the Izard holdings in South Carolina were sold for back taxes.

Elizabeth died in Philadelphia about a year after Governor Izard came to Arkansas. He died in office about two years later and is buried in Mount Holly Cemetery in Little Rock. He was fifty-one years old.

There are several similarities between Governors Miller and Izard. Both were lawyers, both fought in the War of 1812, both attained the rank of general, neither served his full term as governor, neither brought his wife to Arkansas, and Crittenden was a thorn in the side of them both.

Governor Izard was not popular with the rough settlers of the territory, although they respected him and knew that he was a good governor. To them he seemed cold and aloof and they couldn't understand why he spent all his spare time in his library instead of visiting with them. He lived in a small brick cottage on the corner of Spring and Cherry (now Second) streets. The house was torn down years ago, and his library was lost in an accident on the river when it was being shipped home after his death.

George Izard was a learned aristocrat who had been educated in the best schools at home and abroad. He attained high rank in the military, served a tour as Commandant of West Point, had a distinguished career in both law and the diplomatic corps, and moved in the best circles socially and professionally in South Carolina, New York, Philadelphia, and Virginia. One can only guess at the depth of this man's loneliness in frontier Arkansas, where he had few friends, no family, and too much Crittenden.

During Izard's term in office, Robert Crittenden probably reached the peak of his power. One of the contributing factors to his decline was a duel he had with Henry W. Conway.

It was an election year and feelings ran high. The real issue was the presidential election. In Arkansas the Adams-Clay supporters were the Whigs, led by Crittenden, and the Andrew Jackson supporters were the Democratic Party, led by Henry Conway.

Conway was running for reelection to the all-powerful position of territorial representative to Congress. He and Crittenden had been friends in the past, but Crittenden turned against Conway in this campaign year and saw to it that Conway had opposition. The campaign was bitter and vicious to the point that Crittenden called Conway a coward and a thief. When the election was over Crittenden challenged Conway to a duel. The two met on the east bank of the Mississippi River on October 29, 1827. The first exchange of fire caused lint to fly from Crittenden's lapel, and Conway was mortally wounded by a bullet in the chest. He died on November 9, about two months before his thirty-fifth birthday.

In the past, the Family had kept up a semblance of friendship with Crittenden in order to keep down his opposition, but this campaign and Conway's death fueled the fire of the Izards' unrelenting opposition to Crittenden forever.

When Governor Izard died in office, the Family saw to it that President Jackson knew Crittenden had led Jackson's opposition in the Arkansas election. Jackson did not give the coveted appointment of governor to Crittenden. In fact, he did not even reappoint him secretary. Instead he named his good friends John Pope and William S. Fulton as governor and secretary, respectively.

Governor Izard's untimely death made Crittenden acting governor once more. Serving temporarily for someone else was as close as he ever came to realizing his great ambition of becoming governor.

Even though Crittenden was no longer secretary, he had not given up his political ambitions and did not leave Arkansas. He had built a large law practice in Little Rock, owned a great deal of property, and had a political following in the territory. He had gone deeply into debt to build the finest house in Little Rock. It stood on a block of land at Seventh and Scott. It had the usual dependencies of kitchen, storehouse, smoke-house, wellhouse, and slave quarters. The Crittendens lived there in a grand manner, he dispensing cigars, wine, and patronage, and Ann entertaining lavishly. He stayed to lead the opposition to Governor Pope and to further his own political ambitions.

FRANCES WATKINS WALTON POPE
1829-1835

GOVERNOR JOHN POPE was appointed on March 9, 1829, and arrived in Little Rock soon afterward. Frances Watkins Walton Pope was the first governor's wife actually to live in Arkansas. She arrived in May 1829, and to celebrate her arrival Major Nicholas Peay gave a large dinner party at his hotel, The Anthony House.

The primitive pioneer village of Little Rock was then about eight years old. There were maybe a dozen streets with names. There were also taverns, a hotel, a gristmill, a wagon-maker, a gunsmith, a drugstore, a tailor or two, and a few mercantile stores. There were only three or four nice homes scattered among the log and frame houses. The Popes lived in a one-story four-room house on the southeast corner of Louisiana and Cherry streets (now Second Street), and the governor's office was on the south side of Markham. The governor shared the building with the territorial surveyor's office and the post office.

If Frances had kept a personal diary it would indeed make interesting reading. During her husband's term, Little Rock was incorporated as a city, the first mayor was elected, and a second newspaper was established. She probably attended the first theatrical production in the city, which took place November 3, 1834. She saw construction begin on a new Capitol. She lived through epidemics of cholera and smallpox and terrible floods of the Arkansas River. The raging waters washed away entire plantations—houses, barns, people, and cattle—as if they were toys. New channels were cut in the river when the waters swept across points of land. The winter of 1832–33 was the coldest known, with ice four inches thick on the river.

She witnessed the Trail of Tears, the great migration of Indians forced westward from their homes in the eastern states. In the fall of 1832, the vanguard of this army of fugitives arrived at Little Rock five or six thousand strong and made camp on the riverbank. It took several days for these people to cross the river with their cattle, horses, women, and children. Once across they were rushed out of town, for the townspeople did not want them around.

Backed up against Indian territory as they were, Arkansas inhabitants were not as interested in the slavery issue as they were in getting rid of the Indians. This feeling reached all the way to the presidency, for Andrew Jackson said, "The only good Indian is a dead Indian."

In 1830 there were a few more than 30,000 inhabitants of the territory, 25,000 whites and 5,000 slaves. Except for the hardy souls who had followed Stephen Austin into Texas, Arkansas was the westernmost frontier, peopled with a new breed who might well have stepped out of the Middle Ages.

The men were picturesque frontiersmen. They wore buckskin leggings, a blanket cape, deerskin moccasins, long hair to their shoulders, and a knife at their belt. The women matched the men. Their manners were as coarse as their clothing and they were as good as the men with the rifle. Both sexes smoked the corncob pipe and indulged in dram drinking. The heroes of the new breed were men of the people—men such as Davy Crockett, Daniel Boone, and Kit Carson.

Andrew Jackson, who embodied the main characteristics of these settlers, had been elected president. The last of the elder statesmen had been retired from the White House. The people were tired of the Virginia gentlemen presidents and had elected a defender and symbol of the common man as their leader.

The style of candidates changed from "learned" to "good" and from "cultured" to "natural," and the ideal politician changed from an elder statesman or diplomat to a military hero or someone who had served a political apprenticeship. It became popular for candidates to claim they were born in a log cabin.

President Jackson did not choose one of the new breed when he appointed the third territorial governor of Arkansas. John Pope, cousin of George Washington, was the eldest son of Colonel and Mrs. William Pope of Virginia. When he was nine years old his family had moved to Kentucky, where he grew up. He returned to Virginia to earn his law degree from William and Mary College and then returned to Kentucky to enter politics. He was elected to several offices, including United States senator, spent some time as a law professor, and served one term as secretary of state of Kentucky before being appointed territorial governor of Arkansas.

In spite of having only one arm (he had lost the other in a fodder cutter when he was fourteen), he was a handsome man, tall, slender, successful in his profession, and with a fine family background. He was considered a very eligible bachelor, and his success with the ladies was legendary, as borne out by the three he eventually married.

His first marriage to Anne Christian, niece of Patrick Henry, lasted about ten years. Courthouse records of Jefferson County, Kentucky, show that she and John Pope joined in the execution of property deeds in 1806. We do not know the exact date of her death, but John Pope was a widower when he went to Washington in 1807 as a newly elected senator.

There Senator Pope met and married Eliza Dorcas Janet Johnson, daughter of Joshua Johnson, first American counsel general to England. Some of Pope's historians feel that this close tie to the mother country caused the senator's wife to influence him to vote against America's entrance into war with

England in 1812. Whatever the reason for this vote, Henry Clay used it as a tool to defeat Senator Pope in his bid for reelection.

Eliza Pope died in 1818. She and the senator had two daughters, Florida, who died young, and Elizabeth, who grew up and married John W. Cocke.

John Pope's third wife was Frances Watkins Walton, the wealthy widow of General Matthew Walton. After marrying in 1820, they lived in her home, Walton Manor, on her plantation near Springfield, Kentucky. When he was given the appointment as governor of the territory of Arkansas, she sold her land and home and moved to Little Rock, bringing her slaves with her. She remained by her husband's side, running the household and serving as official hostess under difficult circumstances. Her husband did not like his new position. He called the "governorship of Arkansas Territory an inadequate reward—the capitol (sic) mistake of his life."

His days in Arkansas were marked by frustration, defeat, and one great success, a new Capitol. In his first address to the legislature he had given it a constructive program, urging the building of roads, schools, and a suitable statehouse. Nothing was done.

When the legislature failed to appropriate money to build the Capitol, Governor Pope went to Washington and, because of his close friendship with President Jackson and his firsthand knowledge of the working of Congress, obtained a grant of ten sections of land (6,400 acres). Proceeds from the sale of this land were to be used to finance the building of a proper Capitol.

When this land grant became a reality, Crittenden thought he had found a way out of the financial troubles brought on by the cost of his fine home. He dreamed up a scheme to exchange his expensive house for the ten sections of land. A legislative committee was formed for the purpose of selecting and selling the sections. Crittenden packed the committee with his friends and was able to pass a bill that provided that the land be given to him in exchange for his house. Governor Pope vetoed the bill, and the opposition was unable to muster enough support to override the veto.

To get back at the governor, the legislature sent a petition to Congress asking that the governor be recalled and that they be allowed to elect their governor. As a result of all these shenanigans by Crittenden and the legislature, Congress directed that Governor Pope personally supervise the selection and sale of the land and the construction of a Capitol. He did it well. He chose the site and in 1833 started the building that was completed in 1840 and served as our state Capitol for the next half-century.

In 1833 Crittenden ran for Congress. His effort to secure the Capitol lands for himself was an issue in the campaign. He recklessly boasted that he had bribed the legislature with hams from his own smokehouse. He became known as the "canvassed ham" candidate and was defeated—a blow from which he never recovered. He died a broken man after the long and arduous trial of a lawsuit in Vicksburg, Mississippi, in December 1834. No one knows where he is buried. This man, who wanted so much to be governor of Arkansas, never made it. His wife, Anne, who served so often and so well as official hostess while substituting for others, was never honored with the official title of Wife of the Governor.

Governor Pope was not reappointed as governor. He had fallen into disfavor with both the political Family and his longtime friend, President Jackson. The president had sent to Pope a copy of his forthcoming message to Congress. Pope thought he was supposed to critique the speech. Being a man of decisive convictions, he wrote President Jackson and honestly and clearly stated his opposition to the president's stand on certain issues. Jackson was furious at being disagreed with, and only the intervention of Senator Sevier kept Jackson from removing Pope from office immediately. Sevier was not acting out of friendship to Pope; he was looking after the Family's interests, for the Family did not want Pope to be driven into Crittenden's camp. Together, Crittenden and Pope would have been too much to overcome. Pope was allowed to remain in office until the end of his term. Secretary William S. Fulton was appointed as governor and Lewis Randolph, nephew of Thomas Jefferson, was named secretary.

The trickery of Arkansas politics and the harsh pioneer life did not defeat Frances Pope. She and John returned to Kentucky in 1835 and bought back her land and Walton Manor, only to sell it again a few years later when they moved to a new home they had built in Springfield, Kentucky. He again entered Kentucky politics and was elected to Congress, where he served several terms.

MATILDA NOWLAND FULTON
1835-1836

MATILDA NOWLAND FULTON was to the manor born on September 15, 1803, in Hartford County, Maryland. She married her cousin William Savin Fulton in 1823. Their mothers were sisters and their fathers were business partners.

Both Matilda and William belonged to wealthy families of high social standing on the Eastern Shore of Maryland. Matilda's mother was Rebecca Savin and William's mother was Elizabeth Savin, beautiful daughters of William Savin, a prosperous owner of large wheat plantations. Rebecca married Perry Nowland and Elizabeth married David Fulton, partners along with Perry's brother Benjamin in a highly successful mercantile business.

Rebecca and Perry Nowland were fond of the social life and lived and entertained on a grand scale. Invitations were much sought after to their oyster suppers, balls, and parties, and especially to Perry's hunts and Rebecca's fine breakfasts afterward at their country estate. They resided on the Eastern Shore for many years, but the early deaths of several of their children alarmed them. They felt that the climate was the cause of these deaths.

The two sisters received a large inheritance of money and property when their father died. Rebecca and Perry used this money to buy a large farm inland across the bay at Bath, Maryland. William's parents, Elizabeth and David, used her inheritance to move to Baltimore and set up a wholesale grocery business. These two moves separated William and Matilda for the first time in their lives.

At their new home Rebecca and Perry resumed their social life in an even grander style than before. But the War of 1812 came along and ruined their business, and Perry

unexpectedly died soon afterward. The grand bubble of rich living for Rebecca had burst. She sold her country estate and moved with her six surviving children to Baltimore to be near her sister Elizabeth. William and Matilda were once again living close to each other.

After a few years Elizabeth and David moved to Gallatin, Tennessee, where their oldest daughter and her family lived. Being in Baltimore without Elizabeth was too lonely for Rebecca. She packed up and moved her family to Gallatin.

William Fulton, Elizabeth and David's oldest son, had finished college and was studying law in Baltimore when his family moved to Tennessee. He continued his study in Nashville, and upon graduation received an attractive offer to practice law in Florence, Alabama. His father was offered a job with a newspaper in that city and thus the family moved to Florence. Again Rebecca could not bear to be apart from her sister; she moved to Florence too.

The close relationship of the two sisters caused their children to spend an unusual amount of time together. William and Matilda decided they never wanted to part. They were married in 1828.

While a law student in Nashville, William Fulton became friends with Andrew Jackson. A family member says Matilda and William spent their honeymoon with the Jacksons at the Hermitage. In a collection of letters of the Honorable William S. Fulton there are several written by Andrew Jackson; one to the Fultons soon after their marriage commends Matilda's "industry and economy" and advises to her to "learn to live within your means." After William served as General Jackson's military aide in the Seminole War, there was another letter from Jackson in which he told Fulton, "You can count on my friendship." Fulton's political future was assured.

President Jackson appointed his old friend secretary and later governor of Arkansas Territory. Upon Fulton's arrival in Little Rock, he wrote his father on May 25, 1829, that they had arrived safely and been well received by the people in Little Rock, "a pretty little town," that Matilda was "delighted with her new home," and that "she has found female society here, every way equal to any she has ever been acquainted with."

In *Early Days in Arkansas,* Judge W.F. Pope wrote of visiting in the Fulton home and meeting Mrs. Fulton. Calling her a "beautiful and accomplished lady," he said that "a stranger never would have imagined this modest looking cottage to be the seat of such an elegant hospitality, but such was the case." The house he referred to was a cottage situated on Scott Street between Mulberry (Third) and Walnut (Fourth). (Unfortunately this house was destroyed before the restoration of the territorial buildings was begun in 1939. It is interesting that Governor and Mrs. Fulton's granddaughter, Mrs. Fairfax Loughborough, is the person most responsible for restoring these buildings.)

Secretary William Savin Fulton was appointed by his good friend President Andrew Jackson to serve a three-year term as territorial governor, but he was fated to serve only one year, because on June 15, 1836, Arkansas was admitted to the Union as a state. Statehood was no surprise to anyone—there had long been a concerted effort to achieve this, and Congress had granted permission for a constitutional convention two years before. The constitution had been written and plans made for celebration. All that was needed was an act of Congress. This was finally passed after a stormy twenty-five-hour nonstop session.

Governor Fulton had opposed statehood but was persuaded to relax his opposition. As a reward he and his friend Ambrose Sevier

were elected the first two United States senators from Arkansas. This was arranged by the Family. For the most part Family members were all large land- and slave-owners, and it was in their immediate interest that Arkansas be admitted as a slave state. This might not be possible later.

William and Matilda Fulton had lived in Little Rock six years before he became governor. They were community leaders both socially and politically, with a wide circle of friends to join them in celebrating when he received his appointment as governor on March 9, 1835. Their rejoicing soon turned to sorrow, for almost immediately Matilda became seriously ill and their infant daughter died. On May 5 another little daughter died. Matilda's one year as First Lady was spent recovering from her illness and the loss of two precious children. By the time she had begun to regain her strength and overcome her grief, William had been elected senator.

Matilda did not go to Washington with her husband—perhaps because after the events of the past year she did not feel up to the change. Also they were in the midst of building a new house, and someone needed to oversee the completion of this project. Records show that by 1838 she had joined the senator in the capital city.

Matilda Nowland Fulton, as wife of a man elected to high office, did not live a lace-collar and china-teacup life, although she had plenty of both. Instead, she energetically went about the business of providing her family with necessities and comforts, while her husband pursued his career as a public servant. She did not allow the rough pioneer life of Arkansas to divert her from her genteel upbringing; she maintained the high ideals and cultured life she had experienced in her childhood home. She served as a bulwark between the world as she and William had known it and as it was now, fostering a sense of gentleness and culture in her home even though she had to work very hard herself.

Platter that Matilda Nowland Fulton inherited from her mother, Rebecca Nowland. C. 1785. (Photo by Anne McMath)

A letter she wrote to William when he was away from home on February 9, 1832, provides real insight into Matilda's strength and character. She tells him that she and her hands slaughtered and cut up nine hogs in one day. At the end of the day she didn't feel well; she thought it was because she had worked all day in the smokehouse and was only fatigued. The next morning when she still did not feel well, she decided "it was not prudent to stay alone" so she sent for a friend to come and stay with her. As her condition worsened, she sent for three other women, including Mrs. Pope, the governor's wife. After two days of labor she gave birth to a baby boy. In the letter there was not a word of sympathy for herself or a complaint at having gone through this ordeal alone—nor did she berate her husband for being away at butchering time! She accepted her role graciously, expressing joy over her "beautiful" son and concern over William's welfare during his difficult travels.

Matilda Fulton was mistress of her home, but she was also the overseer of land and crops when her husband was away. She and William bought forty acres of land out in the country south of Little Rock and built a home they named Rosewood. In letters that she wrote to him after he went to the senate,

she describes the progress of the construction. She had supervised the proper installation of the windows, and as soon as the roofers were finished, she said, all would be "ready for the whitewash."

She did complain to her husband about the slovenly ways of her houseman, who would not return all day when sent on an errand. She wanted to replace him, but first she had to try out a new man named John who had been recommended to her. In later letters she wrote glowingly of John, saying he was very willing to work and "seemed to take as much pride as she did in how the place looked." He helped her with the gardens and yard. She asked the senator to send her some bulbs and told him she had been able to get only fifty apple trees for the orchard! She told the senator that her sausage and souse meat was very good that year, and that she would be busy all the next day stuffing the sausage.

In later letters we learn that their daughter Elizabeth had gone to Washington with her father and was attending school there. Matilda urged her husband to see to it that Elizabeth should "have as much social life as possible, and learn and change."

They were a warm and loving family. Several times in each letter Matilda expressed concern for William's safety and told him how much he and Elizabeth were loved and missed.

In a letter written at Rosewood in March 1840, Matilda asked her husband to bring winter and summer clothing for both the family and servants because it "would cost six times as much in Little Rock" to buy the needed items. She specified that this clothing be cheap and plain—no finery, for she "had more than she could ever wear." She wanted a plain, black, silk dress and some dark calico for next winter and "white and colored stockings." Apparently Elizabeth was grown up by now for Matilda asked William to bring party clothes for the girl—"supply her with necessary things for parties and companys."

Rosewood was the Fultons' home for the

rest of their lives. He died in 1844; it was thought his death was due to sleeping in a freshly painted room. Matilda lived there until her death thirty-five years later. In his will Senator Fulton directed that this home and property belonged to Mrs. Fulton for her lifetime, but upon her death he willed it to the State of Arkansas to be used as the site of a school for the blind.

Rosewood burned some time after Mrs. Fulton's death and a school for the blind was indeed built on this land. It remained the site of the Arkansas School for the Blind until a new one was built some years later at its present location on West Markham Street. The Fulton property at Eighteenth and Center Street is now the location of the Governor's Mansion.

Of the children born to the Fultons, two daughters survived—Elizabeth (Mrs. Moorehead Wright) and Sophia ((1) Mrs. James Curran and (2) Mrs. George Claiborne Watkins, the third Chief Justice of the Arkansas Supreme Court). The descendants of these daughters have been and still are prominent citizens of Arkansas.

Wives of the Governors of Arkansas
1836–1990

James Sevier Conway. (Photo courtesy of the Southwest Arkansas Regional Archives and the Arkansas History Commission)

Mary Jane Bradley Conway. (Photo courtesy of the Arkansas History Commission)

MARY JANE BRADLEY CONWAY
1830-1840

MARY JANE BRADLEY and her family had lived in the Red River Valley for some time before her future husband settled there in 1823. Her uncles, Captain Hugh Bradley and Fleetwood Herndon, were soldiers in the War of 1812 and were with Andrew Jackson at New Orleans. After the war, Bradley and Herndon came up the Red River in flatboats and settled at Long Prairie, in an area which became Lafayette County. It is not known whether Mary Jane and her parents were with them or whether they came later. Mary Jane Bradley's grandfather was James Bradley, a soldier in the Revolution. He was born in North Carolina and married Jane Davidson of Tennessee. They had two sons, John and Davidson. John married Jane Barton; it was they who moved to Long Prairie and became the parents of Mary Jane Bradley. After Mary Jane's father died as a young man, her mother married William Woodard. All three of these families, the Woodards, Bradleys, and Herndons, were among the established residents in the area when James S. Conway settled there.

Mary Jane was one of the area's most beautiful girls, and it was only natural that the young, handsome James Sevier Conway was attracted to her. They began a courtship that ended in marriage at his home in Long Prairie on December 21, 1825, thus uniting two very prestigious pioneer families.

The Conways were leading citizens of Arkansas and were a part of a political dynasty which controlled state politics until the Civil War. This alliance of Conways, Rectors, Seviers, and Johnsons led the Democratic Party and elected themselves and their friends to the lion's share of offices. From the Family came governors, senators, judges, and various other office-holders.

Mary Jane's husband, James Conway, was the second son of Thomas and Ann Rector Conway, who had seven sons and three daughters. Their oldest son, Henry, was Arkansas's territorial representative in Congress. Their second and seventh sons, James and Elias, were the state's first and fifth governors—the only brothers ever to serve in that office.

Henry and James Conway were the first members of the Conway family to come to Arkansas. They were brought here by their uncle, William Rector, as part of a crew of surveyors who made the original survey of Arkansas. Henry chose not to stay in the surveying business very long. Through the influence of his uncles William and Elias Rector, he was appointed to two powerful political positions in Arkansas. Later he was elected to the influential post of delegate to Congress, and had just been elected to a third term when he was killed in a duel with Robert Crittenden.

James Conway settled in the Red River area on his large plantation. Some historians say he had 2,000 acres, while others claim it was 3,200 and that he added another 1,000 acres of hill land that rimmed his original holdings. Some of this land had been granted to him as a commission or bonus, and he had bought some of it. He immediately set about acquiring the eighty or so slaves needed to farm his acreage and began to raise cotton and corn.

When his brother Henry was killed in the duel, James assumed the role of leader—the beginning of the dynasty in which the Conway name became a symbol of Arkansas politics.

Inauguration of James Sevier Conway as the first governor of the State of Arkansas took place on September 18, 1836, in the unfinished Capitol. Newspaper reports of this momentous event tell of parades, marching bands, escorts, speeches, excitement, enthusiasm, and even fancy clothes, but there is no mention of Mrs. Conway. Apparently, she did not attend her husband's inauguration. This was not unusual for the times. As early as 1808, Dolley Madison had broken precedent and was the first wife of a president to attend her husband's inauguration. Almost thirty years later the custom had not yet trickled down to Arkansas. In the early days of this state women were kept in the background of politics, just as they had been in the early years of our nation. For the most part women fitted themselves into the contemporary model of womanliness. One would assume such was the role for Mary Jane Conway.

Whether home was on the plantation in Lafayette County or in the new house they built at Second and Spring streets, where they lived during his term as governor, the Conways lived in a style of ease and refinement, for they were wealthy people. The First Lady had servants and a six-thousand-dollar carriage, but no public image!

Behind her public reticence must have been a woman of spunk and courage, for Mary Jane lived through her husband's controversial term as governor and then survived him by twenty-three years. His term in office was marked by special sessions, boundary disputes, Indian troubles, problems with the state militia, courts of inquiry, accusations, denial, and a national depression. Not surprisingly, Governor Conway became ill during the last year of his term and seriously considered resigning from office. It was a matter of conjecture whether his failing health was due to a physical condition or the fiscal problems of the state. Arkansas was barely three years old and already $30 million in debt. There was a deficit of $65,000 in the treasury and a hopelessly inadequate income. The State Bank and a Real Estate Bank, established in the first two bills passed by the legislature after Conway took office, allowed money-hungry

people to bleed the state dry. These banks had already failed. It was enough to make anyone ill.

Conway was a happy farmer who took office as governor at a time when only someone of iron nerve, trained in political and governmental affairs, could have foreseen the iniquity of the schemes to establish these two banks and stopped their authorization. Conway failed to use the power of the governor's office, and it backfired on him. From the start he let the proponents of these banks control government, and they left a Pandora's box of debt and troubles that plagued Arkansas for generations to come. Conway's sin in this piracy was one of omission and not commission.

Conway wanted to resign from office, but when his friends influenced him to stay on, he took a few months' leave of absence instead. The president of the senate, Samuel Calhoun Roane, became acting governor—the first of many throughout Arkansas history.

James S. Conway retired from office after one term. He and Mrs. Conway returned to their plantation, where they lived the rest of their lives. He maintained an interest in politics and education, but devoted most of his time to overseeing his extensive farming operations.

Upon returning to Long Prairie they set about building a large, new home on a magnificent location. Because their farm lands along the Red River were subject to seasonal floods, they bought adjoining hill land and selected a perfect site atop a flat-topped hill. There were springs that furnished plenty of water, and woods where game abounded. Since it was set apart from the mosquito-infested lowland, it was cooler and healthier than the site of their present home. It took years to build the house, for the site had to be cleared, logs cut, and lumber sawed. A kiln had to be built to fire the handmade bricks, shingles had to be hand-hewn from cypress blocks, and a blacksmith had to be found to make the needed hardware. Governor Conway hired an expert carpenter who directed the slaves in the building of a large, solidly built house.

Mary Jane's new home had two stories, with four rooms upstairs and four rooms downstairs. Each room was twenty feet square and there was a connecting hall on each floor. This hall was also twenty feet wide and forty feet long, with double doors opening on the front onto a portico on both floors. The heavy oak doors were flanked by side-lights, thus creating an impressive entrance. The porticoes were twenty feet wide and twelve feet deep and were supported by large round columns. Across the back of the house a broad veranda extended the entire sixty-foot width of the building. The walls of the house were logs covered by weatherboard on the outside and plaster on the inside.

The kitchen was a twenty-foot-square building separate from the house. Its fireplace extended the full width of one wall. Three cranes, varying in length from three to five feet, hung over the fireplace. It had an eight-foot-long hearth which was used for baking; on special occasions every available space would be filled. Also in the kitchen were two solid hickory blocks two feet square, polished to a mirror finish—one for preparing pastries and the other for cutting meat. Pans of milk and bowls of butter and cream were kept fresh in a springhouse built over a rock spring.

Being the wife of the governor and living in a relatively small house with only a few household servants probably seemed like a vacation to Mary Jane, compared to her responsibilities as mistress of a plantation home and eighty slaves. The character of Miss Ellen, Scarlett's mother in *Gone with the Wind,* is an accurate portrayal of the life Mary Jane Conway lived. It was her responsibility to train and oversee the household staff. Just keeping supplies for this many people would have been a monumental task in itself. Trips were made to New Orleans twice a year, and supplies were brought back

in barrels, bushels, and hogsheads. If something was needed before the next semiannual buying trip, orders were placed with commission merchants who traveled the rivers bringing supplies to the Indians and settlers.

After Walnut Hill was built, the entertainment schedule increased. The children were growing up and beginning to have visitors and parties. In addition, Walnut Hill was located directly on the military road from Fort Smith to Fort Jessup, Louisiana, and was a prime stopover for travelers.

There exists a detailed description of a ball and reception given by the Conways to honor Albert Pike, Archibald Yell, a Colonel Adams, Charles Pelham, and James F. Fagan, who with their troops were on their way to fight the Mexican War. The soldiers pitched their tents on the Conway plantation and courtesies were extended to all. The guest list for this party included prominent families from south Arkansas and north Louisiana, and the reception was well attended. The feast was served on a fifty-yard plank table set up on the lawn. The table was covered with snowy white damask and set with china, silver, and cut glass. Each end and the center were decorated with a pyramid of three large cakes iced to a snowy whiteness and elaborately embossed. On one end of the table there was a large platter containing a roast suckling pig with an apple in its mouth. The menu for this buffet consisted of

Mary Jane Bradley Conway's china. (Photo by Anne McMath)

Mary Jane and James's daughter Susan and her husband, James Logan, at the time of their marriage. (Photo courtesy of Southwest Arkansas Regional Archives)

platters of wild game, fowls, vegetables, salads, fruits, salt-rising bread, bowls of ambrosia, apple snow, soufflés, syllabub, and many other tempting dishes. White-aproned black waiters passed hot biscuits and trays of roast pork and turkey. Food for these occasions was provided in part from game native to the nearby woods and partly from the family gardens over which old Daddy Ralph presided. It was prepared in the kitchen under the supervision of a turban-topped "Auntie" and her helpers.

In the Southwest Arkansas Regional Archives in Washington, Arkansas, in the Nan Robson Brown collection (she was a granddaughter of Governor and Mrs. Conway), there is a newspaper article written by K.C. Hill, dated August 31, 1941. The article is about "Aunt Elvira," who was believed to be 117 years old at the time of the article. She had been a slave of James S. Conway, whom she called "Marster Conway." She didn't remember how many children she had, but she had pleasant memories of "Miss Mary Jane" coming down to the quarters, bringing apples and peaches to the children. "Miss Mary Jane's" carriage was always driven by Uncle Ned, a slave who looked after "Marster Conway." Aunt Elvira said that once "Uncle Ned" stayed away a long time and when he came back he drove "Miss Mary Jane" down to see them. She had never been told that Mr. Conway was elected governor. The reporter surmised that "Uncle Ned" went to Little Rock with Governor and Mrs. Conway.

In this era a plantation like Walnut Hill had to be largely self-sufficient. Mary Jane Conway presided over a home that served as the setting for a variety of family occasions—birth and death, work, leisure, and celebrations. Many festivities were held in this house that was the center of civilization and hospitality in frontier country.

When the oldest daughter, Nancy, married Valentine Sevier, a feast was served in the lower hall to 125 guests.

When daughter Martha married Dr. James S. Sevier she was regal in a gown of white tarlatan over silk. The dress had a low-cut neck, short sleeves, and a long train. Her accessories of bridal veil, orange blossoms, white silk hose, and satin slippers were brought from Mobile, Alabama.

Of the six children born to James and Mary Jane Conway, five survived to maturity. They were Ann Jane "Nancy" Conway Sevier Turner; Martha Conway Sevier; Frances Conway Bradley; Susan Conway Logan; and Frederick Elias Conway.

Governor Conway died and was buried at Walnut Hill in 1855. Mary Jane died in 1876 and is buried beside her husband.

Manor houses of the old South symbolized the owner's acceptance of the challenge of the land and times, of his pride of possession and the realization of great wealth. Walnut Hill was just such a house—a fine example of a great southern plantation presided over by Mary Jane Bradley Conway, an aristocratic lady in the finest traditions of southern womanhood.

ARCHIBALD YELL
1830-1844

ARCHIBALD YELL SUCCEEDED James Conway as governor. He was worthy and honorable, of unblemished integrity, a sincere devotee of the interests of his country. A man of kindly nature who harbored no secret malice, he was frank, open, and popular. His friends had wanted him to be the first governor, but he had not lived in the state long enough to be eligible. It is said he could be all things to all men, "whether it was in a camp meeting, a shooting match or a treat at the bar." Albert Pike, who opposed Yell during his lifetime, wrote this about Mr. Yell forty years after his death: "What follies most of our piques and resentments, our contentions and wranglings seem to have been, when we look back upon them, and cheerfully admit that those whom we disliked and felt enmity toward were good and upright men!"

Yell is the only former governor to have been killed in action. He met his death in the Mexican War. By that time he had resigned from office before his term was up, and Samuel Adams was acting governor.

Although Yell had been married three times, none of his wives lived to see him elected governor; he was a widower with six children when he served. His eldest daughter, who was a grown young lady when her father was governor, could have been his official hostess, but there is no record that she was. She was reared by her maternal grandparents and it is possible she and father were not close. Since this is the story of only those women who actually served as First Lady, we will leave the three Mrs. Yells to rest in peace! They were Mary Scott, Nancy (or Ann) Jordan Moore, and Maria (or Mary) Ficklin.

CINDERELLA BETTIS DREW
1844-1849

THE STORY OF the third governor and First Lady may be the saddest of all the First Families. When Thomas and Cinderella Bettis were married, both were wealthy, highly respected citizens, but unlike Cinderella and Prince Charming in the fairy tale, they did not live happily ever after. In fact, his term as governor proved to be the midnight hour when their golden chariot turned to a pumpkin! They never recovered from financial problems brought on by serving as governor and never regained the financial security that was theirs when he was elected.

Cinderella's parents, Mr. and Mrs. Ransom Bettis, came from North Carolina in 1815 and settled in Lawrence County in northwestern Arkansas. History is not clear whether she was born in North Carolina or after the family moved to Arkansas. Her father claimed large land holdings for himself and dealt in land speculation, a most profitable business in the early days of Arkansas. He established a trading post on the Black River and built a home nearby. This trading post was called Bettis Bluff and later became the town of Pocahontas.

It would be interesting to know how and why Mr. and Mrs. Bettis chose the name of Cinderella for their daughter. Certainly the circumstances of her early life bore no resemblance to the fairy tale, for she was the somewhat spoiled only child of doting, wealthy parents. She grew into a striking young woman with coal-black hair and lustrous dark eyes, tall and dignified with an air of haughtiness. This attitude of superiority was further accentuated by her use of flowery language and big words. Surely the realities of adulthood tamed this high-spirited, petted daughter accustomed to wealth and fulfilled wishes.

Fate was not kind to Cinderella and

Thomas Drew. In the early years of their marriage their life was happy and secure, their future full of promise. It is possible their financial woes began before Thomas was elected governor, but certainly his term in public office was the end of good times for this family. Their situation worsened as the years went by, and they died owning nothing.

Historians differ on how and when Thomas Drew came to Arkansas. Some say he came here from Tennessee as a very young man driving a wagon from which he peddled housewares to the settlers. Others say he became a peddler after arriving in Arkansas and that it was during his travels in this enterprise that he met the Bettis family. Hallum's history, written in 1887, claims Drew came as a peddler to the state. They all agree that he first settled in Clark County, taught school for a while, and served one term as county clerk there. He also farmed near Camden before he moved to Lawrence County and became wealthy as a partner in the land speculating business with Ransom Bettis.

When Cinderella and Thomas married, her father's gift to the young couple was eight hundred acres of rich farmland across the river in Cherokee Bay and fifteen or more slaves to farm it. They built a home on this land, where it is presumed they lived until he was elected governor and the family moved to Little Rock. (Today the town of Biggers sits on this land.)

Both Cinderella's husband and her father were active in the growth and development of their area. They made donations of land to the little town of Pocahontas, and when Lawrence County was divided into Lawrence and Randolph counties, they led the fight to have Pocahontas named the county seat of the new county of Randolph. The issue was to be decided by a vote of the people. Before the election, Bettis and Drew gave a barbecue for the voters. In his book *Pioneers and Makers of Arkansas* Josiah Shinn describes the barbecues and camp meetings of early days:

The barbecue was a feature of early territorial life, and the pioneers could smell a feast of this kind for fifty miles. The bergue was another great feast and consisted of five hundred squirrels properly cleaned and boiled to the consistency of soup in a twenty-gallon iron caldron. A barbecue or a bergue was the social occasion of the period, but politicians soon turned it into a machine for vote getting and for sampling bad whiskey and worse oratory. When camp meetings began in 1823, another social outlet was created and it was no uncommon thing to see three hundred horses hitched to swinging limbs of trees in the forest, whose riders, male and female, had traveled from forty to fifty miles. When preaching was over and the basket dinners eaten, the men parceled themselves off in squads to attend to more important matters, swap horses, trade land and do the other fellow up before he had time to get in his work on him. One eye always toward the horns of the altar, while the other sought for soft snaps and easy mutton. Thus they prayed and preyed until 4:00, when they struck the trail for a long ride home.

The Drew-Bettis barbecue was not unlike the above description. Tables groaned with an ample spread, and liquor flowed freely. It is said that the outcome of the election was greatly influenced by this picnic, for Pocahontas was chosen as the county seat. Drew and Bettis donated the land on which the new courthouse was built; Drew donated $3,000 and Bettis $1,000 toward the cost of the building. The courthouse has remained on this site ever since, although the original building has been replaced.

Thomas Drew was a successful businessman, farmer, and lawyer and was active in the Democratic Party, but he had no ambition to run for office. His one term as clerk of Clark County had satisfied his desire for public office. Then in 1844 the Democratic Convention elected Elias N. Conway to be the party's candidate for governor. When Conway declined and suggested to the convention they choose his friend Thomas Drew instead, political lightning struck one of Arkansas's best and happiest farmers. Drew, a truthful and open man, won the voters' confidence during the campaign and was elected governor. He served one term and said that because of his personal financial situation he did not want to run for another. The country had come through the panic of 1837; Drew may have lost heavily in railroad investments that were popular at the time. Whatever the reason for his financial woes, he could not support his family on the $1,800 annual salary paid the governor. His friends persuaded him to make the race for reelection, promising that they would see to it that the legislature raised the governor's salary. He won the election, and when the legislature failed to increase his salary he promptly resigned.

Richard C. Byrd became the acting governor and served until a special election was held and John Seldon Roane was elected as Arkansas's fourth governor.

The record of Cinderella Drew as First Lady is sparse. Her husband's inauguration was essentially the same as the two previous ones, with escorts for the governor, a parade of militia, musicians, federal, state, and local officials, representatives of various lodges and societies, groups of private citizens—everybody but the governor's wife. Thus Cinderella finally had something in common with the heroine of the fairy tale; she was left out of the party! The only thing we know about her as First Lady is where she lived. Governor and Mrs. Drew and their children resided on Cumberland Street near Mulberry (now Third) Street.

When Drew resigned in January 1849, it is not certain where the family lived. Presumably they returned to their home near Pocahontas. Records show that on June 1, 1850, Thomas and Cinderella deeded considerable real estate and several slaves to her mother, Mary Bettis, to repay $4,100 they had borrowed from her in 1846.

Drew ceased any political activity, and subsequently his name appears only in deed records where he and Cinderella disposed of their holdings. In 1866 we find him back in Pocahontas, employed as a bookkeeper in a general store at a salary of $200 per month. A part of that was withheld by the store and applied to Drew's overdue account there.

In time he resigned from this job and went back into the practice of law. An arrangement was made whereby the clerk who replaced Drew at the store would board with the Drews for twenty-five dollars a month. This amount was withheld from the clerk's salary and credited to the Drews' account at the store.

Drew was described as being small in stature, kind, and friendly, a gentle and patient man. He was of ordinary ability, but no one ever disputed his integrity. The history of the man is perplexing, unraveled by no amount of prying research. Before he became governor he was an energetic, resourceful businessman and citizen. His life after leaving the governor's office formed a pattern of failure and disappointment. One wonders if the disappointments during the years in office broke his spirit. If not, then what did? This question has haunted historians through the years, but none has come up with a pat answer to the complexities of Drew's life.

Cinderella, the proud, aristocratic lady who began her married life as the mistress of her own plantation and rose to the exalted position of First Lady of the State of Arkansas, was forced in later years to take in boarders to help support her family. It is a matter of record that although the Drews were financially troubled, they were a loving family and their home was a warm and welcoming place. The two daughters were talented musicians, and the home was always filled with the happy sounds of young people. Cinderella and Thomas had six children, five of whom survived to adulthood: Joe, James, Ransom, Emma, and Sadie.

When Cinderella was born no record had been made of her birth, and when she died on November 19, 1869, her death notice was only one line among all other death notices of the day. Yet for a short while she had held one of the highest positions attainable in this state—certainly the highest accessible to a woman of her day.

Fourth Governor (Bachelor)

JOHN SELDON ROANE
1849-1852

WHEN GOVERNOR DREW resigned soon after the beginning of his second term, a special election was held and John S. Roane was elected. He came from a politically active family. One uncle had served as governor of Tennessee and another ancestor had been governor of Virginia. John Roane served as the speaker of the Arkansas House of Representatives and was a brigadier general in the Confederacy. Since he was a bachelor when he served as governor, and history does not name an official hostess for him, we have to skip over this interesting man and his family. He married later and had a family of five children.

ELIAS NELSON CONWAY
1852-1860

ELIAS N. CONWAY served longer than any governor until Orval Faubus. He had a long and distinguished career of public service, and many historians believe he was a better governor than his brother James Conway. Elias had the iron nerve that James lacked, and his long experience in state government enabled him to recognize the state's interest in every situation. He throttled the monster Real Estate and State banks that were bankrupting the state. He practiced rigid economy in government and left the state in a strengthened financial position.

He never married and after retiring from the governor's office lived in virtual seclusion until his death in 1892. He revered his family and surrounded himself with portraits of his brothers and his mother, Ann Rector Conway.

ERNESTINE FLORA LINDE RECTOR
1860-1862

FLORA RECTOR IS described in *The Encyclopedia of the New West* as a

> very highly cultivated musician, of fine intellectual endowments, superior mind, and at once amiable and conspicuous for the devotion to her family, her relations and friends, and for her charity and benevolence. She is a lady of marked personal appearance and beauty. Moreover, she is meritorious, having come from Memphis to support herself rather than be a burden on her father. She taught music and *belle lettres* in Little Rock with great success when a young lady. It was here that Governor Rector met and married her. She has fine clerical capacity, copying thousands of pages without an error, thus being of material help to her husband.

Flora Linde Rector was the daughter of Albert Linde and Felicité Perrine Saubert Linde. Her mother was born in Augen, the so-called Garden Spot of France. She spoke five languages and performed well on the piano, harp, and guitar. Felicité had traveled extensively in Europe and Asia with her father, and they were touring the United States when he died in South Carolina in 1836. Felicité then went to New York, where she married Albert Linde. Later the Lindes moved to Richmond, Virginia, and it was there that Ernestine Flora was born in March 1839.

Flora grew up in Memphis, Tennessee, and was graduated from St. Agnes Academy as valedictorian of her class. Like her mother, she was bilingual and musical. She attended Ripley Female College in Ripley, Tennessee, where she majored in music, and after graduation she became an instructor of music at that institution.

Flora Linde and Henry Rector were married at an Episcopal church in Little Rock on February 11, 1860. The first summer of their marriage was spent in an exciting political campaign, and he was inaugurated as governor on December 15 of that year. Twenty-two-year-old Flora became a bride, mistress of a large house, stepmother to seven children, and wife of the governor all in the same year!

Henry Rector had been born in Kentucky on May 1, 1819, son of Elias and Fannie Thurston Rector. His early years were spent in St. Louis, where his father was postmaster. When his father died and his mother remarried, he lived for a time in northwestern Missouri and worked in the salt mines for his stepfather. Henry came to Arkansas in 1835 to manage the vast land holdings left to him by his father. His property in Hot Springs alone was valued at $250,000.

Rector was a lawyer in Little Rock who carried on an extensive farming operation on his 1,800-acre plantation nearby on the Arkansas River. He and his first wife, Jane Field, niece of Governor John Pope, had built a large home on a half-block of land at Third and Spring streets for their family. Their children were Frank, Ann, William, Julia, Henry, Elias, and Frances. Jane Rector died at the age of thirty-five, after nineteen years of marriage. Three years later Henry and Flora were married.

Henry served one term as United States marshal for the District of Arkansas, two terms in the state senate, one term as a representative, and four years as United States surveyor general of Arkansas, and in 1859 he was elected to the Supreme Court of the State of Arkansas.

In 1860 he was urged to run for governor

against the Family's selected candidate. Although he was indeed related to members of the political Family, he had never become a part of their inner circle. He broke with them, ran as an independent candidate, and won! Some said he won because the other candidates only made pretty speeches, while Rector appealed to the good common sense of the voters. One biographer called Rector a natural orator with a rich vocabulary and a commanding appearance. Many considered him the best debater of his time.

As soon as he was inaugurated, both the Family and the *Arkansas Gazette* took after Rector. The Family usurped powers that rightfully belonged to the governor and interfered with his command of the state militia. They silently and ingeniously rewrote the state Constitution, reducing his term from four years to two. Rector had not intended to run for a second term, but did and was defeated by Harris Flanagin. Disgusted, Rector resigned on November 5 and Thomas Fletcher, president of the senate, served as acting governor until Flanagin took office on November 15, 1862.

When Rector began his term as governor the question of whether to secede was being hotly debated in Arkansas. A secession convention was called but it adjourned when unable to pass a secession ordinance.

The newly completed telegraph service into Little Rock greatly influenced actions in this state during the Civil War period. The first message over the new lines carried an unconfirmed report that additional Union troops were en route to Little Rock to reinforce the arsenal. When the people of Helena heard this they formed up and marched to the rescue. Little Rock residents were met with the surprise spectacle of eight hundred armed troops marching down Main Street. Everyone came out to see the soldiers. Excitement and anxiety filled the air! Governor Rector prevented a battle by calling for surrender of the arsenal to state authorities. The captain in charge of the arsenal was as eager to avoid bloodshed as was Rector. He

quietly withdrew and marched his men to the riverfront, where they boarded a steamboat for St. Louis.

In April 1861 word leaked out that telegraphed orders from President Lincoln directed that all federal funds be taken out of Arkansas. This caused excited speculation that war was imminent. The wires soon crackled with the message that Fort Sumter had been fired upon.

Immediately Governor Rector called for volunteers to go to Fort Smith to demand surrender of that fort, and the secession convention was reconvened. A quiet and subdued crowd gathered in the Capitol and on the grounds to hear the vote counted—sixty-five for and five against secession. After a motion to make the vote unanimous there was one lone hold-out, Isaac Murphy.

On May 20, 1861, Arkansas officially became a Confederate state. Flora Rector watched the city of Little Rock fill up with men willing to go to war, but lacking uniforms. She joined with committees of women who volunteered to gather materials and make uniforms. They worked in shifts day and night, sewing uniforms and underwear and darning socks. Some worked in their homes and others gathered in a store building on Main Street. The women made gallons of salve to treat the soldiers' feet. They arranged musicals to benefit families whose men were away at war. Old men rolled bandages and relayed news. Camp followers came into Little Rock and established brothels, causing a curfew to be imposed on the city. When election time rolled around only a few old men were present to vote; women were not yet enfranchised, and the younger men were away at war.

It was popular to donate goods to a produce-loan run by the Confederacy, and Mrs. Elizabeth Wright, daughter of former Governor and Mrs. Fulton, gave four hundred bales of cotton. Women were urged to donate woolen clothing to be used in the manufacture of cannon cartridges.

Life became progressively worse for women, children, and old men as goods became scarcer and prices higher. Gradually the realities of war began to sink in as loved ones became casualties and the wounded were brought back to Little Rock. They were housed in various buildings over the city, and women were called upon to help nurse and cook. Governor and Mrs. Rector watched Little Rock become one big hospital city with the stench of death everywhere. Women arranged work schedules and organized volunteers as nurses, cooks, and burial crews. More ground was purchased to provide burial space; four buildings on Main Street were taken over for use as hospitals. St. John's College, which had closed from lack of students, offered its building to the state for use as a hospital. St. Mary's, a school for girls, was still operating but offered to close.

After leaving the governor's office, Henry Rector sought to enter the Confederate Army as a commissioned officer. The Family intervened and saw to it that Rector's request was denied. His patriotism was greater than any vindictive feelings he might have harbored, so he simply enlisted as a private and served until the end of the war. His oldest son, Captain William F. Rector, was killed in action at Helena. *The Encyclopedia of the New West* carries a report of his death written by Flora Rector.

He was shot at the head of his command, scaling the breastworks, by a minnie-ball through the lungs. Left on the field in the hands of the victorious Federals he was taken to the house of Mrs. Moore, a friend in Helena, where he shortly afterward died without a murmur of regret, expressing pleasure that he was dying for his country, and in defense of the right of self-government. He was interred in Mrs. Moore's garden, afterwards occupied as a camp ground by the Federals and the grave obliterated, but after the war, his father and brother succeeded in resurrecting the remains and they were re-
interred in the family cemetery in Little Rock. William was a young man of fine appearance and strongly marked character—brave, adventurous, generous to a fault and loving.

Coming as they did during the terrible time of the Civil War, Flora Rector's years as First Lady were among the most difficult of all. In the midst of the trials and trauma of the war and her husband's besieged administration, she gave birth to her only child, Ernestine Flora, in March 1861.

After the war Governor Rector returned home and like everyone else found his business in shambles. He got together a pair of old mules and horses that Union troops had not found worth stealing, and with the aid of two other men he started a freight line to haul cotton. This turned out to be a successful venture. Rector's having to make a fresh start in such a humble manner won for him even greater respect than being elected governor. He turned his attention to farming his lands in Pulaski, Garland, and Hempstead counties, resumed his practice of law, and served as a delegate to the Constitutional Convention of 1874 from Garland County.

This family remained prominent in civic and social affairs of Arkansas all their lives. Mrs. Rector's brother, Dr. Theodore F. Linde, lived in Hot Springs, where he was very active in that city's politics, serving as mayor three terms.

The *Arkansas Gazette* described Flora Rector as "graceful and gracious, universally admired for her graceful accomplishments." After Ernestine's debut into society on December 20, 1879, the *Gazette* reported, "The entertainment given last night by Governor and Mrs. Rector at their elegant mansion on the corner of Spring and Third Streets was one of the most brilliant as well as happy and enjoyable occasions it has ever been our good fortune to attend." The article further reports that the "fashionable young ladies and gentleman" danced until the wee hours and a "most elegant and bounteous supper" was served. A later item in the same newspaper said,

> The party at Governor Rector's last night was like every entertainment at the residence of this distinguished gentleman. An air of enjoyment and greeting of sincerity only found among the class so illustriously represented by Governor and Mrs. Rector, a lady whose presence is a pleasant reminder of southern grace, and Miss Ernestine whose debut into society was characterized by such an acknowledgement some time ago, did not leave unturned a single leaf in welcome's foliage but made everyone enter into the enjoyment which availed all.

Ernestine's wedding to McGehee Williams was the subject of a lengthy article on page one of the December 16, 1880, *Gazette.* The wedding had taken place the morning before at the Rector home. The reporter spoke in glowing terms of the prominence of this couple and their families. The attendants were named and the ceremony and setting were described in detail, including the elegant breakfast and the numerous gifts. The bride was exquisitely dressed in "cream satin trimmed with point lace, orange blossoms and lily of the valley. She wore diamond ornaments."

Flora Rector was loved and respected by her children and her community. When she died in her home on April 3, 1899, after a few days' illness, her stepson, E.W. Rector, a member of the Arkansas House of Representatives at the time, was instrumental in having a resolution passed memorializing her.

Governor Rector died in the last hours of 1899, just before the turn of the twentieth century.

MARTHA ELIZABETH NASH FLANAGIN
1862-1865

MARTHA ELIZABETH NASH Flanagin is the only wife of an Arkansas governor whose husband did not have a long campaign for office. Colonel Flanagin was with the Confederate forces in Tennessee when his friends nominated him as a candidate for governor. Some say he knew nothing of this until the day before election, and others say he learned of his nomination three weeks before the election and came home and campaigned the last few days. However it happened, Flanagin became Arkansas's seventh governor on November 15, 1862.

Martha was born in Prince Edward County, Virginia, on April 3, 1830. When she was four, her parents moved to Tennessee and later to Hempstead County, Arkansas. She was descended from Abner Nash, who with sons John and Thomas immigrated to Virginia from Tenby, in south Wales, to escape religious persecution. Thomas died in 1737 but John and Abner became men of wealth and power in early Virginia. Abner served in the House of Burgesses and John owned a 4,000-acre plantation on the Appomattox and Bush rivers in Prince Edward County. Here he built his home, Templeton Manor, where he lived in grand style. He became justice of the peace, a position of importance in colonial days, and rode to court in princely fashion in his coach and four. He married Anne Owen and they had eight children, one of whom was John Nash, II, the great-grandfather of Martha Nash Flanagin. Martha, whose nickname was "Pat," was the daughter of Phineas Nash and Phoebe Haskins Ligon Nash, and was also one of eight children.

Martha grew up on the plantation established by her parents on the Red River near Harmon, Arkansas. As a young lady she attended an academy in nearby Washington, never thinking that she would someday return to that little city as the wife of the governor.

She became the wife of Harris Flanagin in true fairy-tale fashion; he came riding out of the next county to claim her hand. A friend had reprimanded Harris for never having married, and told Harris that Martha Nash was just the girl for him. The very next day Harris went to her home, introduced himself, and told her family that he had come courting, with marriage in mind! The handsome, successful young lawyer was invited to stay to supper and he proposed that very evening to the tall brunette. She accepted and they were married three weeks later, on July 3, 1851, in an elegant wedding.

Harris had taught school as he made his way from his home in New Jersey, finally settling in Arkansas. He was virtually penniless when he arrived here, but in a few years he had become the owner of almost three thousand acres of farmland, thirteen town lots, and six slaves. He was able to build a lovely colonial home for his bride and to furnish it properly. He ordered hand-carved walnut furniture from Philadelphia which came by boat to New Orleans and up the Ouachita River to Arkadelphia. Many pieces of this museum-quality furniture are still in the hands of family members. Their silver tea service was also ordered from Philadelphia. It had the unusual monogram of "HMF"—"H" for Harris, "M" for Martha, and "F" for Flanagin. He provided her with gold-banded china to serve her family and guests. Martha was cordial by nature and loved to entertain. She was a real asset to her husband, for she was related to many leading families in Arkansas and was herself a leading citizen.

Martha and Harris had three children:

Hand-carved walnut chairs (with seats reproduced from the original) that Harris Flanagin had made for his bride, Martha Elizabeth Nash. The chairs were made in Philadelphia and shipped by river to Arkadelphia, Arkansas. (Photo by Anne McMath)

Jewelry given to Martha Nash Flanagin by her husband. (Photo by Anne McMath)

Duncan, named for Harris's business partner; Nash, named for Martha's family; and Laura, who became the wife of a distinguished Presbyterian minister.

Martha Flanagin was the daughter of a long line of Presbyterian ministers and was a charter member of the Presbyterian church that was organized in Arkadelphia in 1859. She was devoted to her church and her home was always open to any minister. Family history quotes one of the children as saying that Mama got out the "tin frings" (meaning the silver service) when the preachers came to visit!

Martha was talented in music and enter-

tained the children of the family, even after she was quite old, by playing and singing old-time reels and tunes. She was a gracious hostess and a superior cook. One favorite white cake was served so often at Presbyterian socials it became known as the "White Synod Cake." She had learned her baking at her girlhood home where the unusual ingredients of bear grease and partridge eggs were often used. She was artistic in her culinary efforts, and after frosting the cakes with white icing she decorated them with vines, flowers, and rail fences. Another of her specialties was watermelon rind preserves, which she carved in fancy shapes and served in clear cups of citron. The citron cups were intended only as table decoration but were often eaten by guests unfamiliar with the delicacy. Many prominent persons enjoyed Martha's elegant dinner parties.

Mrs. Flanagin must have felt grave concern for her husband as he took office during the troubled war years. State government was in great disarray. It mattered not what new laws the legislature passed, because there was absolutely no money to carry out corrective policies. Tax collections had been suspended. Lawlessness abounded and many people fled the state for points farther west. Flanagin made little headway in coming to grips with the pressing problems.

The people of Arkansas were suffering not only from attacks by bushwackers and guerrillas, but from a real shortage of necessities—especially medicines and clothing. Even the weather became their enemy. The winter of 1863 was famous for its bitter cold. Temperatures remained below freezing for weeks. Several sub-zero readings were recorded, and at Little Rock the Arkansas River remained frozen solid for months.

In January 1863 Arkansas Post surrendered, and that summer so did Vicksburg. On September 10 the first Union troops entered Little Rock. They took control of the government and the newspapers. Shipping routes were reopened and food became more abundant. The Union Army brought

Martha Elizabeth Nash Flanagin. (Photo courtesy of the Southwest Arkansas Regional Archives)

hospital equipment and trained personnel. Little Rock women were relieved of their nursing duties.

When Little Rock fell, Governor and Mrs. Flanagin fled to their home in Arkadelphia and a short time later they went on to Washington, Arkansas, where he set up a government in exile. This became the first of several times in Arkansas history when two men claimed to be governor. A Unionist government had been established in Little Rock, and in March 1864 a new constitution was ratified and Isaac Murphy was elected governor. He sat as governor in Little Rock and Flanagin sat as governor in Washington. Flanagin offered to call a legislative session to repeal all acts of secession and war and then to resign. The Federals refused to negotiate but instead ordered Flanagin to return the state archives to Little Rock. One can

only imagine Martha Flanagin's anxiety as her husband left to meet the enemy. She could not be really certain that he would not be taken prisoner. However, he was allowed to return home safely. He immediately set about to rebuild his law practice. This was a trying time in his and Martha's life. It is widely believed that his early death was brought on by overwork during the next few years. Flanagin died in October 1874 soon after serving as a delegate to the Constitutional Convention, where he assumed a leading role.

Martha, thirteen years younger than he, survived him by thirty years. On April 18, 1904, she died in the home to which she had gone as a bride—a lady much revered for her contribution to the cultural, educational, and religious affairs of her community.

ANGELINA LOCKHART MURPHY
and MALILLA ELIZABETH JANE MURPHY BERRY
1864-1868

ARKANSAS'S EIGHTH GOVERNOR is the same Isaac Murphy who cast the lone "no" vote on the resolution to secede from the Union. Originally the vote was sixty-five for and five against secession. When asked to change their vote in order to make it unanimous, four delegates did so, but Isaac Murphy said, "I have cast my vote after mature reflection, and have duly considered the consequences, and I cannot conscientiously change it. I therefore vote 'No.'" Obviously he was a man of strong will, resolute and unchanging once his mind was made up. He found a girl with the same characteristics in Angelina Lockhart, of Clarksville, Tennessee.

Angelina's parents objected strenuously to Isaac's courtship of their daughter. To Mr. and Mrs. Lockhart, Isaac was a poor itinerant schoolteacher who also claimed to be a lawyer. He came from somewhere up north, had no family or background, was sixteen years older than Angelina, and although he was over thirty was still wandering over the country—not at all an acceptable suitor for their daughter.

Angelina saw a man of quiet good looks, well-educated, kind and genteel; a person of strong character, high ideals, and a great loneliness. She made her decision to marry him no matter the cost. They eloped, and her parents banished her from the family. If, through the years, she longed to see her parents or hungered for a visit with her brothers and sisters, she kept it to herself. Years later one of her brothers did pay her a visit in Fayetteville—the only time after her marriage she saw any of her own family.

Angelina had been born in Tennessee in 1813, the oldest of eight children born to William and Elizabeth Lockhart. Even though all family ties were broken for Angelina Lockhart Murphy, she remained proud of her family name, as well she might. The first Lockhart of record was Sir Simon Lockhart of Lee Castle in Scotland. Clifford Stanly Sims, in his book *The Origin of Significance of Scottish Surnames,* writes that

> the name was originally Locard. The family descended from Sir Simon Locard of Lee, in Lanarkshire, who, in 1329, accompanied Lord James Douglas with the heart of Robert Bruce to Palestine, from this circumstance he changed his name to Lockhart as it was formally spelled, and took for his arms a human heart proper, within a padlock sable, and for a motto "Corda serata pando," which signifies "Lay open the locked hearts."

It is assumed that all Lockharts descend from this man whether the name is spelled "Lockert," "Lockhert," or "Lockhart."

Isaac Murphy was born October 16, 1799, near Pittsburgh, Pennsylvania, to wealthy parents. His father died when Isaac was a small boy and his mother died when he was fourteen. Except for the money spent on education, his guardian made off with his entire inheritance. Penniless, he had come south, where he was to spend the rest of his life.

Angelina and Isaac were married July 30, 1830, in Clarksville, Tennessee, and four years later they and their two children moved to Mount Comfort in Washington County in the Territory of Arkansas. Here they established a home and a school. When the school burned, they moved to Fayetteville, where Isaac set up a law practice and began his political career in addition to teaching. He continued in these endeavors for the next twenty years. When he moved the family to Huntsville, he continued in the practice of law and again established a school, where his two oldest daughters assisted in teaching duties. He was elected to the state senate from this district.

Isaac and Angelina had eight children. Their two sons died in early childhood and three of their six daughters died in early womanhood. The three who survived were Mary, who married H.C. Lowe; Lockhart, who married Reverend Thomas M. Thorpe; and Malilla Elizabeth Jane, who married James R. Berry.

Records show that the Murphy daughters' weddings were held at home. In at least one instance, the attendants were named but no other details were given. However, Josiah Shinn in *Early Days in Arkansas* describes a typical home wedding of that time:

These were the great events of the neighborhood and were celebrated with all the pomp and ceremony. . . . The wedding supper then, given at the house of the bride, meant something to eat, something substantial, wonderfully tasteful and altogether abounding. In the center of a long table, running diagonally across the large old-fashioned generous room, cake stands were placed one above the other to the height of three feet, containing cakes of the most toothsome kind, made at home by cake makers and not bought at a bakery, each tier of cake flanked by rows of small glasses, each filled with a different colored jelly, all topped with a bouquet of hundred-leafed roses, sweet pinks and lilacs. At one end of the table was a young pig cooked whole lying in a dish as you have seen live pigs in a trough, flanked by dressing made savory with sage, thyme and parsley, with a small nubbin or roasting ear held between its feet and nose, and its tail curled saucily over its naked back;

this pig being a thoroughbred of early Arkansas days before modern degeneracy had developed the razorback and straighttailed variety. At the other end a turkey hen sat in state upon a gorgeous platter surrounded by stuffing with hardboiled eggs protruding, as though the foul were preparing to hatch a glorious brood. This was not the modern "nature study" of imitation eggs and learned palaver, but the real turkey on a nest of real stuffing and eggs equally as real and altogether true to nature. Then there was a great platter of cold ham, and that other of sliced lamb, and numerous dishes of chicken salad. . . .

Time fails to enumerate the pyramids of cream potatoes, the bountiful dishes of butter beans and cucumbers, and the huge tureens of gigantic roasting ears. All down the aisles of these substantials were tumblers of stick candy of all colors and sizes, very much like the barber poles that grace the avenues of our city. The only new thing advertised for the occasion were egg puffs, known today as sugar kisses. These were an innovation brought up from New Orleans, and were carried home as souvenirs to furnish social diversion for the following month.

For dessert another huge tureen, holding about ten gallons, contained that savory production called in those days "float" which modern learning classifies as "egg-nog" . . . .

An exact copy of the wedding feast came the next day at the infare, which was held at the home of the groom.

The Murphys might well have celebrated when they could, for the decade that began in 1860 was a nightmare for this family.

1860. Angelina died on February 15 and was thus spared the horrors and heartaches that were to befall her family during the next ten years.

1861. In May, Isaac Murphy cast the only vote against secession, and as a result was so maligned by his neighbors he was forced to leave home and join the Union forces in Missouri for protection. He spent the next eighteen months as a civilian member of General Samuel R. Curtis's staff.

1862. Daughter Mary's husband, H.C. Lowe, died in May as a result of an illness he contracted while fighting for the Confederacy. The fact that he fought for the rebel cause did not prevent neighbors from making life miserable for the family who remained in Huntsville when Isaac Murphy was forced to leave. Daughters Laura, Louisa, Lockhart, and Mary Lowe and her two sons, Willie and Augustus, were victims of much gossip and harassment.

1863. Isaac Murphy was a member of the command staff of Union forces who stopped over in Huntsville for several days. While there, these soldiers took many prisoners, some of whom were leading citizens of the community. The night before this army left Huntsville, twelve of these prisoners were marched out of town and shot by a firing squad. As a result, a new wave of hatred was directed toward the Murphy daughters. Their home was raided and many of their household goods were taken. They were forced to leave their home under guard of a company of Federal troops who saw them safely aboard the train for St. Louis. The trip was so rigorous in the cold weather that Louisa, Laura, and the child Willie became seriously ill. Louisa died on March 1 and Laura and Willie both died on March 13.

1864–1868. Isaac Murphy was elected governor, despite his widespread unpopularity, because only Unionists could vote. He found little pleasure in serving as chief executive of the state, for his term came during the terrible time of transition from war to peace. His was the unenviable task of uniting a people still filled with hate, and of reestablishing a government that had become virtually nonexistent. He met with opposition on all sides.

1870. This tragic decade for the Murphy family ended with the accidental drowning

Angelina Lockhart Murphy. (Photo courtesy of the Arkansas History Commission)

of Geraldine, the youngest daughter. While attempting to cross a swollen creek, her carriage overturned and she was trapped beneath it.

Had Angelina lived to be First Lady, she surely would have been filled with pride in seeing her husband elected to the highest office in his chosen state, and would have fulfilled her duties with characteristic grace and strength. Her family remembers her as a high-spirited woman of courage, who spent her life in loyal devotion to her husband and children.

During his four years as governor, Murphy made his home with his oldest daughter, Malilla Berry, who served as his official hostess. She must have been cut from the same cloth as her mother, for she reared her family and ran her home with the dignity befitting her husband's and her father's positions. The Berry family had moved to Little Rock several years before Murphy became governor. James R. Berry held various positions with the state legislature and was appointed state auditor when Murphy was appointed provisional governor. They both were elected for only two-year terms. At the end of his term as auditor, Berry became private secretary to the governor and served in that position for the balance of Governor Murphy's term.

In his later years James Berry dictated a forty-nine-page memorandum to his granddaughter which is a superb source of information about the life and times of people in Arkansas during this period of our history. It is filled with genealogical history of the Berry, Murphy, Lowe and Lockhart families, and details the arrangements that were made to enable Governor Clayton to become United States senator. He tells of the shenanigans of the election of 1872, when Baxter was declared winner over Brooks in the race for governor.

Berry describes the sparsely furnished governor's office as having a pine desk, one table, a few split-bottom chairs and no carpet. When Governor Flanagin returned the state archives to Little Rock, Berry says for the most part they were dumped into his office and he and his clerks had the responsibility of sorting and returning them to the proper office. He further states:

The expenses of carrying on the Governor's Mansion were for the most part met by me—my wife having in charge, the duty of entertaining etc. In those times we had much company abroad, as well as old friends and neighbors and but little pay for any of it. I had the benefit of getting commissaries at Government prices, but how I passed through those trying times, I scarcely know.

From this we know that Malilla fulfilled her duties as hostess for her family, but there are no details of their social life. Apparently they had a nice home and lived well, even going into debt to do so.

Isaac Murphy died on September 8, 1882. Both he and Angelina were buried in the Huntsville cemetery. Despite the difficulties encountered in the beginning of his term as chief executive, his administration ended on a positive note. He had won the respect of much of his opposition and had rebuilt the state government. It is largely due to his efforts that legislation was passed that established the public school system and the University of Arkansas. Twelve days before he went out of office, Arkansas was readmitted to the Union.

ADELINE McGRAW CLAYTON
1868-1871

ADELINE McGRAW MET her future husband during the Civil War when he was the commanding officer of the Union troops occupying her hometown of Helena. It is believed that they met when the Union officers took over her father's hotel. Adeline, a Rebel to the core, made so much mischief for these men that Colonel Powell Clayton had her arrested, but probably not jailed. Just how this situation turned into romance is not known, but the spunky girl apparently caught the colonel's eye. Soon after the war was over, they were married.

Adeline was one of three daughters born to Captain and Mrs. Ben McGraw. Her father, a hotel keeper and steamboat captain who sailed the Ohio and Mississippi rivers, moved his family to Helena when the daughters were quite young. Two of the girls were born in Virginia, but Adeline was born in Paducah, Kentucky, on January 26, 1843.

Powell Clayton, the son of John and Ann Clayton, was born in Bethel County, Pennsylvania. He is a prime example of the old saying "the acorn does not fall far from the tree," for he followed the example of his forebears by achieving high rank in both the military and politics. Clayton became brigadier general in the Union Army and later served as governor of Arkansas, United States senator, and ambassador to Mexico.

Adeline's life as the wife of Powell Clayton was one of varied experiences, status, and more than her share of strife and turmoil. During the Civil War, Colonel Clayton invested in cotton and realized a sizeable profit which enabled him, along with his twin brothers, to buy Linwood, a large plantation in Jefferson County near Pine Bluff. When he and Adeline married she became mistress of this plantation.

Two years later Adeline was the mistress of a large brick home overlooking the river in Little Rock, the mother of a baby girl, Lucy, and First Lady of the state, for her husband had been elected governor! Still, all was not as idyllic as it sounds. The home was situated on Lincoln Avenue, the street that in those days was called "Carpetbaggers Row" by longtime residents of the city. The street came by this name because many former Federal soldiers who settled in Little Rock after the war lived in the fine homes there. Adeline's friends came from this group of neighbors. She was not accepted by the old established families. To these loyal Confederates she was not only a turncoat, but a Republican turncoat. At times she must have felt very lonely. The Reconstruction period was a time of great political conflict, and her husband was the most controversial figure in Arkansas politics. The years of public service were unusually rugged for Powell Clayton and his family.

Clayton's inauguration as governor took place on July 2, 1868. He and the outgoing governor, Isaac Murphy, rode to the State House in an open carriage drawn by six black horses and were escorted by a troop of mounted soldiers. In his book *The Aftermath of The Civil War,* Clayton describes how the front-row seats at the inaugural ceremonies were occupied by fashionably dressed ladies, chatting and waving their fans, but he does not mention Adeline. It would be reasonable to assume that she was among this group. The other rows of seats were occupied by well-dressed carpetbaggers and scalawags. Standing under the shade trees apart from the crowd, a group of ragged ex-Confederates looked on with contempt.

In a state where bitter campaigns were the norm rather than the exception, the gubernatorial campaign of 1868 was violent in the extreme. As the nominee of the newly formed Republican Party, Clayton endured slander, ridicule, and terrible name-calling from his Democratic opposition. They felt he was a radical opportunist who meant to enrich himself at state expense, and they said so. A suave sophisticate and able speaker, Clayton in turn charged the Democrats with terrorism and scare tactics.

His term in office began in a time of great violence in Arkansas. Most Democrats had lost the right to vote by virtue of having served the Confederacy. Angered at having lost the ballot, they took to the bullet. Murder and terrorism were so widespread that Clayton resorted to the drastic action of calling out the militia to prevent anarchy. The Ku Klux Klan fanned the fires of hate and fear. One of Clayton's militia captains, a congressman, and a Confederate general were among those murdered. Mrs. Clayton knew that her husband's life was in danger, for his bravery often bordered on the foolhardy. She also knew that the political opposition was dedicated to getting rid of him one way or another. Clayton turned to Washington and to the neighboring states for help to stop the killing, burning, and robbery, but no one would provide him with additional arms for his militia. When he finally bought arms he had to charter a steamer to deliver the cargo. The steamer was run aground and the arms pirated. The situation finally cooled down but Clayton's opposition did not. A split within the Republican Party caused him more trouble. The lieutenant governor banded together with several senators and brought criminal charges against Clayton. His three years as governor were filled with serious criminal charges, accusations, investigations, and impeachment proceedings. An Arkansas grand jury indictment even followed him to Washington after he became senator. In later years Clayton said that all these investigations served to enhance his position with the national party. He had shown himself to be a fighter and a survivor. He was a man of steel, of questionable scru-

ples, and he pushed people around as though they were pawns on a chessboard. In spite of his imperious manner, or maybe because of it, he was able to get some very constructive legislation passed during his term in office. Taxes were passed to support free public schools, and funds were provided to reclaim swamplands and build flood control levees along rivers.

Clayton's election to the senate was clouded by a special congressional investigation of "Allegations Against Senator Powell Clayton." Clayton became senator only after it was "arranged" that Secretary of State White and Lieutenant Governor Johnson should resign from office. Johnson then became secretary of state and O.A. Hadley became president of the Arkansas Senate for the express purpose of becoming governor when the state legislature elected Clayton to the United States Senate. These changes were made because Clayton had promised his supporters he would not leave the state in the hands of the hated Lieutenant Governor Johnson. During the congressional investigation of these actions, it was brought out that money had indeed changed hands but testimony indicated that the resignations came about only to "promote party harmony" and that the money was given for legitimate reasons. No one was supposed to notice that one of these men suddenly had no desire to remain in Arkansas and the other was the proud owner of a new plantation!

Adeline Clayton was not the type to turn a deaf ear to the many serious accusations against her husband. She knew of the investigations and of the shady manipulations that took place before her husband's nomination to the senate. This courageous young woman, who had not feared all the Union Army in Helena, who had stood up for her beliefs without thought of consequences, would have demanded to know the truth from her husband. The governor had plenty of explaining to do at home. She was shamed and embarrassed by much of it, and according to family lore the marriage was as stormy

Adeline McGraw Clayton. (Photo courtesy of June Westfall)

as the political career!

Both Adeline and Powell Clayton were strong people, and there were enough good times mixed in with the bad times to keep the couple together. They were thrilled over the birth of their first child, Lucy, born the year he was elected governor. Their son, Powell Jr., was born in 1871, the year Governor Clayton resigned to become United States senator. A second son was born two years later in Washington, D.C., but died in infancy. Two daughters, Charlotte and Kathleen, completed the family.

While living in Washington, the Claytons enjoyed a position of prominence among the nation's leaders. In 1877, when his term as senator was up, the family returned to Little Rock. He had become president of a railroad and it was in this connection that the family moved to Eureka Springs. The years spent there were the happiest of Adeline's life. Her youngest children were almost grown; her husband was free from the tensions of elective office and was a leader in the community. Here, as in her hometown of Helena, she once again had many friends of her own. One woman, Charlotte Luce, became her best friend for the rest of their lives.

Governor Clayton and several other prominent businessmen formed the Eureka Springs Improvement Company. This company was involved in many business ventures—land, hotels, railroads, a gas company, and a stone quarry, to name a few. The activities of the Improvement Company did indeed contribute to the growth and economy of Eureka Springs and made wealthy men of these business partners. Clayton was a leader in this group. They built the magnificent Crescent Hotel, Clayton's brainchild. Through his Washington contacts their limestone quarry received government contracts to provide stone for many public buildings.

The Claytons lived at the Crescent Hotel in the Governor's Suite. The grand opening of this hotel was a gala affair attended by four hundred guests, including the Republican presidential nominee James G. Blaine.

Adeline Clayton was a leader in the sophisticated social life of this small resort city in the Arkansas Ozarks. The ladies of the community lavishly entertained the wealthy people who came to vacation at the fine hotels and to take the healing waters. In typical Gay Nineties style, the visitors would reciprocate with elaborate entertainment at their hotel.

Many people who came to take the waters had very little money and no means of support. To relieve the oppression of these people, Adeline Clayton called on some of her friends to join her in forming the Ladies United Relief Association. This club provided clothes, food, and housing for the needy and even burial for some. So great were the needs of these people, the ladies opened a hospital to care for them, but closed it when they suspected they were inheriting indigents from other communities.

The club was a flourishing organization for the nine years Adeline was its president and leader. When Governor Clayton (she always called him General Clayton) accepted the post of ambassador to Mexico, she continued to send money to her beloved project, LURA. Without her leadership, the club began to flounder and finally disbanded because the caseload was too heavy for the few remaining active members. Out of loyalty to Adeline, they did eventually reorganize.

Powell Clayton served as United States Ambassador to Mexico from 1897 to 1905. He was offered a choice of positions, but selected this post because it would allow him time to retain his position as Republican National Committeeman and to control all political appointments and patronage in Arkansas. He resigned as national committeeman and retired from politics when the Democrats again came into power with the election of Woodrow Wilson in 1912. The Claytons lived in Washington, D.C., until his death in 1914. He was buried with full military honors in Arlington National Cemetery.

Adeline remained high-spirited and direct almost all of her life. In a letter written at the time of the Spanish-American War to her good friend Charlotte Luce, she states in no uncertain terms her opposition to our entry into this war and concludes by saying that "General C. thinks it dreadful the way I feel and think and has forbidden me expressing my opinions outside the family. . . ."

In January 1916 in a letter to the daughter of her friend Mrs. Luce, she shows that she had begun to feel old and tired:

My dearest Lizzie,

Since getting your letter, Kathleen has come to us. Charlotte and Powell knew she was coming. I did not. Looks a lot like she did when here two years ago. Has three months leave of absence from her Red Cross work. Says she has come to take me back to England with her.

I think with dismay of such an upheaval at my time of life. Was 73 the 26th of January. Am like an old cat or some wounded animal that wants to hide before dying.

Can't you understand me? I love my children, each the same but this coming separation from Powell is positive agony, feeling as I do that I shall never see him again.

Adeline and her children maintained a very close, loving relationship all their lives. The daughters were solicitous of her and often expressed their respect for her. The oldest daughter, Lucy, was first married to Fred F. Gilbert, a broker from Chicago who died in 1890. She later married Samuel G. Jones, a career military man who attained the rank of brigadier general in the army. The other two daughters acquired titles when they married men in the diplomatic corps. Charlotte married Baron Ludovic Moncheur, Belgian Minister to the United States, and Kathleen married Sir Arthur Cunningham Grant Duff, an English diplomat.

Powell Clayton, Jr., married the daughter of distinguished Virginia families, Nancy Tayloe Langhorne. Powell Jr. chose a career in the army and was killed in action while stationed at Fort Sam Houston, Texas.

Adeline, the spunky girl from Helena who survived the Civil War, her husband's turbulent political career, and a marriage that was far from tranquil; who held on when her child died; who took in stride the Washington social life; who as wife of the company president traveled the country in queenly style in the luxury of their private railroad car; who presided graciously as the ambassador's wife; who filled her role as mother of Baroness Charlotte and Lady Kathleen, finally had something she could not handle. She often described her relationship with her son as a "closed corporation," and when news came of his death she took to her bed and died. Her obituary in the *Arkansas Gazette* bore a Washington, D.C., January 1917 dateline and gave the place of death as Oxted, England, where she was living with her daughter. The obituary further stated, "Her two weeks illness was ascribed by physicians to shock over the death of her only son, Major Powell Clayton, of Sixteenth U.S. Infantry from injuries received in service at the border." She was survived by her three daughters and a daughter-in-law. She was buried in England.

As far as can be determined, all the descendants of Governor and Mrs. Clayton are the children and grandchildren of Baron and Baroness Moncheur, and all live in Belgium.

The letters I have quoted from Adeline are the property of Mrs. Bernice Cole, a family friend. Adeline's family gave a portrait of her to the people of Arkansas, and commissioned Mrs. Cole to decide where it would hang. She chose the museum in Eureka Springs, the place where Adeline was happiest.

HARRIET PATTON BAXTER
1873-1874

BOTH HARRIET AND Elisha Baxter were born in Rutherford County, North Carolina. Elisha was the sixteenth child in his family of seventeen children, the sixth son of his father's second marriage. His parents were William and Catherine Lee Baxter. Harriet was born in 1830, the third child of Colonel and Mrs. Elijah Patton.

Harriet and Elisha were married in 1849 when she was nineteen and Elisha was twenty-two and already a prosperous merchant. Their future looked bright and secure. Like many people his age, Elisha became restless and decided he wanted to do something different. He blithely gave his interest in the mercantile business to his partner, and took up farming. Of this venture it is said that he did little damage to the land and added nothing to his material wealth! After this unsatisfactory experience, he packed up Harriet and their young son and moved to Arkansas. They settled in Batesville where he and his brother, Taylor R. Baxter, established another mercantile business.

Elisha soon learned that it had been his partner who was responsible for the success of their business back in North Carolina. By nature Elisha was not cut out to be a merchant. He could not say "no" to anyone. Most of his customers owed him money, and few paid their debts. In a little over a year Elisha's ledger showed him to be short on cash and long on experience in the frailties of his fellow human beings. In 1855 he closed his business and used his inheritance and savings to pay his debts. He took a $20-a-month job with the local newspaper to provide a bare living for his family while he studied law.

During these years life was very difficult for Harriet Baxter. Her responsibilities were to establish and maintain a home in this rugged country and to help her husband provide for the family and further his political career, which he had begun when they first moved to Batesville. If Harriet did not complain, it must have been difficult not to. In the six years of their marriage her husband had failed in three attempts at making a living, their savings had been spent to cover his losses, and he had moved her to rough country hundreds of miles from home and family. Her days were filled with the multiple tasks and hardships that faced every settler's wife. It must have seemed a sorry trade for the comfort and security she was accustomed to back home in North Carolina and which she thought was hers when they married.

Gradually, as Elisha's law practice became established, life became a bit easier. They became respected citizens and leaders in the community. He was popular with voters and was always elected by large majorities. He belonged to the Whig Party as long as it was an active national party and then became a Democrat until the Civil War, when he was forced into becoming a Republican.

Baxter did not take part in the events leading up to the secession, for he felt secession would be ruinous to the South. He was a patriot who loved his country, and as he stated in his autobiography, to secede "would be unjust to the Federal Government." A conscientious Union man, he tried to live in the South and remain on neutral ground—not reckoning with the passion of the masses who, in the whirlwind of revolution and war, lost tolerance for anyone not fighting for their all-encompassing cause. When General Curtis, with 20,000 Federal troops, marched into Arkansas and through Batesville, he offered Baxter command of a Union regiment, which Baxter refused. As word of the offer spread after the departure of the Federal troops, Baxter's neighbors and former friends advised him in no uncertain terms to leave also. In fact, they were very explicit in saying where he could go. They, who were giving husbands, fathers, and sons to the Cause, drove Baxter from home and family. He escaped into Missouri, where later he was captured by Confederates and arrested as a traitor. He evaded the hangman's noose by breaking out of prison and stealing away like a convict. He lived off the land until he reached Union lines in Springfield, Missouri, where he joined the Union Army. The quiet noncombatant finally realized he had to join the fight. He raised the Fourth Arkansas Mounted Infantry for the Union Army and served as colonel in command. Through the power of the bayonet, Baxter returned to Arkansas in triumph when Little Rock was occupied. Governor Murphy cut short Baxter's military career by appointing him to the state Supreme Court.

Shortly thereafter, the legislature elected Baxter and William Meade Fishback to the United States Senate, but they were not allowed to take their seats. There is no record of how Harriet felt or thought during these heartbreaking and perilous times. We do not know what misery the neighbors dealt her and the children after they forced Elisha to leave home. It seems unlikely that they would have treated her kindly. Whatever the situation, she survived it and was by her husband's side when he took office as governor.

The decade of the Civil War and Reconstruction were the worst times in the history of this state. Elisha Baxter's term as governor ended the Reconstruction Era. He had been elected in a bitterly fought campaign against Joseph Brooks, a fellow Republican from a different faction within the party. It took two months to count the vote, and after the vote was thrown out from several counties, Baxter was shown to have the majority. He took office on January 6, 1873.

The women who served as First Lady dur-ing this decade faced trials not experienced before or since. There is no way to accurately determine which governor's wife had the most difficult time, but Harriet Baxter had more than her share of tribulations. It could be argued that her husband's time in office was the worst of all. After he had been governor for a year, the politicians learned they could not control him and decided they had supported the wrong man. All his opposition banded together and took action to have him removed from office and Brooks installed as governor. This resulted in a month-long bloody war known as the Brooks-Baxter War. Brother was pitted against brother, Democrat against Democrat, Republican against Republican. One Confederate general headed the Baxter troops and another headed the Brooks troops. To quote the historian Josiah Shinn, "It was the devil to pay and no pitch hot!" This sad chapter in our history will not be retold here. There are several sources of detailed accounts available.

Harriet Baxter had to live through the horror and mortification of having her husband physically removed from office by an armed band of the Brooks men. Brooks was sworn in as governor by the same man who had sworn Baxter in a year earlier. Brooks then took over the governor's office in the Capitol, and Baxter set up a governor's office in St. John's Seminary and war headquarters in the Anthony Hotel. Harriet Baxter was reliving the hideous nightmare that was hers during the Civil War. Once again she feared for her husband's life, and once again that threat came from fellow citizens. Once again she and her children were not safe in their own home. She feared to open her door to anyone, for she did not know who was friend or foe. Yet she had to answer any knock, for the only way she could get news of her husband was by messenger—and that wasn't often, because it was unsafe for anyone to be on the streets of Little Rock. The Baxters lived at Fifteenth and Spring streets, an isolated area. The house was surrounded by woods and situated some distance back from the road. The location had been selected to give the family privacy, but during the political war it would have been comforting for Harriet to have had a sympathetic neighbor.

Baxter's advisers worked around the clock and some did not return to their homes until the war was over a month later. Baxter was again declared governor, but not before fifty people were killed or wounded. A congressional investigation of this upheaval concluded that things were best left alone in Arkansas! Arkansas politics was not only the hottest thing north of the equator, it was positively dangerous. Harriet Baxter no longer felt any thrill or honor in being the governor's wife. She just wanted to go home to Batesville, where she felt safe and knew who her friends were.

Harriet Baxter, the mild-mannered lady whose only interest was home and family, was probably much relieved to be out of public life. Although Elisha Baxter served as a Republican governor, the Democrats nominated him as their candidate to succeed himself in office. He declined, probably at the behest of Harriet. She probably told him, "No thanks, I don't care for any more!"

When the children were all grown and married, the Baxters moved from their plantation home into the town of Batesville, where they lived the remainder of their lives. They both died near the turn of the century and are buried in Batesville. They had six children—Millard, George, Edward, Catherine, Fannie, and Hattie. Edward was a highly respected doctor in Melbourne, Arkansas, and outlived all his brothers and sisters.

Mrs. Jacoway quotes a granddaughter as saying,

> In regard to my grandmother's life we can give you nothing of great interest, as she was just the sweetest, quietest, and the most home-loving and home-keeping

woman in the world, her husband and children absolutely making her entire universe. The fact that they adored her speaks volumes for her life as a wife and a mother.

The Encyclopedia of the New West describes Governor Baxter as a man with a strong natural sense of goodness and a dread of violence that was manifest throughout his life. He was a "good and upright judge but when aroused he is a man of courage, and has the will to follow his own judgment." Harriet is described as a domestic woman of the old style—lacking much interest in society, but "esteemed by all within the circle of her associations." She is further described as having "every trait that constitutes the excellent wife, mother and neighbor."

It is striking how many times in Elisha Baxter's life he was forced to do something. He was forced into the study of law when he failed to earn a living by either farming or merchandising; he was forced to take a job in the newspaper business in order to support his family; he was forced to change his political affiliations, not once but twice; he was a gentle man who did not want to fight with anyone but was forced to become a military man; he, who as a lawyer and a judge was accustomed to upholding and enforcing the law, was forced to live outside the law like a common criminal; he was forced out of the governor's office, and won it back by force. Harriet, who is often described as compliant and domestic, may have been forced into those attitudes in order to survive. The hand that fate dealt her husband was a hard hand to play. The only way for her to survive it was to concern herself completely with her home and to remain aloof from the firing line that was her husband's career. She undoubtedly was a woman of great courage and enormous inner strength.

SARAH VIRGINIA SANDERS GARLAND
1874-1877

THE EMINENT ARKANSAS historian, Dallas T. Herndon, described Augustus Hill Garland as one of the ten most important men in early Arkansas history.

Augustus Garland served in both the house and senate of the Confederate Congress and was governor of Arkansas, a United States senator, and United States attorney general, the only Arkansan to hold a cabinet post. He was a leader in the Secession Convention of 1861 and exercised great influence in the 1864 and 1874 Constitutional Conventions.

During the Brooks-Baxter War, Garland more than any one man was responsible for the restoration of order and the return of Baxter to the governor's office. He persuaded President Grant to intervene in this civil war, but Grant passed the final decision to the Arkansas legislature. This played right into Garland's hands. For some time he and his friends had been filling any vacancy in the Republican-held house and senate with fellow Democrats. The legislature, now controlled by Democrats, held that Baxter was the rightful governor. The Democratic Party was returned to power and Garland was acclaimed a champion of freedom and democracy.

He won national fame as a result of his case, *Ex Parte Garland,* in which he challenged the constitutionality of the Iron Clad Oath Law. Under this law any southern attorney who had been loyal to the Confederacy was barred from practice in federal court. With the help of United States Senator Reverdy Johnson of Maryland, Garland had obtained a presidential pardon, but the disbarment still rankled. He filed suit to regain his rights. When he argued and won his case in the Supreme Court, he restored the rights of all southern lawyers. This decision won national recognition for Garland as a lawyer

and set a precedent for undoing much of the *ex post facto* legislation passed during the latter part of the Civil War and immediately afterward.

Garland's success on behalf of Baxter, his newly acquired national fame, his outstanding record in the Confederacy, and his leadership in both the secession and constitutional conventions made him the logical choice as leader of the Democratic Party in Arkansas.

In 1874 he ran for and was elected to the office of governor of Arkansas.

When Garland took office as governor, he found that Reconstruction had left the state $17 million in debt. When he left office this debt had been substantially reduced. He reorganized state government to comply with the new constitution; he was an active supporter of the Arkansas Industrial University at Fayetteville and had legislation passed that established Branch Normal College in Pine Bluff and the schools for the deaf and blind. He appointed a large number of blacks to fill important posts in his administration, including W.H. Gray, whom he named commissioner of state lands.

Augustus Garland was known for his humane spirit. He was possessed of strong convictions and doggedly pursued an objective until he conquered. His innate abilities plus his heritage and training made him exceptionally well-qualified to assume a position of leadership on either state or national levels. A skilled speaker, he was a willing servant of the people even to the detriment of his own law practice. His untiring efforts on behalf of good government and his devotion to the Democratic Party made him in demand by the people for public office. Immediately after the Civil War, he was elected to the United States Senate but was not allowed to take his seat. He served two terms as governor and then was once again elected to the United States Senate. He resigned as senator in 1885 to become United States Attorney General when appointed by President Grover Cleveland. He refused all offers to run again for the senate when his term as attorney general was over. Instead he chose to remain in Washington, D.C., to resume his practice of law and to spend time writing. On January 26, 1899, he collapsed while arguing a case before the Supreme Court and died a few minutes later. He was buried in Mount Holly Cemetery at Little Rock.

Gus Garland's parents, Barbara and Rufus Garland, moved to Arkansas in 1833 and settled on the Red River in Lafayette County (now Miller). Rufus died a young man. They had eight children, four of whom reached maturity: Elizabeth, John, Rufus, and Augustus. Barbara Garland's second marriage was to Major Thomas Hubbard, a prominent lawyer in Washington, Arkansas. He was a very attentive stepfather to Barbara's children and was a guiding force in Augustus's decision to study law.

Augustus's mother was a highly respected, well-educated lady of keen intellect. She was urged to run for governor in her own right, a rare compliment during the mid-nineteenth century when it was considered improper for women to concern themselves with anything outside the home. She equated education with success and gave her children every advantage. At fourteen Augustus had finished all the local schools and was sent to boarding school to continue his studies. He graduated from college with honors at the age of seventeen and returned home, where he taught school for one year, studied law, and worked as a deputy clerk under his future father-in-law, Simon Sanders.

Sanders had moved his family from North Carolina to Arkansas, first to Columbus and then to Washington, where members of his wife's family had settled. Dr. James Walker, Ephriam Myrick, and their families were leading citizens of the area. The future First Lady, Virginia Sanders, grew up in a warm circle of parents, siblings, aunts, uncles, and lots and lots of cousins.

By the time Virginia had become a teenager, life in her hometown of Washington had reached a high degree of sophistication and ease. The little town was enjoying the golden years prevalent over the South before the Civil War. The five hotels had dinner menus and wine lists; there was talk of building an opera house for the many theatrical troupes that came there and used the courthouse as their auditorium. Streets teemed with buggies and carriages pulled by teams of fine horses in shining harness. The newspaper advertised a new shipment of ladies' clothing from New York, Boston, and New Orleans—laces, silks, doeskin gloves, and French kid boots. For the gentlemen of the town there were vests of either black or printed satin, white Marseilles or embroidered linen to go with linen shirts, and doeskin or French Cassimere pants. Mary Medearis, in her book *Washington, Arkansas,* describes the town's social life: "There were fox hunts in the moonlight. There were formal-dress balls in the houses on the plantation—more balls in the houses in Washington—there were hoopskirts and candlelight, shining silver dishes on the rosewood and mahogany sideboards. . . ."

Life in Arkansas had progressed past the point of mere survival. Time, effort, and money could now be spent on a good education, and the wealthy could afford to travel. Such was the case with Simon Sanders. In 1851 he took daughters Virginia and Zenobia, then sixteen and fourteen, on a trip east. They stopped over in Culpepper, Virginia, to visit relatives, and the girls were thrilled with their cousin, Zenobia (Nobia) Simms, who joined them for the remainder of the trip and returned to Arkansas with them. They arrived back home in December 1851. After spending weeks bumping over rough roads in a stagecoach it would seem unlikely that these girls would care for any more travel

Home where Virginia Sanders spent happy girlhood years in the then-flourishing town of Washington, Arkansas. (Photo courtesy of the Southwest Arkansas Regional Archives)

soon, but the very next day they rode the nine miles to Dr. Walker's home to reunite with their cousins. A series of welcoming and holiday parties began. To quote Mrs. Medearis again, "there were balls in the plantation home of the Walkers at Columbus, and musicales in the parlor of the Myrick home out on the Southwest Trail, and literary readings in the library of the Sanders home in Washington." This round robin of socials kept up, and Cupid must have attended every function, for in February the weddings began. Augustus and Virginia were not among the twosomes, but his brother Rufus married Isabelle Walker and Zenobia Simms married Robert Walker—Dr. Walker's son by his first wife. When sixteen-year-old Nobia wrote home to tell her parents of her pending marriage to young Robert, the news was met with consternation. Her father immediately dispatched Captain Joe D. Brown, a bachelor cousin, to ride to Arkansas and bring the young lady home. Once he arrived in Washington, he had such a good time he

stayed to dance at their wedding! When he returned to Virginia he gave a glowing report of the bridegroom, and all opposition to the match vanished. Virginia was a bridesmaid at this double wedding and Augustus was his brother Rufus's best man.

Virginia Sanders, a belle of Washington society, and Augustus Garland were married the next year—1853. He was admitted to the bar the same year, and began the practice of law with his stepfather. A few years later he was invited to become a law partner of Judge Ebenezer Cummins in Little Rock. Judge Cummins had a large practice, and when he died one year later, Gus Garland came into possession of one of the most lucrative law practices in Arkansas. He interrupted his practice to serve in the Confederate Provisional Congress, moving his family from Little Rock to Richmond, where they lived during the four years of the war.

After returning to Little Rock he built a large two-story home at Fourteenth and Scott streets (now known as the Garland-Mitchell

Governor and Mrs. Augustus Garland and child. (Photo courtesy of the Arkansas History Commission)

House). During the early days of the Brooks-Baxter War, Virginia was disturbed one evening by a late-night knock on the door. Gus had retired early, but she had stayed up to write letters. She took a lamp and answered the door to a delegation from the Baxter forces. She invited them in and awakened Gus, who dressed and came downstairs to meet with the men. They had come to solicit his help in returning Governor Baxter to office. He reluctantly went with them to a meeting at their headquarters at the Anthony Hotel and did not return home for six weeks!

Virginia spent many restless days and sleepless nights worrying and wondering about her husband, for these were perilous days of actual war in the streets of Little

Rock. Finally Gus returned home, quite the hero for his valiant efforts in returning peace to the city and restoring faith in the future.

In 1870 he bought a 12,000-acre plantation he named Hominy Hill, a few miles southwest of Little Rock. He and Virginia Garland spent many happy days in seclusion there.

Augustus Garland was elected governor in 1870 and remained in that office until he was elected to the United States Senate in 1877.

Virginia Garland was a pretty woman, a true Old South aristocrat. Her girlhood days in the highly cultivated society of Washington prepared her well for her role as wife of a prominent lawyer and First Lady. She was quite at ease in assuming her duties as wife, mother, and hostess. Although always somewhat frail and retiring, she was a source of strength and inspiration to her husband and family. She was never able to fill her role as wife of the senator, for she died at her home on Christmas Eve 1877. Augustus Garland never remarried. He was a romantic and a sentimentalist. Some time after Virginia's death he returned to visit Dr. Walker's old home, where he and Virginia had courted. In her book Mrs. Jacoway reports that Senator Garland told his young host on that day: "Boy, this yard is holy. My wife sat under this tree and talked to me. She gave me a rose from this bush, and by that right hand column of the front porch she sat when she promised to marry me. It will some day be yours. Never do a thing to mar it."

SUSAN ELIZABETH BEVENS MILLER
1877-1881

SUSAN ELIZABETH BEVENS was born at Morgantown, North Carolina, on June 20, 1829, the daughter of Catherine Elizabeth McGuire Bevens and William C. Bevens, descendants of early settlers of this country. Through her mother, Susan descends from William Sharpe, one of the fifty-five delegates to the Continental Congress. Her father was a native of South Carolina, and was a descendant of some of that state's earliest settlers.

William Read Miller was Arkansas's first native-born governor, but his wife, Susan, had lived in North Carolina and Texas before the family finally settled in Batesville, Arkansas. Susan's father was orphaned at an early age and his was a lonely struggle of survival. He was an ambitious young man and succeeded in getting a good education. He began the study of law, but gave it up for a gold-mining venture that failed. He then entered the mercantile business in Greenville, North Carolina, and was phenomenally successful. In Susan Bevens Miller's personal memoirs she told about these happy years in Greenville. She remembered driving out to their farm with her father behind a pair of high-stepping bob-tailed ponies, her first days at school, and her first piano recital.

The crash of 1837, coupled with the loss at sea of an entire cargo of merchandise, was a severe blow to her father's business. He decided to sell out and move to the new Republic of Texas, where he hoped to make another fortune. In 1840, when Susan was eleven, they left Greenville, traveling by carriage, steamer, and train, and arrived in New Orleans one day too late to take the packet to Texas. There was a smallpox epidemic in New Orleans, and rather than wait two weeks there for the next packet, Bevens booked passage for his family on a schooner bound for Matagorda Bay, Texas, a port about halfway between Galveston and Corpus Christi.

They sailed into the path of a hurricane and were tossed about like a toy in the rough seas for days. When the sailors gave up all hope of surviving the storm, they gathered in the cabin to drown their sorrows before they drowned at sea! Susan's father bribed the helmsman to go back on duty and sat with him all through the night to make sure the man didn't rejoin the drinking party. Susan and her mother and sisters spent the night below in a pitch-dark cabin with one of the children who was seriously ill. There was fear the little girl would not live through the night. The next morning the storm had abated somewhat, the sick child was better, and the passengers were able to gather together for breakfast. The feeling of deliverance was soon broken by the cry of "Man overboard!" Little Susan looked out in time to see a man with arms outstretched in a plea for help, just before he was swamped by the heavy seas—a shattering image for a little girl already scared out of her wits.

After fourteen days at sea the little schooner finally landed at Matagorda. Bevens had invested heavily in foodstuffs both to feed his family and to sell at a profit to the frontier people. This investment had been lost in the storm—most of it had been thrown overboard to lighten the ship and the rest was soaked with salt water and ruined. The loss caused the family to be quite short on supplies and money. They made their way overland, reaching Austin around the middle of the summer. Bevens went to work for the government, and the family could have been on the road to prosperity again except that the change in climate caused them all to fall ill, as Susan said, "terribly ill—too sick to even wait on each other."

Bevens realized his situation in Austin was not going to produce the future he desired for his family. When they were all finally well, he made the difficult decision to leave them in Austin and went to Houston to resume his study of law. Mrs. Bevens found it very hard to adjust to frontier life, but did what she could to ease the family's financial distress by taking in sewing and selling her draperies, linens, and silver.

In Austin the family continued to suffer illnesses, but a worse threat was Indian raids. One day a neighbor running past their house told them what the alarm meant and that they should hurry to the fort for safety. Her father grabbed up Susan's little sister, who was ill, and her mother snatched up the baby. Although Susan was very sick, she had to run to safety on her own. They made this mad dash several times that fall, and became rather accustomed to the overnight stay in the fort. Indian raids would not have caused the family to leave Texas, but the threat of a Mexican attack did. People in Austin had heard about the siege of the Alamo, and when word came that a Mexican attack was imminent, the town emptied in one day. Those who could, rode, and those who could not ride walked out of town. The Bevens family could not leave because sister Harriet was very sick and Papa was away. He showed up the next morning during breakfast with a carryall. They hurriedly packed a few necessities and put a bed in for Harriet, and the family of six piled in the carryall and left as fast as they could. They left breakfast dishes on the table, the cow and chickens in the yard, and abandoned their home and furniture, never to see it again. Her father rode all day with a loaded gun across his lap lest trouble with Indians arise along the way. They arrived at the home of a relative in Louisiana and remained there two weeks while Harriet recovered. From there they went to Batesville, Arkansas, where they lived with Mrs. Bevens's brothers for a year while Bevens returned to Houston to finish law school. When he was admitted to the bar,

the family established a home at Liberty, Texas, on the Trinity River.

The new law practice soon became very prosperous, the country was beautiful, and the family was again together, their hopes raised for a bright future, when tragedy struck—malaria! The entire family was stricken. Susan's mother almost died; she was expecting a child at the time. When little Loutie was born in March and Mrs. Bevens had not recovered by May, her doctor advised the family to return to the East. On this trip, the fourth crossing of the Gulf by the family, sixteen-year-old Susan had the full responsibility of her invalid mother and her new little sister. She became a second mother to this child, and a strong bond formed between the two that lasted until Loutie's death years later. When the family arrived in New Orleans they found the Mississippi River overflowing in the great flood of 1844. As they sailed up the river, they were saddened by the sight of houses and barns floating past them down the river. When it was necessary to change boats they had to wait two weeks for the floodwaters to recede, because they were changing to a smaller boat that could not handle the flood. After a few days at a hotel, a near relative invited them to be her guests. They accepted and were royally entertained. Finally they embarked on a tiny steamer called "The Bee"—the smallest steamboat Susan had ever seen. She said that after two weeks, most of which was spent tied to a tree, they finally arrived at her Uncle Ed McGuire's plantation eighteen miles below Batesville. He was their "rich uncle" who owned thousands of acres of rich bottomland and nearly a hundred slaves. After a few days' visit they went on to Batesville, where they eventually settled.

Bevens established a law practice that afforded a good living for him and his family. He became a leading citizen of Batesville and was elected to the state legislature and later a circuit judgeship, a post he held for several terms. Judge Bevens was a strict Presbyterian who saw to his children's proper upbringing and education. The children grew up and married in this small, peaceful, southern town.

After Bevens was elected judge, he bought a farm in the Oil Trough Bottoms and built a large house set well back from the White River. Susan and William Read Miller were married in 1848. They bought a farm adjoining her father's, and when her husband received an appointment to fill an unexpired term as state auditor, Susan and the children remained in their home. Her two sisters were not yet married and the girls had a happy time visiting back and forth between the two houses only a mile apart. Susan's house was close enough to the river to be in danger during flood times. Once she and Harriet were caught in the rapidly rising waters and had to wade knee-deep to get back to her parents' home—two very frightened girls.

In 1857 when William Miller was elected to a full term as auditor, he and Susan and the children moved to Little Rock. In December 1859 Susan's little daughter Harriet died of diphtheria and a few months later her sister Harriet died. The next December her son Laddie died of the same disease; in quick succession came the death of her daughter Kate and her beloved little sister, Loutie. Susan was left with only two children, Lou and Effie, and Lou was ill. In desperation, she gathered up her children and went home to visit her parents.

The Civil War had begun and a regiment of Confederate soldiers was camped nearby on the Bevenses' farm. Two-thirds of the regiment came down with the measles, and Judge and Mrs. Bevens took twenty-five of them into their home. They and Susan joined in the nursing duties until Susan's mother caught pneumonia and nearly died. During her recovery word came that the Yankees were marching toward Batesville, so once again the Bevens family had to flee the enemy and abandon home and property, never to return.

They packed two wagons and a carriage and were joined by others for the hazardous trip to Little Rock. They were following the route used by the Confederate Army when crossing Arkansas. The heavy traffic of the army coupled with the spring rains had turned the roads into an impassable mire—mules had been known to drown in some of the mudholes. Somehow this valiant group managed to survive, and when they arrived at Susan's home in Little Rock, it looked like heaven to them. They thought they would never leave. In preparation to wait out the war, Susan, her sister Kitty, and their father unstacked a pile of firewood, hid 1,500 pounds of meat, hams, and bacon in it and restacked it all in the darkness of night. This was to supply the family while the menfolk were off to war. When it came time to part, the men decided that it was not safe for the women and children to remain in the city and persuaded the ladies to leave. Each lady was allowed to pack her own wagon with one carpet, three rocking chairs, her beds, dishes, and crockery, and all the books there was room for.

They left Little Rock in June and went as far as Chalybeate Springs, where the state government had taken refuge. Susan was reunited with her husband, who was then state auditor. In September the government and all the families moved to Hempstead County when they heard that the Federal army was closing in. In this new location their servants built cabins for everyone, and the groups remained there long enough to make a crop. Again word came that the Federals were advancing, and it became necessary to move on. They did not want to leave, for they were comfortable and had made many friends in the area, but they also felt they should take the servants to a place where later on they could be self-supporting. The family of refugees headed for Texas.

William Miller joined his family for this trip. Once when they stopped to make camp, they felt they were far enough into Texas to be safe without posting overnight guards. Bevens and the servants who had been shar-

A miniature of Susan Bevens Miller. (Photo courtesy of William Read Miller)

A portrait of Governor William Read Miller painted by his wife, Susan. (Photo courtesy of William Read Miller)

ing this duty needed a good night's sleep. It was the custom to separate a week's supply of provisions and put them in the cook's wagon, and also have the servants cook enough on Saturday to last through Sunday and thus give them a day of rest. When the group awakened on this Sunday morning they found the cook wagon had been robbed of provisions and Sunday dinner. Miller's horse was gone, as were certain other items such as boots and shoes. The worst of all was that the sifter and all the pots and pans had been taken. Preparing meals the remainder of the trip was a double nightmare. From this they learned to station their wagons in a circle for protection.

Refugees from all over the South had swarmed into Texas like blackbirds and it was very difficult to find a home. This group finally settled in Corsicana, where Bevens used his teams to run a freight line to support the family. The women spent their time learning to make do and make over, for by now their supply of necessities had dwindled to a dangerously low level. Susan even learned to make shoes! At Christmas they wanted to invite guests to dinner, but they had no oven large enough to cook a turkey or roast a pig and refused to have a "dining" without one or the other. Finally Susan remembered that her cedar chest had a tin lining, so an oven of sorts was fashioned and they had an elegant Christmas dinner even though they had to borrow a few dishes. Susan said these were happy days and that she loved to think back on those last days with her parents.

When they realized the war was almost over and the Rebel cause was lost, the group considered going on into Mexico to live. Sick children delayed their departure, and by the time the children were well they had decided to remain among their own countrymen rather than go into a strange land. They once again headed for Arkansas in spite of Susan's and her sister Kitty's urgings to stay in Texas. The girls liked the area and were tired of moving.

William Read Miller was born on a farm near Batesville, Arkansas, one of seven children in the family of Mr. and Mrs. John Miller. In 1814 a small colony of four families migrated from Virginia and settled in the Batesville area. Governor Miller's grandfather, Simon Miller, was one of these four early settlers. Thus Governor Miller was the third generation of his family to live there, and the first governor of Arkansas who was born and brought up in the state that he was destined to lead. He was a precocious youngster and expressed an early interest in law and politics, much to his parents' chagrin. During the presidential campaign in 1836, when William was only thirteen, he saw Mr. C.F.M. Noland, an enthusiastic Whig, on the street in Batesville and shouted, "Hurrah for Van Buren!" Mr. Nolan replied, "Hurrah for a jackass!" Whereupon young Billy promptly called back, "That's right, Fent, you holler for your candidate and I'll holler for mine!" These actions by a young upstart won him the lifelong devotion of his fellow Democrats. His admirers predicted that someday the boy would be governor, and his detractors thought the young whippersnapper would never amount to a hill o' beans!

William was twenty-three and already making a name for himself when Susan's family came to live in Batesville. He became county clerk in 1848 and he and Susan were married the following year. He resigned as county clerk in 1854 to accept an appointment from Governor Elias Conway as state auditor, an office Miller held off and on for years.

Unlike many who are elected governor, the Millers were not faced with the problems of moving to the capital city and becoming established in a new community. They had lived for years at their home on the southwest corner of Third and Arch streets, were longtime members of the Second Presbyterian Church, and had a wide circle of friends. It was an easy matter to add the duties of the governorship to their lives when he was elected in 1877. Having served in public office for so many years, both were prepared for the demands that would be made on them when Miller became governor. Susan was a charming First Lady who graciously handled her official duties.

At the end of Governor Miller's term an *Arkansas Gazette* editorial described him as a distinguished son of Arkansas who as an orator had many superiors. However, it said, as "a man of judgment he has no superior in the State and few equals." This glowing editorial further stated that no governor had a better record and that Governor Miller left "not a single blot on his record book." He was always elected by a large majority. His popularity was due to his integrity and executive ability—qualities attributed to him by friend and foe alike. His fellow citizens honored him by electing him to public office over and over. He was respected as a man with the courage of his convictions who did not wait for the political weathercock to give him direction.

Susan Miller was a devout Christian and a tireless worker in her church. She was a student of the Bible, with a talent for teaching which she used in the Sunday school department of her church. A son described her as being "gentle—gifted—good" and above the average woman of her time in intellect and education. She strived to improve herself and to use her talents, yet she did not aspire to leadership. She never wavered from her proper upbringing even through all her difficulties, running her home with grace and gentle firmness. She met her responsibilities not out of a sense of duty, but because she loved being a wife and mother. She and Governor Miller had seven children, four of whom lived to maturity: Louisa, Effie, William Read, and Hugh.

When Governor Miller died in November 1887, Mrs. Miller moved to Richmond, Virginia, to live with married children until her death in that city on August 10, 1905. She and Governor Miller are buried in Mount Holly Cemetery in Little Rock.

ANNE MARIA SEVIER CHURCHILL
1881-1883

WITH THE EXCEPTION of the Izards, the Churchills were the most sophisticated and worldly of any of the gubernatorial couples who had held the office up to this date.

Anne Sevier was born in Little Rock, attended a fashionable girls' school in Georgetown, socialized at the White House, made her debut in Kentucky, and returned to Little Rock for a stylish wedding to her dashing army lieutenant, Thomas Churchill.

Thomas Churchill was born on the family plantation near Lexington, Kentucky. He graduated from St. Mary's College at Bardstown and received his law degree from Transylvania University in Lexington. When the Mexican War broke out he enlisted as a lieutenant. If he had any vestige of boy left as he rode off to war, it was lost in the saddle between Kentucky and Mexico City. A Mexican military prison provided further sobering effect and erased the last trace of small-town Southerner. Churchill returned from the war lean, tall, tan, and tough, with a look in his eye of having seen things that could not be talked about.

En route to Mexico, he stopped over in Little Rock, where he was entertained in the home of Federal Judge Benjamin Johnson. Here he saw a miniature of Anne and was charmed by her beauty. Judge Johnson explained that this was his granddaughter and the daughter of United States Senator Sevier. The lieutenant remarked that he would like to meet her, little realizing that someday he actually would.

After graduating with honors from finishing school, Anne went to Lexington, Kentucky, to visit relatives who sponsored her formal debut into society. It was at the Presentation Ball that she met the handsome lieutenant. He immediately fell in love with the girl with the sparkling eyes whose picture he had seen in her grandfather's parlor in Little Rock. The social whirl of debutante parties afforded him many opportunities to pursue his enthusiastic courtship. It was all cut short when word was received that Anne's father, who had retired and was living on his plantation near Little Rock, was seriously ill. She immediately made plans to go home. Thomas would not allow her to make the dangerous boat trip alone. He went with her and they were grieved to learn that the senator had died on New Year's Eve just before they arrived at the plantation. The year was 1848. Thomas served as a pallbearer at the funeral and remained for some time to comfort Anne through this time of sorrow. The two were very much in love, but Anne was only nineteen and she felt that a long engagement would be proper. Thomas reluctantly agreed to the two-year wait and returned home to Kentucky. Within months he heard rumors that Anne had another suitor. Thomas Churchill buckled on his long-barrelled pistol and came to Little Rock to eliminate his rival, real or imagined. The rival disappeared when Thomas appeared on the scene, and Cupid won out, for soon—on July 31, 1849—there was a wedding in the rose-bedecked parlor of Anne's grandfather's stately home.

This house has appeared earlier in these pages. Judge Johnson bought it from Robert Crittenden after Crittenden's unsuccessful campaign for Congress in 1833. Judge Johnson further enlarged and embellished the house, making it even more beautiful. There were flower and vegetable gardens and an orchard on the estate. An alley of cedars led up to the imposing front door. Gaslights had been installed, the first in any residence in Little Rock. It was a spacious home and the scene of entertainment for many famous visitors.

The wedding trip was a two-day stage-coach journey to the village of Hot Springs. In an article by Christina Williams McCorkle, published in the *Arkansas Gazette* on July 28, 1957, she quotes a Churchill daughter who tells an amusing story that Anne delighted in relating through the years. The bride and groom stopped overnight at an inn in Malvern called Halfway House. All the guests slept in one large room in this hotel, and it was the custom for the women to retire first and blow out the candles. To locate their beds, the men entered the room and called out their wives' names. On this particular night, one man entered the room and called out to his wife, "Mary?" Voices from opposite sides of the room answered, "Here I am," and the poor fellow did not know which one was his wife!

Anne enjoyed telling another story about her honeymoon. In the early years the Hot Springs thermal waters ran unhindered and uncovered down the mountainside. The water was brought into the bathhouse by the bucketful and poured into washtubs for bathing. Just as one lady was about to step into her tub, a bucket of water was poured and out wriggled a snake. The nude lady ran out of the bathhouse screaming for help!

The Churchills' first home was Blenheim, on their plantation on the Arkansas River, seven miles from Little Rock. They lived there until he was appointed postmaster of Little Rock in 1857, a position he held for the next four years. After Arkansas's secession, he personally raised a regiment, the First Arkansas Mounted Riflemen, which went into service under his command as colonel. Churchill's record during the Civil War is one of distinction. In March 1862 he was promoted to brigadier general, and in December of that year he was given command of the Arkansas-Texas troops whose mission it was to defend Arkansas Post.

When her husband went off to war, Anne packed her china, silver, linens, and family portraits, closed her plantation home, and with her two children, Abby and Sam, moved into her Little Rock home.

Whenever possible, she and the children joined General Churchill during the four years of the war. They were with him at Arkansas Post when it came under the attack of superior Union forces. The officers rushed their wives and children on board a boat to get them to safety. Suddenly Anne realized they were being fired upon. They managed to escape, but as they sailed away she witnessed the fury of the Battle of Arkansas Post and her husband and his men fighting desperately to hold the fort against improbable odds. After three days of fierce fighting the Confederates were forced to surrender, and once again General Churchill was a prisoner of war. After three months at Camp Chase, Ohio, he was freed in an exchange of prisoners and reported back to duty. He was promoted to major general in 1863. One of the proudest moments of his military career came when he was invited to be a pallbearer at the funeral of General Stonewall Jackson. When the war ended Anne, the courageous wife, was with General Churchill at Minden, Louisiana, living in a tent.

When they returned to their plantation, they found that the Federals had burned their home and had used Anne's piano for a horse trough. Undaunted, they built a log cabin and started over.

After Reconstruction the Democrats elected Churchill state treasurer. In 1880 he was elected governor, and his inauguration on January 13, 1881, was a time of rejoicing for the people of Arkansas. They had been too long under Republican and Reconstruction rule. At this point in time, they could finally believe that was all behind them. The following is the *Arkansas Gazette*'s report of the festivities:

The Inauguration: Magnificent Parade— Imposing Ceremonies—Music and Military

The scene presented on our streets

and at the Statehouse yesterday, upon the occasion of the Inauguration of Governor T.J. Churchill, was one that will long be remembered by our citizens. It marks a new era in Arkansas legislative ceremonies, and points how evenly we are keeping stride with our much older sister states. Heretofore, since the Democrats have regained the political government of the state, the inaugural ceremonies have not been very impressive. Our governors have gone quietly in, taken their oaths and entered upon the discharge of their duties, which duties they have well and faithfully performed. The clouds of reconstruction and radical rule were still dimly visible and too fresh in the memory of all, for their effects not to be keenly felt. But now the clouds have disappeared and the bright sun of democracy shines on a happy and prosperous state. We have been in mourning long enough. We lay aside the weeds and resume the bright colors of prosperity.

The battalion, composed of the two military companies, proceeded (sic) by the colored brass band, approached the residence of General Churchill; at eleven o'clock a line was formed in front of the gate, and when the governor appeared he was greeted with a military salute. The procession was then formed and proceeded down Sixth Street in the following order: First the band, then the companies, preceded by Major Waters, Adjutant Johnson and Chaplain Tupper on horseback. The governor followed in a carriage, accompanied by his wife, Mrs. Governor Blackburn of Kentucky, and his brother, Mr. Churchill of Kentucky. Then came other carriages containing distinguished citizens and relations of the governor. The procession proceeded down Sixth to Scott, north on Scott to Markham, and west on Markham to the statehouse, where the companies stacked arms and disbanded, and the governor was met by a joint committee from the

senate and house, who conducted him, together with the other state officers, to the hall of the House of Representatives.

The crowd inside of the house was very large. Beautiful ladies were crowded in among old sober-sided judges and grim law makers. The galleries groaned under the immense weight.

After the inauguration the crowd retired to the statehouse yard to witness the dress parade by the military companies. The boys acquitted themselves in a manner that surpassed the expectations of their best friends. They were cheered heartily. The contrast between the two beautiful uniforms was striking—and equally pleasing—the one in blue and the other in grey. The beautiful flag lately presented to the Quapaw guards by the young ladies of Little Rock was much admired. As the boys were marching around the yard, which was densely crowded with men, women, and children, the martial heart of many an old veteran throbbed with responsive measure to the even tread of the soldier boy's feet. Little Rock is justly proud of her military boys. They deserve praise and should be encouraged.

The inaugural ball was likewise reported in glowing terms:

Inauguration Ball The Most Brilliant Assemblage Ever Seen in Little Rock

A fitting termination of the impressive inauguration exercises yesterday was the exceedingly brilliant ball at Concordia hall last night, given under the auspices of the Thalian Club. Over 750 invitations had been sent out, and a large number of those invited were present. Many of the toilets worn on this occasion had been sent from Paris, and the scene was one of joy and festivity. The large hall was filled with the happy crowd of spectators and participants, and during many hours dancing was kept up to the inspiring strains of an excellent orchestra. The supper was an elegant affair and was thoroughly enjoyed. The military gentlemen who had drawn so many flattering comments during the day, as escorts of Gen. Churchill during the inauguration exercises, were present in all the dazzling brilliance of their pretty uniforms and added to the effect in the ball room. There were many guests from abroad, and it is not too extravagant to say that the entire number of persons moving in the best society circles were present. Lack of space prevents further comment, but the ball was undoubtedly one of the most magnificent that has ever been given in Little Rock.

In the article about the inauguration, the reference to "Mrs. Governor Blackburn of Kentucky" identifies Governor Churchill's sister, who was the wife of the governor of Kentucky. The awkward manner of identifying her is a good example of why the term "First Lady" has evolved through the years.

The Churchills were well received in Little Rock social circles. They had lived in the city before being elected and had many personal friends. Anne Churchill performed her social duties graciously, but the only mention in the press of any social events given or attended by the Churchills is a squib announcing their thirty-third wedding anniversary. They held a reception in their home which was attended only by members of the family and a few close friends.

During his term as governor, the Churchills lived in a house at Sixth and Arch streets. This three-bedroom house was ample for official entertaining. On the first floor there were a parlor, a library, and a large dining room all opening off a wide hall. The spiral staircase was at the back of the entrance hall. The kitchen was in a separate building, and the grounds were shaded by oak, cedar, and magnolia trees. They rented the house from a Dr. Jennings. Because Governor Churchill's family descended from John Churchill, the first Duke of Marlborough, and Dr. Jennings descended from Sarah Jennings, wife of the Duke, the governor and the doctor jokingly called each other "Duke" and "Duchess."

The Duke of Marlborough was commander of all of Queen Anne's armed forces at home and abroad. His military successes were rewarded with many grand gifts from his country, one of the most lavish being the estate in Oxfordshire on which a palace was built. The Duke named his new home Blenheim Castle, in honor of the Battle of Blenheim he had so successfully fought in 1704. Through the generations the Churchill family has named their homes or estates Blenheim. (Governor Churchill chose this name for his Arkansas plantation.) The American branch of the Churchill family were people of wealth, accustomed to the amenities that money can provide. Historically they had large, well-furnished homes, servants, china, silver, and carriages imported from England.

Anne Sevier was also of noble heritage. The Seviers came to this country from France, where they had held positions of honor in both church and state for hundreds of years, tracing their lineage back to King Henry of Navarre. They fled France to escape the persecution of the Huguenots by Louis XIV. The name changed from the original Xavier in France to its anglicized form of Sevier after coming to America.

Anne Sevier was one of four children born to Ambrose Sevier and Juliette Johnson. Her grandfather, Judge Benjamin Johnson, was federal judge of Arkansas during its four years as a territory, and he continued in the same post thirteen years after statehood. Judge Johnson was a cultured, well-educated man, wealthy both in worldly goods and in the esteem of the people of Arkansas. His brother was vice president of the United States when Martin Van Buren was president. His son, Anne's uncle, was a United States senator from Arkansas.

Anne's father, Ambrose H. Sevier, was the son of John Sevier, the founder of the state of Tennessee and six times governor of the state, and Anne Conway, sister to our first and fifth governors. When Henry Conway was killed in a duel with Robert Crittenden, Ambrose Sevier was elected to take his place in Congress. Ambrose was reelected three times, and it was he who introduced in the United States House of Representatives the measure for statehood for Arkansas. Ambrose Sevier and William S. Fulton were elected as the first United States senators from this state.

A fond memory of Anne's and one she liked to tell in her later years was the drama of the day Arkansas received word of the long-awaited statehood. When word finally came, on cue by the ringing of a bell, all lights over the city were extinguished and homemade tallow candles in turnip holders were placed on window sills and lighted all over the city. They burned for an hour until the bell rang again and the candles were extinguished.

Senator Sevier took his daughter Anne to Washington with him when she was twelve and enrolled her in the fashionable Miss English's School for Girls in Georgetown. She did not return to Little Rock for six years— the trip was long and hazardous by boat and coach. At Miss English's School she was subjected to the customary strict academic discipline. Anne had a sharp mind and applied herself studiously, excelling in both the liberal arts and science. She read and spoke French with the ease of a native. She could recite pages of poetry from memory and sometimes won the extra credit that was given to students who could honestly say they had not looked at their lessons since study period the night before. This was to strengthen their memory. Students were forced to go to church, and the Bible was one of their textbooks. If they tried to escape church with the excuse they had nothing to wear, the headmistress made them wear something from her unfashionable wardrobe.

They did not use that excuse a second time!

Anne's years at Miss English's School were not all drudgery. Her father was a close friend of President Polk, and because of this friendship Anne was afforded the rare treat of White House visits. Twice a month a carriage was sent to her school and she was allowed to invite several friends to accompany her on a visit to the presidential mansion. On each of these visits Anne was extended the courtesy of choosing the dessert. Family lore says that it was always ice cream.

Among her closest friends in Washington were Varina Howell (the second Mrs. Jefferson Davis) and Dolley Madison. In typical teenage fashion, they gathered with other young friends and practiced the popular dances of the day to Varina's piano playing. Her position as the senator's daughter and a frequent visitor to the White House swept Anne into the center of the Washington social scene. She caught the eye of Senator James Buchanan. Although she resisted his courtship, they remained friends throughout their lives. It was to him she turned for help when he was president and her husband wanted to become postmaster of Little Rock. President Buchanan saw to the appointment.

The *Encyclopedia of the New West* describes Anne Churchill as

> a petite brunette, of beauty, sparkling intellect, vivacious, and admired by a large circle of friends. Time and cares of wife and mother and war did not rob her of these charms which pertain to the gracious lady and holds [sic] the respect of those who knew her. . . . She is in every sense a most elegant lady, and well educated. She spent much of her early life in Washington while her father was Senator. As a girl she was handsome— fine looking. She is a superior woman— has a superior cast of mind and is superior in manners and character.

Thomas and Anne Churchill had six children: Abby, who died at the age of twenty-one; Samuel; Ambrose S., who died in infancy; Juliette; Emily St. Aubert; and Mattie Johnson. Only Samuel—who married Kate Hooper, daughter of a distinguished surgeon of the Confederate Army—and Mattie—who married Edward Langhorne of Virginia—had children. Samuel had three and Mattie had two.

Mrs. Churchill was a communicant of Christ Episcopal Church and was active in church work and patriotic societies all her life. She and the governor celebrated their fiftieth wedding anniversary on July 31, 1899. He died on his eighty-first birthday, March 10, 1905, and she died on February 20, 1917. Both are buried in Mount Holly Cemetery at Little Rock.

ELIZABETH QUAILLE BERRY
1883-1885

ELIZABETH QUAILLE ELOPED on horseback to marry her future governor and devoted the rest of her life to a tender watchfulness over this man on crutches. Lieutenant Berry, a veteran of the battles of Shiloh and Corinth, was captured and spent months as a Union prisoner. When he was finally released, he was given an honorable discharge from the Confederate Army and spent the remaining months of the war in Texas. Upon returning to Arkansas he found a teaching job in the small town of Ozark. Here he began the study of law and the courtship of Elizabeth Quaille.

Her parents disapproved of him as a suitor for their daughter. They felt great sympathy for this severely handicapped young man, who had certainly proved himself to be a man of valor and courage—but they were concerned about how he would support a wife and family. He was barely subsisting on the meager teacher's salary that would last only a few months. Then what? He obviously had no money, he was twenty-four years old, he had very little formal education, and his handicap would prevent him from engaging in any type of manual labor. His prospects for the future were dim indeed.

Nothing could dissuade Elizabeth from marrying the man of her choice. A headstrong, courageous young woman, deeply in love, she took matters in her own hands: she ran away. She and James Berry were married October 31, 1865, at her sister's home in Ozark. The wedding created a schism between daughter and parents that existed for almost twenty years.

During the first years of their marriage, life was extremely difficult for the Berrys. After the wedding they went to live with the bridegroom's sister, Mrs. Sam W. Peel, in Carroll County. Mrs. Peel's log cabin home was so small the newlyweds had to sleep in the wellhouse.

No hardship was too great to overcome for Elizabeth. Fired by her parents' rejection of her husband, she let nothing distract her and James in building a successful career for him. The young couple persevered, and within the year their fortunes took a turn for the better. James found another teaching job, was admitted to the bar, and was elected to the legislature. After practicing law in Carrollton for two years, he and Elizabeth moved to Bentonville, where they established a permanent home and had their family of six children. A large white frame house was home to this close-knit family. James Berry was again elected to the legislature, became speaker of the house, was next elected circuit judge, and resigned in 1882 to run for governor. He won that election and was inaugurated as governor on January 13, 1883. In contrast to the elaborate inauguration ceremonies of Governor Churchill two years before, Governor Berry's inauguration was simply reported in the newspaper as having happened! In his address to the General Assembly he outlined a constructive program that was well received. His term as governor earned him the name "Honest Jim."

The Berrys did not establish a home in Little Rock for the two years that he was governor. Instead they lived at a boardinghouse on Louisiana Street near Fourth and Fifth. It can be assumed that under the circumstances Mrs. Berry did little if any entertaining as First Lady. She was not the social sort. A son describes her as being absolutely devoted to husband and children. She kept the children in line by threatening them with a peachtree switch, which she never used. Although at times she suffered from violent headaches she was always even-tempered, kind, and serene. She dedicated her life to watching over her handicapped husband. As much as possible she was always at hand to guard against accident. His welfare was uppermost with her.

She was of medium height, dressed neatly, and wore her long brown hair pulled straight back and coiled in a bun. Her appearance was as straightforward as her character. All her life she maintained the same indepen-dence of mind that she exhibited when she eloped. Regardless of the public office held by her husband, she never changed. She saw no need to adapt to politics or society; her standards remained the same. She spent a great deal of time working on behalf of the poor and never let a needy person go in want if she knew about it.

James Henderson Berry, one of ten chil-dren, was born May 15, 1841, in Jackson County, Alabama, the son of James M. and Isabelle Orr Berry. The family left Alabama and moved to Arkansas in 1848, settling in Carrollton in Carroll County, where they bought a farm and established a general mer-chandise store. James attended the local schools and entered a private academy nearby but was forced to drop out after one year. This ended his formal education. He was self-taught from this point on, and must have been endowed with a keen mind in order to accomplish as much as he did.

Elizabeth Quaille Berry was the daughter of Frederick Quaille and his wife, Frances Quisenberry. She was born September 29, 1848, the first of eight children, and was called Lizzie by family and friends. Her mother, Frances Quisenberry, was a member of a proud German family who traced its lineage back to the late 1300s in Germany, where the name was spelled Questenberg. In 1467 Henrich Questenberg committed the unpardonable sin of marrying an Englishwo-man, was forced to leave Germany, and lived in England from then on. Thus began the migration of this proud family, some of

whom became early settlers in this country. Thomas Quisenberry settled in Virginia in 1608.

Lizzie's father, Frederick Quaille, was born in France in 1815, the son of George and Catherine Quaille. Frederick Quaille immi-grated to America, settling in Louisville, Ken-tucky, in 1824. He moved to Arkansas, where he finally settled in Ozark and established a general merchandise store, a business that turned rich profits in those days. He and Frances Quisenberry married in 1845. He provided well for his children, and daughter Lizzie enjoyed a carefree antebellum girl-hood. It is perhaps understandable why these parents objected to the marriage of their daughter to a penniless, handicapped man who apparently had so little to offer. His fine war record and smiling open coun-tenance did him no good with Lizzie's stern father.

After the elopement, Quaille refused to speak to or recognize the young couple. Angered and hurt by her father's actions, Lizzie firmly resolved that her husband would be successful. She recognized his intellectual and moral worth and was the inspiration that pointed him ever onward and upward. Her determined loyalty and support were rewarded when he was elected to the highest office in the state and she wore the title "First Lady of Arkansas." This gentle woman, strong of will and firm of purpose, had succeeded in realizing her goal of great success for her husband.

Just before the inauguration her parents asked for forgiveness, and the reconciliation that came about between the two families was Lizzie's consummate reward. All the deprivation, hard work, planning, and heart-aches washed away when her parents saw her husband as the noble man she had always known him to be. Her belief in him was vindicated.

Governor Berry always gave her the credit for his success. After serving as governor, he was elected to the United States Senate and served two terms. Berry received warm praise from his constituency for his faithful service in the senate. He was defeated for reelection by the colorful and dynamic Jeff Davis. They returned to their home in Bentonville, where Governor Berry died in January 1913.

The town of Berryville was named for James Henderson Berry. This town is situated in a beautiful valley, a natural amphitheater surrounded by rolling mountains and crossed by two rivers. The valley was settled by hardy pioneers whose families have given Arkansas many prominent historic characters.

Governor Berry's rapid and unchecked political success was aided by his fine appearance, his open and frank personality, and a great deal of personal magnetism—powerful factors to all except his father-in-law. It took him eighteen years to convince Frederick Quaille of his worth!

ANN BLAKEMORE HUGHES
1885-1889

ANN BLAKEMORE AND Simon P. Hughes both lost parents early in life. The exact date of her father's death has not come to light, but in January 1845 the probate court of Monroe County, Arkansas, appointed William A. Harvich legal guardian of orphaned eight-year-old Ann Blakemore. From the 1850 census we learn that Ann's mother and her guardian, William Harvich, had married and that Ann was living with them. In 1851 her guardianship was changed from stepfather William to John A. Harvich, the sheriff. Both these Harvich men played important roles in Ann's life, over and above their duties as guardians. William became a father figure to her and provided for her until her marriage—even after Ann's mother died and William remarried. John Harvich was not only Ann's guardian, but became the mentor and closest friend of the man she would marry.

Ann's parents were Lucinda Maddox, of Kentucky ancestry, and George W. Blakemore, descendant of Major George Blakemore, officer of the American Revolution. Ann's father was a prominent planter in Monroe County, Arkansas, and at the time of her birth, November 30, 1836, he was postmaster for "Mouth of Cache." The name of this settlement was later changed to Clarendon, Arkansas. Ann was the only child born to George and Lucinda Blakemore. She attended the Young Ladies Model School in Sommerville, Tennessee, where she was schooled in academics and social graces.

Governor Hughes was orphaned early in life. He was the seventh child born to Mary Hubbard and Simon P. Hughes. When his mother died, his grief-stricken father left the children with relatives and moved to Texas, where he died two years later. Simon Jr. was fourteen.

As was the custom in those days, the Hughes children attended school only a few months in winter and worked on the farm during planting and harvest time. At the age of fourteen Simon came to Pulaski County, where for two years he hired out as a farm hand. He returned to Tennessee and under the tutelage of a great teacher, his maternal uncle Professor Peter Hubbard, studied Latin and mathematics for two years at the Sylvan Academy. He entered Clinton College, but the burden of school and self-support became too great, and he returned to Arkansas, where he settled on the White River near Clarendon, again supporting himself by doing farm work. John A. Harvich, the sheriff of Monroe County, admired young Simon for his strong character and straightforward manner. When Sheriff Harvich decided to retire, he suggested to Simon that he run for the office. Simon was flabbergasted. He was twenty-two and not well known, was only a farm hand, and couldn't afford the bond required to hold the office. The sheriff assured him that people would soon see that Simon was a man of courage and integrity and that he, the sheriff, would make a bond for Simon.

Simon loved the campaign, the barbecues, the large crowds, the public speaking, and the challenge that came from his opponent, a bully who ridiculed him. At the supreme moment Simon faced down the bully and demanded and commanded respect in such a manner the bully quickly backed down. This act of moral and physical courage gained Simon the admiration and respect of the crowd, and word of it soon spread over the county. He won the election. Simon began the study of law while in the sheriff's office, and he and Ann were married in 1856. At the same time he was admitted to the bar and began the practice of law.

Simon Hughes, a man of peace who had spoken out against secession before the Civil War, did not hesitate to join the fight when war broke out. He was elected captain of Company F of the 23rd Infantry Regiment and eventually was promoted to lieutenant colonel. When the regiment was reorganized after the Battle of Shiloh, Hughes did not retire, but joined with Morgan's Texas Battalion of Calvary as a private and remained with that unit until the end of the war.

At one time during the war he was badly in need of a uniform that was not available. Ann Hughes, ever resourceful and efficient, managed to get the necessary materials and with her own slender fingers sewed every stitch of the new uniform for her husband. A daughter later marveled at her having performed this task, which seemed to dwarf her even more: Ann Hughes was not quite five feet tall and her normal weight was eighty-seven pounds. This petite woman was the mother of nine children: William B., Simon P., Lucinda, Ann, Sarah, Robert C., Lillian, George, and John. Lucinda, Ann, and Simon all died during the Civil War. Robert Carlton Hughes was the only one of the nine children who had children. His daughter, Alice Ann Hughes Coffman Edwards, is the only one of Robert's children still living at this writing, and she has furnished much of the information in this chapter. She well remembers the governor's son and her uncle, Dr. William Hughes, who was a prominent ear, nose, and throat specialist. He took training in the medical schools of America, Vienna, and London, practiced in Little Rock, and died in 1924. Lillian Hughes, a daughter of Governor and Mrs. Hughes, was an accomplished musician and composer well-known in musical circles in Little Rock. She often spoke of her mother's musical talent and said she inherited her own ability from her mother.

Ann Blakemore Hughes was a person of high ideals, and her appreciation of the finer things in life greatly influenced her children.

She had an imaginative and creative mind well-versed in classical literature, and she maintained a keen interest in current events. She was cultured, serene, and dignified in manner and was a charming and gracious hostess to the many dignitaries, friends, and relations she and her husband entertained. They lived in Clarendon until he was named attorney general in 1874, at which time they moved to Little Rock, where they made their home in a large colonial house at Sixth and Arch streets. This house was adequate to the needs of the family and the official entertaining required while Hughes was attorney general and again as governor. The house had been the home of the Churchills when he was governor.

Hughes was inaugurated as governor on January 17, 1885, in a simple ceremony. The inauguration date for his second term was January 15, 1887. Hughes's two terms as governor were successful and he enjoyed great popularity with the people. He was late in making his decision to run for a third term, and by the time he threw his hat in the ring others were running hard and a split in the party had occurred. James Philip Eagle emerged as the victor. The story of this state Democratic Convention is an interesting bit of Arkansas political history. The balloting continued for five days before a deadlock was broken and Eagle was nominated. In his acceptance speech Eagle did much to heal the break in the party by praising Governor Hughes and his administration. Hughes very graciously stumped the state on behalf of Eagle, who won the election.

This couple, ever faithful to their family, their duty, their friends, and each other, left a lasting impression on the state in which they lived and served. While Hughes was governor, their son John died and the family had to carry on despite their grief, but carry on they did.

Ann Hughes found great strength through her religion. She was a Methodist and a devoted reader of the Bible. Family history tells us that she read it through more than once and that each chapter in her personal Bible bears a trembly X at the end of each chapter to indicate that she had finished reading that portion.

Governor Hughes died in 1906 at the stately family home at Twelfth and Cumberland. Ann Hughes lived six years after his death. Both are buried at Mount Holly Cemetery in Little Rock.

Ann Blakemore Hughes's grandchildren were Blossom, who married J.H. Stanley; Robert, who never married; William, who married Helen Hutson Riffel; Lillian, who married Fred D. Weniger; Simon P., who married Maude Etta Robinson; Charles, who married Mai Patterson; and Alice Ann, who married first Marshall B. Coffman and later Julian Edwards. Mrs. Edwards says the "P" in the name of Simon P. was only an initial—that it never stood for any name.

MARY KAVANAUGH OLDHAM EAGLE
1889-1893

NO ONE IN the family remembers how or why Mary K. Oldham Eagle became "Mamie," but that is what she was called by family and friends. James Eagle was called "Uncle Chunk" by his nieces and nephews because, they said, he was built like a chunk—short, stocky, and strong. A clipping in a family scrapbook describes Mamie Eagle as being elegant in appearance, tall and slender, with a fine figure and a graceful, erect carriage. A family portrait of her bears this out. She had long brown hair which she wore in a loose coil on top of her head with waves and soft curls framing her face. With her fair complexion and dark gray, very expressive eyes, she was a real beauty.

Another family portrait shows her at the age of four to be a chubby-cheeked little girl with brown hair parted in the middle and combed straight down to frame her face. She is wearing a blue silk off-the-shoulder dress in the style of frocks in Old World portraits. In her lap is a leghorn hat filled with roses. The artist captured the very arresting, direct gaze of the dark gray eyes.

Mamie Oldham was born February 4, 1854, to William K. and Jacintha Kate Brown Oldham and grew up in Kentucky. Her well-to-do parents provided for her early schooling at home with private tutors. Later she attended Science Hill Seminary for Girls in Shelbyville, Kentucky, and graduated with distinction.

She met her future husband when he came to visit her parents in 1866. She was twelve and he was twenty-nine, a veteran of the Civil War, prosperous businessman, and plantation owner. He became enamored of the lovely young lady and vowed then and there to marry her someday. He carried on a protracted courtship through the years by periodic visits to her home. He waited six-teen years for his chosen bride to grow up, finish school, and have a teaching career. When they finally married at her parents' home on January 3, 1882, she was twenty-eight and he was forty-five! He brought his bride to his plantation home south of Lonoke, which they named Eyrie. Here they lived in the gracious style of the Old South, as befitted a prosperous plantation owner of that time. It was not necessary that Mamie Eagle work, but she chose to join her husband in all his endeavors. She became bookkeeper for his various enterprises, assisted him in his duties as a Baptist minister, and campaigned with him in election years. Ten years before their marriage James Eagle had begun his political career when friends, without his knowledge, placed his name in nomination as their candidate for the House of Representatives in the Arkansas state legislature. Even though his introduction to politics was not of his doing, he became hopelessly bitten by the political bug.

In 1880 he resisted his friends' urging to run for governor, but eight years later he actively sought the office. In May 1888 the state Democratic Convention met in what proved to be a bloody intraparty fight that lasted five days. Eagle, Governor Hughes, and two other very strong contenders, Col. John G. Fletcher and William M. Fishback, were the major candidates in the race to be the party's nominee for governor. Women rarely if ever attended this convention, but Mamie Eagle attended every session.

On the first ballot the count was Hughes 122, Fletcher 113, Eagle 97, and Fishback 25. As the days and balloting wore on, first one candidate and then another withdrew. The Eagle forces were working furiously to pick up these votes for their man, and a calm and composed Mamie Eagle was advising her

A portrait of Mary Kavanaugh Oldham Eagle. (Photo by Anne McMath)

husband's friends and supporters and directing the floor fight for votes during the five exciting days. James Eagle was declared the party's nominee with 248 votes on the 126th ballot.

Mamie Eagle traveled over the state campaigning with her husband. Eagle won the election but his opponent demanded an investigation of the vote count. Nothing came of his request, and the inauguration took place as scheduled, but it differed from others in that only after the crowd gathered in the galleries and House Chamber did the speaker and sergeant-at-arms begin a vote count county by county—three hours of tedium that usually took place before the ceremonies began. When the governor and other state officials were declared elected, the speaker appointed an escort committee to wait upon the officers. At this point Mrs. Eagle and two relatives, Mrs. J.L. Gentry of Sedalia, Missouri, and Miss Willie Hocker of Pine Bluff, were escorted to seats near the speaker's desk. (Miss Hocker designed the Arkansas flag.)

After he was elected, Governor and Mrs. Eagle purchased the Crittenden-Johnson home at Seventh and Scott streets and lived there the rest of their lives. This beautiful house provided a proper setting for the many social activities of the Eagles. Recognizing the political value of a personal invitation, Mamie entertained often for her governor-husband.

Their social calendar the first year is indicative of their official entertainments during the years he was in office. Soon after taking office the Eagles entertained their friends and supporters and members of the legislature at a reception held at Concordia Hall, a downtown club that was the center of social life in Little Rock. The *Arkansas Gazette* reported that "it seemed that all 500 or 600 people who had received invitations were in attendance." The hall was decorated very simply with only a pyramid of greenery (probably a backdrop for Governor and Mrs. Eagle as they received their guests) and a few pots of flowers on the stage in front of the orchestra. When the guests began arriving at nine o'clock, Sarlo's orchestra began and the music continued until midnight. At one point, some of the younger couples took the floor for two or three dances before they were stopped. Mrs. Eagle did not approve. In the article reporting this splendid affair, the *Gazette* described the ladies' dresses as

> models of loveliness. Mrs. Eagle's costume was one of the most exquisite and handsome ever worn in this city. It was made of white princess royale silk, plain and brocaded combined. The brocade figure was a delicate running vine of the pompadour character in nankin yellow and formed the low necked waist and the train. Plain royale silk formed the balance of the dress, which had liberal trimmings of filmy point d'Alencon. There was hardly a costume in the assemblage that does not deserve special mention.

Supper was announced and Speaker

Hudgins escorted Governor and Mrs. Eagle to the table. One hundred guests were seated at the time and served a splendid supper at the beautifully decorated tables. "In short the reception was a successful and brilliant affair and afforded much pleasure to their many guests."

Another important event on the Eagles' social calendar was a dinner party at their home on Thanksgiving evening. Quite a large number of guests were treated to a ten-course dinner of delicacies of the season.

Christmas week the doors of the grandest house in Little Rock were again thrown open in gracious hospitality when Governor and Mrs. Eagle entertained the state officers and their wives and a few friends. The spacious rooms and wide halls sparkled in Christmas dress and were brilliantly lit by the city's first gaslights. An orchestra seated in the back of a hall filled the house with music all evening. The thirty-two guests were seated promptly at ten o'clock and served an elegant supper. The feasting continued until midnight and it was long after the midnight hour when the last guests departed.

Mamie and James Eagle were rarely apart. While he was governor she attended political meetings with him rain or shine. When he was a delegate to the Democratic National Convention she went with him. It was Eagle's belief that as a minister he should preach to the small outlying communities who were unable to have a regular minister, and Mamie went with him on these missions. They were sweethearts and best friends the twenty-one years of their marriage. He revealed in his memoirs of her that every day of their lives they spoke their love for each other, and if they were forced to be apart they wrote to each other every day declaring their love.

He served as president of the Arkansas Baptist State Convention for twenty-four years. Much of the credit for the length of his term should be given to Mamie, for she was as involved as he. She was instrumental in organizing the Women's Central Committee,

A portrait of Mary Kavanaugh Oldham as a child. (Photo by Anne McMath)

an auxiliary to this organization, and served as its president until a few months before her death. She studied parliamentary procedure and taught him the rules of presiding. James Eagle was president of the prestigious Southern Baptist Convention for two terms and declined a third. Again Mamie was by his side taking an active part in his work. She was vice-president of the Woman's Union Auxiliary of that organization.

At the end of his term as governor, James Eagle was ill and unable to write his final address to the General Assembly. He asked Mamie to write his speech, which she did. He told her the points he wished to cover and she prepared the entire text, except for one section which she only revised. Obviously Mamie Eagle was well acquainted with

Water urn from the Eagle family. (Photo by Anne McMath)

her husband's administration, for only an informed person could have written the speech.

Mamie was not just an appendage or an alter ego of her husband. She was a highly respected, capable person in her own right. In addition to her activities on behalf of her husband's career and her volume of church work, she was influential in organizing the Federation of Woman's Clubs and often served as a delegate to either the state or national conventions. She was a founder of the Women's Co-operative Association and a member of the Aesthetic Club. Mamie Eagle gained national recognition when she served as a member of the Board of Lady Managers of the Columbian Exposition, an event held in Chicago from May to October, 1893, to commemorate the 400th anniversary of Columbus's discovery of America. Two women from each state were selected by the United States Congress to serve as "lady managers." Mamie Eagle and Mrs. R.A. Edgerton, wife of the postmaster of Little Rock, were the two women chosen from Arkansas. Mrs. Eagle soon took a position of leadership on this

board. She was one of seven selected to arrange for a variety of congresses to be held during the exposition. She was chosen to edit and publish in book form the papers read at these congresses. Because of her knowledge of parliamentary procedure she was often called upon to preside over the meetings, for she had no peer in dispatching business. The national press praised her in this respect and credited her, more than anyone else, for promoting harmony among the many different personalities on the board. At the close of the exposition Mrs. Eagle was one of two women chosen to procure and place a portrait of the board president in the Assembly Hall of the Woman's Building, and was one of the speakers at the unveiling of this portrait.

Although Mamie spent a great deal of time in community and church work, she was an excellent housekeeper. Her home was always tastefully and artistically decorated and her tables well appointed. She dressed in quiet good taste and was gentle in manner, but was a person of strong convictions and never hesitated to speak her opinions. She was unshakable in her belief of what was right and wrong and was loyal to any cause she espoused. She was well-informed and possessed acute reasoning abilities. When she spoke, her opinions carried weight. In 1938 historian Dallas T. Herndon named Mamie Eagle one of the state's ten most famous women.

She was a charming hostess. According to her husband, she felt that "friends should be able to entertain each other for an hour or two without having to resort to cards, games of chance or other lower forms of entertainment. Under no condition was wine served or cards played in her house."

She was her husband's most congenial companion and valued counselor whether in politics or religion. One historian stated that she tried only once to influence him in his actions as governor, and that was in the interest of a convict.

A few months after Governor Eagle took office, the *Gazette* carried a short editorial stating, "Governor Eagle is creating the impression by the very firm and positive course he is pursuing that the law against pistol-toting and illegal liquor selling in Arkansas was enacted to be enforced and that is an excellent impression to cultivate." After careful study of Mamie Eagle one has to believe that if she didn't influence him in this, she certainly approved!

She died of cancer at home on February 15, 1903, at the age of 49. She had been ill for several months, and when all efforts failed to restore her health, she planned her funeral services, which were carried out exactly as she wished. James Eagle sat by her side day and night until she smiled and said "Good-bye, dear," and closed her eyes in death. Two columns on the front page of the *Gazette* were devoted to her obituary, and Governor Jeff Davis issued a proclamation that the Capitol would be closed for a day and a half in her honor, saying "death has claimed one of the purest, noblest and grandest women of Arkansas."

James Eagle described Mamie "as gentle as an evening breeze; pure as a snowflake; tender as the smile of the rose; firm as the granite hills." He was devastated by her loss, spent the next two years writing his memoirs of her, and then died. They are both buried at Mount Holly Cemetery.

There were no children.

WILLIAM MEADE FISHBACK
1893-1895

WILLIAM MEADE FISHBACK was elected governor eleven years after the death of his beloved wife, Adelaide. His oldest daughter had married and moved to another state and his next daughter was too young to serve as his hostess; therefore the state was without a First Lady during this term. Governor Fishback lived at a hotel in Little Rock and his younger children visited him there.

Adelaide Miller was born in Fort Smith, Arkansas, the daughter of Mr. and Mrs. Joseph Miller. She grew up in a large red-brick house located on property that later became the site of the Belle Grove school. She was very active in church, civic, and cultural activities and was a driving force in the establishment of a public library in Fort Smith. She was a devoted wife and mother and a devout Episcopalian. At the time of her death it was said that Fort Smith lost a great force that had contributed to the building of the city. She was from one of its oldest and most esteemed families and had maintained a position of prominence in social and civic affairs of the community. Had she lived to serve beside her husband, obviously she would have been a valuable asset to his political career and a gracious and capable First Lady.

SALLIE WARREN MOORE WOOTEN CLARKE
1895-1897

IT WAS NOT easy to research Sallie Moore Clarke even though her two granddaughters are today prominent citizens of Little Rock. When they were contacted they very regretfully said they have no family files, nor have any been uncovered at the Arkansas History Commission or the university libraries.

Apparently Mrs. Clarke was not the sort to keep scrapbooks and mementoes. Nor did she impress on her daughters the magnitude of her work or of their father's accomplishments. Success was accepted as a matter of course in this family and was simply not talked about.

Little Rock benefited greatly from Sallie Clarke's works. There was much to be done in this city around the turn of the century, and she busied herself with the needs of the community. She was much concerned about underprivileged children and very interested in the Working Woman's Home. She served as president of the Board of Management of this institution.

Mrs. Clarke and her fellow members of the board of the Arkansas Federation of Women's Clubs lobbied the legislature for the preservation of the former Capitol. Their plans were for the building to house an Arkansas museum. All relics of interest and everything connected with the history of Arkansas would be placed in the building. It was their plan for the headquarters of the Arkansas Historical Association and the state headquarters of the Colonial Dames to be located here.

Along with her friends, Sallie Clarke was interested in the decoration of the new Capitol and recommended that a painter of note be found to create murals on the interior walls of the building.

She joined in asking the legislature to pass a pure food act and a child labor law which would keep children under fourteen or sixteen in school and prevent their employment in factories.

Sallie Clarke had a great concern for the public schools of Little Rock and was one of a small group of women who saw the need to develop a better relationship between parents and teachers and to make improvements at the schools. These women decided to meet and talk about ways and means of meeting these needs. They held their first meeting in 1908 in the home of Mrs. T.P. Murray. From this meeting came the Little Rock SIA—School Improvement Association—the forerunner of Arkansas's Parent Teacher Association. When these ladies held their first meeting it never crossed their minds that their idea would be so eagerly accepted that it would spread like wildfire across the state. This simple organization brought parents and teachers together and created a sympathetic understanding between the two groups. They worked together to bring about many needed changes. Through the SIA (sometimes referred to as Sunshine in Arkansas) the school cafeteria was established to insure that all children had milk or a bowl of soup at noon. This organization was responsible for having sanitary drinking fountains installed in the schools, and saw to it that the buildings and grounds were kept clean and attractive. Mrs. Clarke was a generous and interested supporter of the SIA and served as chairman of one of its committees. She was largely responsible for placing a copy of Houdon's *Statue of Washington from Life* in the Little Rock High School, which was then located at Fourteenth and Scott streets.

Governor and Mrs. Clarke were members of Little Rock's First Methodist Church, located then as now at Eighth and Center

Sallie Warren Moore at age sixteen. (Photo courtesy of the J.N. Heiskell Historical Collection/ UALR Library Archives and Special Collections)

streets. Sallie Clarke was devoted to her church and for years served in the capacity of communion steward.

Sallie was born at Moon Lake, Mississippi, at the plantation home of her grandparents, Mr. and Mrs. William F. Moore. Her parents were Mr. and Mrs. Francis Marion Moore. She attended Logan Female College in Russellville, Kentucky, where she majored in art. She had considerable talent as an artist, producing many creditable paintings in her early years. There is no evidence she kept up her painting.

Much of her girlhood was spent in Helena, Arkansas, in the home of her uncle, Mr. Bob Moore. Here she fell in love with and married Alonzo Wooten. They had one son. Mr. Wooten died after a few years, leaving Sallie a very young and beautiful widow.

In 1879, having earned a law degree from the University of Virginia, James P. Clarke moved to Arkansas, finally settling in Helena, where he opened practice. Sallie Moore

Wooten soon caught his eye. He courted her with the same unwavering determination he used in reaching success in any endeavor. The successful lawyer and the young widow were married on November 15, 1883. During the next ten years he launched his political career and Sallie had three children—James Paul Clarke, Jr., and daughters Julia and Marion.

In 1892, when he was elected attorney general, the Clarkes moved to Little Rock. They selected an imposing home located on Little Rock's first paved residential street, at 1312 Scott Street, a house well suited to their needs and social life. Sallie Clarke was an efficient young matron who made her home a haven for her family and a gracious and hospitable place to entertain the many dignitaries who came to call. It has been said that James Clarke was not a popular man but had a "mighty mind." He was known to be a very demanding person with a high temper which he did not always control. However, at home under Sallie's influence and watchful eye he was a model of decorum and chivalry.

James Clarke was elected governor in 1894 and took office in January 1895 in a simple ceremony in the House Chamber. Surely Sallie attended, but there is no mention of her in newspaper reports of the occasion.

Detailed information is not available of Sallie's life as First Lady. It can be safely assumed this gracious, civic-minded lady satisfactorily carried out her duties as the wife of the governor.

James Clarke chose not to run for a second term as governor. Instead, in the 1896 election he ran for the United States Senate. After suffering defeat in several county primaries, he withdrew from the race and practiced law in Little Rock until the next senatorial election. With the support of Governor Jeff Davis, he won the senate seat and took office in 1903. From then on he and Sallie divided their time between Washington, D.C., and Little Rock. Being a senator did not tame James Clarke—he took his temper and independent ways with him to

Washington. The *Arkansas Gazette* described him as having a "tongue like a scythe blade that can cut and carve." This criticism probably didn't bother Sallie, who was always fiercely loyal to her husband. It certainly didn't deter the senator from speaking his mind and going his independent way. Sometimes he voted with his party and sometimes he sided with the Republicans on issues. He had friends on both sides of the aisle and was elected by his party as president pro tem of the senate in 1913 and again in 1915. In 1916 his health began to fail, and on October 1 of that year he died at his home in Little Rock.

At the time of Senator Clarke's death, the eulogy given on the senate floor by a colleague was testimony to the relationship between James and Sallie Clarke and their children and to the happy home created by Sallie for her family. The spokesman said in part,

> No man was ever regarded by his own family more as the prince of all men than was Senator Clarke. On one occasion while a guest in his home an opportunity was afforded to judge his life from this angle. I shall never forget the beautiful scene of domestic happiness that was mine to enjoy while there. His home seemed to be the center of his affection and the fountain of mutual joy. In the sitting room, at the dining table, he was the embodiment of all those refinements that were chivalrous and tender and which go to make the home the universe for those that dwell within it. In a mood brimful of merriment and repartee he

> was the suitor and courtier to the mother of his children, a cavalier in conduct toward his gracious daughters, while every word addressed to the son that bore his name, and every lineament of the Senator's face, proved the extent of that great love which he bore his only boy . . . .

James Paul Clarke greatly influenced the history of his adopted state. He rendered service both on the local and national level and many honors came his way. Probably the greatest came after his death when he was chosen as one of two men to represent Arkansas in Statuary Hall in the United States Capitol.

Through her devotion to the public schools, her family, and her church, Sallie Clarke made a real contribution to her community. Organized social welfare work came into its own during her lifetime, and this remarkable woman did not hesitate to commit herself to new causes. Her tireless efforts made many people's lives more tolerable.

Sallie Clarke lost both her sons and her husband within a short time. James Paul Clarke, Jr., died of peritonitis while serving the army during World War I. The family remembers that although Sallie lived seven more years, those years were spent in grief. Both Senator and Mrs. Clarke are buried at Oakland Cemetery in Little Rock.

Daughters Julia and Marion were the only survivors. Julia married Joseph Warren House and they had one daughter, Ellen (Mrs. James D. Simpson). Marion married Robert Monroe Williams and they had one daughter, Frances (Mrs. Everett Tucker).

MARGARET PARKIN HADLEY JONES
1897-1901

MRS. DANIEL WEBSTER Jones was christened Margaret Parkin, but this cheerful, fun-loving Irish lass was called "Maggie," a name more suited to her personality. Maggie loved people and people loved her. There was always a crowd around her, a virtual parade of guests marching through her house. In addition to being a good hostess, she was an efficient housekeeper and an excellent cook. Maggie is the only twin among Arkansas's First Ladies. She and her twin sister, Molly, were born in Tipton County, Tennessee, on February 11, 1845, and were fifteen months old when the family moved to Arkansas and settled at Hamburg in Ashley County. Molly died at the age of fifteen, but Margaret lived to become First Lady of Arkansas. She was one of seven children born to James and Hannah Holmes Hadley.

Daniel W. Jones came to Arkansas from Texas. His grandfather immigrated from Scotland to North Carolina, where he eventually became a Continental soldier and fought under General George Washington. Daniel's parents were Dr. Isaac and Elizabeth Littlejohn Jones. They moved from North Carolina to Texas where Dr. Jones became a member of Congress from the Republic of Texas. When Daniel was a small boy, his parents decided to leave Texas and come to Arkansas to live. They bought a large plantation in Lafayette County and established a home in Washington, Arkansas, where Daniel grew up. Due to a very unusual circumstance Daniel never lacked for playmates during his boyhood days. When James Black, the inventor and maker of the Bowie knife, had begun to lose his eyesight, he had moved into a small house on Dr. Jones's property in the hope that through protracted treatment Dr. Jones could restore his eyesight. Whenever a young boy became restless or too

much to handle, the mothers of Washington would tell them to "go play with Jim"— gentle Jim Black, who would spin entertaining stories by the hour. Thus the Joneses' yard was always full of little boys. The eye treatments didn't help, but the Jones family took care of Jim Black for many years. He had promised to tell Dr. Jones how he made the Bowie knife, but postponed the telling of it for so long that he couldn't remember the exact formula and it was lost forever.

When the Civil War broke out Daniel enlisted, was severely wounded, was captured twice, and returned home a colonel at the age of twenty-three. In 1864 troop movements took him to Hamburg, Arkansas, where he met and fell in love with the vivacious Maggie Hadley. She was smitten by the dashing young Confederate officer. The pressures of war created a sense of urgency for the young couple and after two weeks' courtship they were married, on January 9, 1864. Dan Jones took his nineteen-year-old bride to his home in Washington and left her with his widowed mother. The two women developed a rare affection for each other which lasted through many years of living in the same house.

Daniel Jones returned home to Washington and his bride. He studied law and discovered he liked politics. He was elected prosecuting attorney, and when he was elected attorney general in 1885 the family moved to Little Rock. He was elected governor and served two terms. The first inauguration took place on January 18, 1897, in a simple ceremony before one of the largest crowds ever assembled in the House Chamber. There is no mention of Mrs. Jones's having attended. Surely she did. Newspaper reporters didn't spend much time or effort reporting these inaugurations. For several years in a row the inauguration was reported in the exact same language except for the name of the governor. It was almost as if the reporter did not attend, but simply copied the article from the preceding one.

The Jones family lived at 1100 Louisiana Street. When her husband became governor, Maggie could tell little difference in her already heavy schedule of entertaining—it was simply an excuse to keep on with what she was already doing! Her naturally winning ways and capacity for making friends would have been great assets in her husband's race for governor, but for some reason she did not campaign with him.

She was a devoted wife and mother. She had a great sense of humor and loved a joke, especially Irish jokes. Her home was a happy-go-lucky place. She loved to read, especially the classics and the Bible, and was well versed in both. She belonged to the Episcopal Church and to the Memorial Chapter of the Daughters of the Confederacy. As the wife of one who had recently served in the Confederacy, she had firsthand information to contribute to the annals of that organization. Governor and Mrs. Jones attended several Confederate reunions. After attending a reunion of the Blue and the Gray—even though she was a loyal Rebel—Maggie came home with the opinion that Yanks weren't all that bad! It was not a surprising reaction for a person of her outgoing and loving personality.

One of the more exciting things that happened to this family while in office was daughter Bobbie's selection to christen the battleship *Arkansas*. The launching took place at the shipyards at Newport News, Virginia, and both Governor and Mrs. Jones accompanied their daughter on the very special mission. (This ship, later retired from duty, was sunk off Bikini Island in the Pacific in a test bombing exercise after World War II.)

After he left the governor's office, Daniel Jones returned to the practice of law in Little Rock, and Maggie continued running her house and looking after her family. She died after three months' illness in their home on February 10, 1914, one day before her sixty-ninth birthday, and one month after she and Daniel celebrated their fiftieth wedding anniversary. Governor Jones died on Christmas Day 1918. They both are buried at Oakland Cemetery in Little Rock.

They were survived by four of their seven children—two daughters, Elizabeth (Mrs. Edgar W. Holman) and Bobbie, and two sons, Claudius and Dr. Daniel W. Jones. Daughters Belle and Josephine died in infancy and son Howard Hadley died in 1902.

INA McKENZIE DAVIS
1901-1907

INA MCKENZIE DAVIS was the only child of Mr. and Mrs. Duncan G.L. McKenzie. She was born October 6, 1862, near Monticello, Arkansas, at the plantation home of her aunt, Mrs. John Kimbrough. Her father, a native of Scotland, immigrated to the United States as a young man and became a Methodist minister. He died when Ina was three months old. Faced with the necessity of earning a living, her mother took up teaching. She taught in rural schools and at the Arkansas Female College in Little Rock until it closed. Ina had continued to live on the plantation with her aunt, but when the college folded her mother moved to Russellville and took Ina with her. They were befriended by the Thach family and later her mother married Captain Frank Thach, a young army officer. There were four children born to this marriage and Ina grew up in a happy household surrounded by brothers and sisters.

A good student, Ina finished the Russellville schools and in 1878 entered the University of Arkansas at Fayetteville. A fellow classmate at the seven-year-old university was young Jefferson Davis. He and Ina were born the same year, both their families moved to Russellville, they both were children of ministers, and when they were sixteen they were freshmen at the university together. After two years there, Jeff Davis transferred to Vanderbilt University, where he completed a two-year law course in one year but was denied his diploma because he failed to meet a residency requirement. He returned to Russellville and applied for admission to the Arkansas bar. Although he was technically under age, his influential father managed to have the age limit waived and in 1881 Jeff Davis was admitted to the bar. He spent one more year studying law at

Cumberland University in Tennessee before he began practicing with his father in partnership—L.W. Davis and Son, Attorneys at Law.

Ina McKenzie transferred to Peabody Normal College in Tennessee for teacher training, but her college career ended when she and Jeff decided to marry. The wedding took place in October 1882 at the Methodist church in Russellville. The ceremony was performed by the bride's uncle, Dr. Augustus Winfield, a renowned Methodist minister.

The early years of their married life were spent in Russellville. Ina was a happy young matron, her husband was a successful, hardworking attorney who had entered politics, and their family was growing with the years. Jeff continued his climb up the political ladder, and when he was elected attorney general of the state, the family moved to Little Rock.

When Jeff Davis decided to run for the office of attorney general he was thought to have little chance of winning. He was in a weakened condition due to a slight stroke that had partially paralyzed his left arm and side. However, he persisted, and his campaign took on new life when one of his opponents died suddenly. Davis was elected, and his term in this office has been described as the most controversial of all attorneys general.

If his term as attorney general was controversial, then as a candidate for governor and as governor, he gave new meaning to the word. He called the Arkansas Supreme Court "the five jackasses"; his Little Rock opposition were "high-collared roosters"; and the press were all "squirrel heads." In turn he was called "immoral," "a demagogue," and "a drunkard." Nevertheless, he carried seventy-four of the seventy-five counties in the Dem-

Ina McKenzie Davis. (Photo courtesy of the J.N. Heiskell Historical Collection/UALR Library Archives and Special Collections)

ocratic primary and soundly defeated his opposition in the general election, in spite of strong opposition from within his own Democratic party.

He was inaugurated on January 18, 1901, in the customary joint session of the General Assembly in the House Chamber. A sign of the intensity of the anti-Davis feelings was evidenced by the outgoing Governor Daniel Webster Jones, who broke custom and did not attend the inauguration.

Governor Davis's inaugural ceremony was starkly simple—no brass band, no parade, no reception. The audience attempted to give three cheers for the new governor but the presiding officer rapped for order after the first cheer. There were many prominent citizens, including women, in the crowd that filled the House Chamber to overflowing. Mrs. Davis and daughters Lina and Bessie, as well as the governor's father, Judge L.W. Davis, witnessed the proceedings.

After Davis was elected he rocked the Democratic Party on its heels by breaking

the unwritten party rule of non-interference in senatorial races. He openly supported James P. Clarke, and when he and Clarke were elected, a powerful statewide political machine was born.

During his second term he picked a fight with ex-Governor James P. Eagle and demanded that Eagle resign from the Capitol Commission. This issue was a burr under Davis's blanket; he was determined that the new Capitol would be built his way, but only succeeded in delaying its construction by several years. When Eagle refused to resign, church politics became involved in civil politics: Both men belonged to Second Baptist Church; Eagle was president of the Arkansas State Baptist Convention and Davis was vice-president. Davis resigned as vice-president of the convention and formally removed Eagle from the Capitol Commission. In less than a week a church disciplinary committee, made up of distinguished citizens, drew up a list of formal charges against Davis. He called it a witch-hunt but nevertheless he was "de-churched"—formally expelled from the congregation.

Only a man with Davis's wiles could have turned this to advantage. He had himself reinstated in the Baptist church in Russellville and called on the people to strike down "those high-collared pharisees" in Little Rock, proclaiming his love for the Baptist Church and saying a "few canting hypocrites of this Church cannot drive me from its blessed folds!"

Davis's morals and his drinking continued to be issues during his political career. In one campaign he answered the charge by declaring, "I want all of you fellows who ever took a drink to vote for me, and all those who haven't may vote for Judge Wood!"

Much has been written about this volatile, unbridled, controversial, and talented man, who was the first in the history of the state to be elected governor for three terms. He was a well-educated, upper-middle-class man who chose to become a Southern backwoods politician. He was unpredictable. With Jeff

Davis, when things seemed to be going along smoothly it was time to beware, for that was only the calm before the storm!

Ina McKenzie Davis was talented in both art and music. Her home was decorated with her own paintings, some of which are highly prized by descendants. She was a devoted mother and made her house a haven for her husband and children. She was a highly intelligent woman, a well-informed helpmate to her husband. She knew of the charges against Jeff, but she believed strongly in his destiny and always upheld and encouraged him. She stood proudly by his side and was always ready to give her valued advice when he needed it. Sometimes she was the only person who could get his attention.

We do not know what manner of man Davis was at home—the genteel, educated man he was brought up to be or the rough-hewn character he played. In his speeches he praised Ina highly and proudly admitted his dependence on her. A grandson says that after the death of these two people, a relative went to the house and destroyed papers and correspondence which would have revealed that things were not always as they seemed in that household. If so, Ina never let it be known. She was a Christian of deep and abiding faith.

She was not disheartened by impeachment proceedings against her husband, which fell short by one vote; she shared his pride in being elected to an unprecedented third term; she rejoiced in his victory for a seat in the United States Senate; she somehow survived the loss of four children as infants. But it all took its toll. She became violently ill on the train coming home from Russellville and died a few weeks later, on April 10, 1909. She was thirty-eight. She was buried at Mount Holly Cemetery, and a large crowd attended her funeral.

Davis was elected to a second term in the United States Senate. Two months before his first term was up, he suffered a stroke and died on January 3, 1913. He was fifty.

When Senator Clarke gave a eulogy for Jeff Davis on the senate floor, he paid tribute to Ina Davis. He said of her,

> I enjoyed abundant opportunities for knowing personally that she was a woman of masterful mind, strong convictions, and of gentle and powerful personality. She was the only person I ever knew who could influence Senator Davis against what appeared to be his settled and fixed whims or purposes. With a woman's intuition she knew exactly what he ought to do, and where her judgment conflicted with his she generally found means to cause her views and wishes to be respected. She was not an unsexed woman who ruled by force of command, but she employed in her conquest womanly qualities only. These she possessed without limit, and by the exertion of them was able to control in such a way as to be in fact the helpmate of her husband, and to become the head of a family of children whose habits, character and demeanor testify to the fact that while she was familiar with the controversies and methods of affairs outside of the home circle, above all she was at her best in her home.

Charles Jacobson, private Secretary to Governor Davis for several years, says of Mrs. Davis,

> I could not help being profoundly impressed with her wonderful intuition, her keen sense of discrimination and unerring conclusions . . . . Her sense of right and wrong was so highly developed and accentuated, that she often criticized her husband for being at times, as she thought, too vindictive, too vitriolic in discussing his opponents. He discussed with her every measure of importance coming before him for action and while at times she did not understand the technicalities involved, she decided everything by her simple rule of justice and

right.

He further said Davis was the "beneficiary of much good luck and many fortunate contingencies, but in my humble opinion none of them have so profoundly affected his career as the circumstances which directed his course across the pathway of Ina McKenzie and united his destiny with hers."

ELIZABETH JANE IRWIN LITTLE
1907-1909

JOHN S. LITTLE was inaugurated as governor almost thirty years to the day after he and Mrs. Little were married. Their thirty years had been busy and full, and it is hoped they were happy years, for terrible troubles stalked this woman before her marriage and again after her husband's election. The thirty years of their marriage were all spent in the world of politics—not always an easy life. John Little was prosecuting attorney of the Twelfth Judicial District when they married January 4, 1877. After serving three terms in that office and a term in the Arkansas House of Representatives, he was elected circuit judge and held that office until he ran for Congress in 1890. During that campaign he withdrew from the race because of ill health. It was rumored that his illness was both mental and physical. By 1894 he was fully recovered and back in the political mainstream.

After serving twelve years in the United States House of Representatives, Congressman Little ran for and was elected governor. He took the Oath of Office on January 18, 1907, before a large crowd of both men and women in the House Chamber. Mrs. Little attended and sat near the speaker's desk. He delivered his forty-five-minute address in clear, distinct tones easily heard throughout the hall. Two days later he collapsed. Again it was thought the problem was both mental and physical. He left his son Paul, who was his secretary, in charge of the governor's office and returned to the family home in Greenwood, Arkansas. In February it was decided that Governor Little should go to the Gulf Coast for rest and recuperation. He officially requested the president of the senate to become acting governor. When Governor Little had not recovered by the time the legislature was ready to adjourn in May, the newly elected president of the senate assumed the office of governor and served the remainder of the term.

Elizabeth Little's life became a nightmare, for her husband spent the rest of his life in and out of hospitals and died in the Arkansas State Hospital for Nervous Diseases. He was buried at the City Cemetery in Greenwood.

Historians praise this man highly. He was born March 15, 1851, on the family farm in Sebastian County, the son of Mary Elizabeth Tatum and Jesse Little. He was given the middle name of Sebastian because he was the first male child born in that newly created county. By the time he was ready to go to school the Civil War had caused the schools to be closed. He spent his early years working on the farm and was seventeen years old before he had the opportunity to attend school. He was bright and eager to learn and advanced rapidly. He later borrowed some law books, retired to his father's farm, and began the study of law. He was admitted to the bar in 1873, moved to Paris in Logan County, and opened up a law office, beginning a remarkable career. He was eminently successful as a prosecuting attorney, a highly respected judge, and a very able and popular congressman, and as governor it was hoped he would restore political peace and harmony to the state. He is described as a man of wit with magnetic manner and tremendous understanding of human nature: a combination that made him a great favorite of the electorate.

Elizabeth Jane Irwin was one of three girls born to Mr. and Mrs. Pleasant Irwin. She was born April 3, 1861, a year of extreme hardship in Arkansas and the South. Her father, who was not physically able to join the Confederacy, was a casualty of the war just the same. Bushwhackers lured him out of the house and shot him. Confederate soldiers riding by the house learned what had happened and were able to track the bushwhackers because one of their horses had only half a shoe. The culprits were found and hanged.

Materials and money were so scarce during the war years that people had to make do in all sorts of resourceful ways. There was no lumber to build a casket for Elizabeth's father's burial; her mother solved the problem by taking the boards off the ceiling of the house. With the men off to war, it was up to the women and children to work for their survival. Even Elizabeth, who was only a small child, had responsibilities: she picked cotton during the day, and at night removed the seeds from it. Her assigned quota was enough cotton to fill her shoe with seeds every night. These early hard times taught her to be stoic and strong; nothing ever got the best of her. She never threw anything away, but found a way to reuse everything. Not surprisingly, her lifetime hobby was the handwork she had been forced to learn as a girl.

Elizabeth's mother eventually moved off the farm to Paris, Arkansas, where she ran a boardinghouse. One of the boarders was the enterprising young lawyer John S. Little. A courtship began between him and Elizabeth, and they were married when Elizabeth was barely sixteen.

John and Elizabeth Little had five children: Montie Olivia, Lizzie Lou, Paul, Thomas Eugene, and Jesse Edward.

Elizabeth was a devoted wife and mother. During the nine years of her husband's illness she followed him from hospital to hospital. She was ninety-two years old when she died on September 15, 1953. She was survived by a daughter, Mrs. M.W. Wallace of Van Buren, Arkansas; two sons, Thomas Eugene Little and Jesse Edward Little, eighteen grandchildren, and fifteen great-grandchildren.

LOUVENIA WALLACE DONAGHEY
1903-1913

ACCORDING TO GOVERNOR Donaghey's auto-biography he and Louvenia Wallace met in Conway, Arkansas, during the Christmas holidays of 1879.

He had come to live in Conway by a fascinating series of events. George Washington Donaghey was born in Union Parish, Louisiana, the son of Christopher Columbus Donaghey and Elizabeth Ingram Donaghey. When he was nine years old his father joined the Confederate Army and went off to war. George was the oldest child in the family, and the mantle of responsibility for the family and farm weighed heavily on the boy's shoulders. The return of his father gave the boy little relief, for Christopher Donaghey came home an alcoholic.

The family lived on a road heavily traveled by families moving from war-torn Mississippi and Alabama to the sweet promise of Texas, a state that had been spared the ravages of war. Often wagon trains would camp on or near the Donaghey property, and young George made his first money running errands for the travelers. He would go hunting and sell his kill to them. He joined them round their campfires at night and heard exciting tales of life out west in Texas. By the time he was ten, he had vowed to go someday to Texas. It became an obsession with him. His dad's drinking, coupled with the lure of the unknown, created an irresistible urge. He bedeviled his parents for permission to leave, but they would not consent. When he was fifteen, one spring morning he went to saddle his horse and the animal was pawing the ground. Young Donaghey thought to himself, "He wants to go too." He simply saddled up and rode off—no money, no food, and no clothes. In the months he was away he endured some rough times, and when he finally returned home he had left

his boyhood in Texas.

The next few years were divided between home, visits to relatives in Conway, and a second trip to Texas. By December 1879 he had returned to Conway with the idea of making that bustling little town his home. He had been there only a few days when he met Louvenia. The Terpsichorian Club was having a grand Christmas reception. Every invited guest was given transportation to the party in a closed carriage, courtesy of the club. Donaghey's uncle owned the livery stable in town and was furnishing transportation to the event; when one more driver was needed, George Donaghey agreed to help out. One of the pairs named on his list was a Miss Wallace and her escort. In the dim light he could see the graceful form that came down the steps on the arm of her escort. When Donaghey heard her soft South Carolina accent he was all attention. In his words, "She had an unusual voice, rich and rare with warm overtones, and the gay lilt of young laughter." All the way to the ball he listened to her as she chatted and laughed. He strained to see her face but "saw only the graceful form and movement as she stepped forward lightly in her swaying hoops and bustle."

The next day, when he learned she was a guest of his cousin, Mrs. John H. Hartje, he finagled an invitation to Christmas dinner at the Hartje house. When he met Louvenia she was even more beautiful than he had imagined. "The bluest eyes I had ever seen danced and melted under a shining bang of warm brown hair. She was just the kind of girl every young man wants to marry." He saw her every day of her visit and asked permission to write to her when she went back home.

Now more than ever he felt pressed to find

his life's work. He became a carpenter and was soon earning forty dollars a month, more money than he had ever dreamed of making. Later he was thrilled to be asked to work in a cabinet shop, for carpenter's bench work was the highest class of work known to the trade.

He decided to go to Carlisle and visit Miss Wallace. Arriving unannounced one Sunday morning, he was bitterly disappointed to find another beau already there. They all went to church and came back to the Wallaces' for a bountiful Sunday dinner. Dessert was a delicious layer cake baked by Louvenia. To learn that this beautiful girl was also a good cook was almost too much for the young man.

With her scintillating wit she kept the group of young people in high spirits all afternoon. He was shy and envied the others' careless banter, feeling he wasn't making any headway with Louvenia. He was amused when she and her sister Maggie told how together they had gotten rid of an unwanted suitor. The young man called so often he had outworn his welcome. He rode a ridiculous white mule. The girls sneaked out and used pokeberry juice to paint red zebra stripes all over the mule's body! Needless to say the young man never came back.

When it was time for George Donaghey to leave, he was thrilled beyond measure when Louvenia asked him to call again. She came to Conway to visit and he saw her every day of her stay. Often traveling theatrical troupes came from Little Rock to Conway to perform—giving residents occasions to wear their finery. At such a performance George created quite a stir when he walked down the aisle with the beautiful Louvenia on his arm. She wore a "sweeping Gainsborough hat trimmed with black and blue plumes, that set off her fair skin and blue eyes." He and Louvenia became engaged. He decided he needed an education in order to provide for her as he wished.

At the age of twenty-six he entered the University of Arkansas, intending to stay until he earned his degree. At the end of the

first year his cousin Susie Hartje came to commencement and persuaded him to come back to Conway. He lucked into a teaching job, so it was July before he went to see Louvenia. He planned to release her from the engagement because it would be unfair to ask her to wait until he graduated. When he saw her, all his intentions melted away. They sat in his buggy and talked and at the end of that evening knew they would be married soon. His teaching job was over on September 10. They were married September 20, 1883.

In his autobiography written fifty years later he described the event:

> For two years Miss Wallace had been preparing for marriage. She had made feather beds and quilts, dainty linens, and all the gewgaws a bride loves. I borrowed a buggy from Uncle William Ingram's livery stable and drove to Little Rock for my Prince Albert coat and wedding trousers. . . . The dress of my bride was typical of those thrifty days when a wedding dress was made to serve many post-wedding occasions. It was rich oxblood satin, made in the fashion of the day, with hoops and bustle.

The young couple made their first home in Conway, where George Donaghey worked as a carpenter. Their home was simple and their life spartan. As a poor man's wife Louvenia worked hard and practiced strict economy. He was again working in the cabinet shop and every day at noon she walked to the shop and took him a pail of hot lunch that she had prepared. She knew her husband was a hard-working man of talent and ambition. She shared his dream of success and was a willing helpmate every step of the way. The partnership of George and Louvenia Donaghey was so close it is impossible to separate their stories.

As a talented carpenter he soon became a partner in the cabinet shop. A great fire burned most of downtown Conway, including the cabinet shop. Donaghey was once again out of work, his investment had burned up, and he still owed $250 of the cost of buying into the partnership that no longer existed. He was despondent. Louvenia took in boarders and sewing to help with the finances. But in the aftermath of loss, some good did come; the fire served as a catalyst that launched Donaghey into the contracting business. Although he made a few bad contracts in the beginning, George Donaghey was an astute businessman. When he began turning a profit, he invested in farms and timberland, but it was through his construction business that he became a wealthy man. The Donagheys are among the few really wealthy couples who have served as the First Family of Arkansas.

In downtown Little Rock, George Donaghey was the builder and owner of the Donaghey Building, the Waldron Building, and the Wallace Building, so named to honor Louvenia's family name. He supervised the building of the Main Street and Broadway bridges across the Arkansas River. He built the first bank building in Conway, the main building of the new Hendrix College, courthouses in Arkansas and Texas, train stations, water towers for the railroads (piping water to them was always an interesting challenge), a new Arkansas insane asylum, roads, and the Arkansas Tuberculosis Sanitorium. It was said that no one invested more time and effort in the building of the new state Capitol than George Donaghey—an interesting story by and of itself.

In 1908 the controversy over the building of a new state Capitol had reached such proportions that George Donaghey ran for governor and was elected on the promise that he would complete the building. He took office on January 14, 1909, in the old statehouse—the last inauguration held in this building until 1975 when David Pryor held his inauguration there.

The Donaghey inauguration took place in the afternoon before a joint session of the house and senate. The *Arkansas Gazette*

reports that five hundred spectators were packed into the House Chamber. "Just below and to the left of Governor Donaghey sat Mrs. Donaghey and a party of about twenty-five ladies who were her guests and who were given special seats by the joint session." There was no reception following the inauguration. He spent a few minutes shaking hands with well-wishers in the House Chamber and in his office.

Both Governor and Mrs. Donaghey were committed to improving the educational opportunities for the young people of Arkansas. It was primarily through his efforts and influence that Conway became the home of three colleges: Hendrix College, State Normal College (later State Teachers College and now the University of Central Arkansas), and Central College. Our four agricultural colleges were created during Donaghey's administration. The Donaghey Foundation was established for the benefit of Little Rock Junior College (now the University of Arkansas at Little Rock). Mrs. Donaghey was present and participated in the formal signing of the papers that created the trust. Later, one of the trustees, banker Alfred G. Kahn, said, "Her enthusiasm for the foundation matched that of the governor, and I believe it was her idea." The foundation's original endowment consisted mainly of the Donaghey Building and the Waldron Building.

Now that the property was given away, Louvenia asked her husband what he planned to do with his time and was stunned when he reminded her of his plantation. Surely a man his age would not assume that burden! It was three thousand acres of problems. But he did. He had drainage ditches dug, put many additional acres under cultivation, and sold it for a profit.

Governor Donaghey was born July 1, 1859, and died on December 15, 1937.

Louvenia Wallace was born in Darlington, South Carolina, in 1862. When she was seventeen her parents, J.G. and Eunice Wallace, moved the family to Arkansas and settled in

Louvenia and George W. Donaghey on the steps of the new Capitol, 1910. (Photo courtesy of the J.N. Heiskell Historical Collection/UALR Library Archives and Special Collections)

Old Austin near Carlisle in Lonoke County. Four years later she and George Donaghey were married. All descriptions of Louvenia speak of her eye-catching style as a young woman. There isn't a clue why, as a mature woman, she changed so completely. A niece remembered her fondly as a plain woman, straight of stature, who always wore low-heeled, sensible shoes, black stockings, and dark dresses with demure lace collars, with her black hair pulled severely back and done up in a knot on her head. She remembers going places with "Auntie Donaghey" and being required to sit up straight "with hands folded primly in my lap. I was so little, my feet wouldn't reach the floor, but stuck straight out in front of me. I'll never forget those black patent leather shoes of mine! I never saw the big diamonds Uncle George gave her until I was grown because 'Auntie Donaghey' always wore white gloves."

Governor and Mrs. Donaghey had no chil-

dren of their own but befriended and educated several children of the family. One niece lived with them much of her life and was treated like a daughter. They adopted Raymond Donaghey, son of the governor's brother.

When George Donaghey was elected governor, they moved to Little Rock and made their home there the rest of their lives. After his death, Mrs. Donaghey spent the remaining ten years of her life running her house and looking after their business interests. She often attended meetings and advised with the Board of the Donaghey Foundation. Upon her death the assets of this trust had increased to approximately one million dollars, and it would be debt-free in five more years.

Louvenia died at her home at 2109 Gaines Street on July 28, 1947. She was stricken while canning food—at eighty-four still the hard-working, frugal housewife. She spent

Governor and Mrs. Donaghey at home, November 23, 1936. The governor is wearing the suit in which he was inaugurated. (Photo by Waff's Photo Shop; courtesy of the Arkansas History Commission)

her married life as her husband's staunch supporter, advisor, and loving wife. She said, "My highest aim in life was to do what I could for his comfort and to assist and encourage him in every way I could."

He dedicated his autobiography thus:

To Louvenia

The sweetheart of my youth,
The helpmate of my young manhood,
The partner of my maturer years,
The Companion who smoothes the path of age
This Biography
Is affectionately dedicated by—
George W. Donaghey.

Governor and Mrs. Joe T. Robinson. (Photo courtesy of the Arkansas History Commission)

EWILDA GERTRUDE MILLER ROBINSON
January 1913

EWILDA "WILLIE" ROBINSON was wife of the governor only fourteen days before her husband was elected senator and she became the wife of a senator! Her husband had been a member of Congress since 1902, but was elected to the office of governor in the fall of 1912. He resigned from Congress on January 14, 1913, and was inaugurated as governor on the 16th and elected to the United States Senate on the 28th. Thus in the space of two weeks Joe T. Robinson held the offices of congressman, governor, and senator.

This short term in the governor's office was brought about by the sudden death of Jeff Davis, who had just been reelected to a second term in the senate. His death created a vacancy for the full term in the senate, and Robinson decided he would rather be senator for six years than governor for two. He was elected to the senate by the Arkansas legislature, the last time a senator was elected in this manner—from that time forward the senators have been elected by the people. Governor Donaghey appointed J.N. Heiskell, editor of the *Arkansas Gazette,* to fill out Senator Davis's unexpired term of twenty-three days. The Arkansas legislature elected W.M. Kavanaugh to serve until March 4 and Robinson to become senator for the full term on that date.

Though Willie Robinson's term as First Lady was short, she should be included in this story because her husband was a duly elected governor. He did not immediately resign and from January 28 to March 10 was both governor and senator. He chose to stay in the governor's office in order to push through the legislative program he had campaigned for and believed in.

Probably because his election to the senate was already pretty much a certainty, his inauguration was very simple—in fact, spar-

tan. A committee from both houses of the General Assembly escorted him to the speaker's rostrum in the House Chamber where he was sworn in before a large crowd of both men and women. It is assumed that Mrs. Robinson attended, although no mention of her was made in the report of the ceremonies by either of the Little Rock papers.

As wife of Joe T. Robinson, Willie Robinson traveled much of the world. They were jet-setters of their era, though their mode of travel was by ship and train—pleasant but time-consuming. A list of the countries visited leaves the impression this senator spent little time on the floor of the senate, and in fact, only one major piece of legislation bears his name. They traveled to Istanbul, Rio de Janeiro, Uruguay, Argentina, Peru, and Chile; to Paris, Copenhagen, England, and Scotland. Most of the trips were on government business, but some were for pleasure. They spent one summer grouse hunting in Scotland, where they lived in an old castle near Aberdeen, and another summer enjoying the hunting season in Czechoslovakia. They went to Panama many times for deep sea fishing. There were two trips to Hawaii and one to Alaska, and in 1935 they were a part of Vice President Garner's entourage to the Philippines to attend the inauguration of Manuel Quezon as the first president of those islands. The Robinsons spent four months in London where the senator was a delegate to the London Naval Peace Conference. While in London they were the guests of King George and Queen Mary at Buckingham Palace several times.

Willie Robinson had the thrill of seeing her husband preside as permanent chairman of the Democratic National Convention in 1928, at Houston, Texas. At this convention Sena-

Ewilda Gertrude Miller Robinson. (Photo courtesy of the Arkansas History Commission)

tor Robinson received his party's vice presidential nomination on the ticket with Al Smith. Herbert Hoover won.

When Franklin Roosevelt became president, Robinson was senate majority leader and his strong supporter. He led the fight to pass the president's court-packing plan, the Judiciary Reorganization Bill. It was rumored that if Robinson were successful in getting this legislation passed, he would receive an appointment to the Supreme Court. Political rumors have a life of their own—sometimes full of purpose but often meaningless, or even mean. In a campaign they can be a tool to influence the public, and can be deliberately started. Sometimes they begin when someone simply wonders aloud about something, or when a newspaper columnist surmises and supposes in order to fill a daily column. Regardless of how they start, they should be taken for what they are worth—nothing! If during the Brooks-Baxter War bullets had flown as thick and fast as rumors, it would have been a bloody battle with no

survivors. The rumor of this presidential promise could have been true or it could have been one of the opposition's tactics to defeat the legislation.

Whether or not there was a promise, Senator Robinson died of a heart attack during the fight to pass the legislation. Willie was left a widow with no income, for there were no pensions or retirement plans for senators in those days. The Robinsons had lived high and well. She had a twenty-one-room home at 2122 Broadway, but little else. Friends and party loyals rallied round and got her the appointment of postmistress of Little Rock. She held this office until her death.

Willie Robinson was a good political wife. This petite person was every inch a lady, dignified but not aloof. She liked people and was well-liked and respected in return.

The cosmopolitan Robinsons had their beginnings in Lonoke, Arkansas. Willie was the daughter of Sarah Evelyn Grady and Jessie Miller. Her father served in the Confederate Army and was wounded in both the battles of Shiloh and Atlanta. After the war he left his native Tennessee and came to Lonoke, where he engaged in the mercantile business until his retirement forty years later.

Joe T. Robinson was the fourth son in a family of ten children. His mother was a part Indian girl from Tennessee, Matilda Jane Swaim, and his father was Dr. James Madison Robinson, a country doctor and Baptist minister. Joe T. attended schools in Lonoke County and for two years at the University of Arkansas, studied law with the eminent jurist Judge Thomas C. Trimble, and received his law degree from the University of Virginia. He and Willie were married December 15, 1896, in Lonoke. They had no children.

IDA VIRGINIA YARBOROUGH HAYS
1913-1917

IDA VIRGINIA HAYS descends from James Yarborough, an Irish immigrant who came to this country before the Revolutionary War. He joined his fellow Americans in their fight for freedom and settled in North Carolina after the war. His descendants gradually moved westward. In 1849 William Yarborough came to Arkansas and settled in Ouachita County ten miles south of Camden. He became a prosperous farmer, and was the father of nine children. One son, Elbert S. Yarborough, married Prudence Winfrey Ross, thus uniting two prominent south Arkansas families. Elbert and Prudence moved to Camden (then called Ecore Fabre, the name the French gave to the settlement) and lived there for several years. After the Civil War, Elbert bought a farm at Buena Vista, set up a mercantile store, and later became postmaster of the little settlement. Elbert was active in church and civic affairs, running for and being elected to various political offices. He and Prudence had three children: Annie Evalyn, Asa Edward, and Ida Virginia, born on August 24, 1873.

Ida lived all her young years at Buena Vista and graduated from high school there. She helped her father in his mercantile business and for a time was his assistant in the post office. She had plans to go to college, but handsome George Washington Hays came along and erased all thought of college from her mind. On February 24, 1895, she married this young lawyer who was a native of Ouachita County.

George and Ida Hays made their home and raised two children in the community that was by then Camden, a cultural center of south Arkansas. They were prominent citizens of the enterprising town. George moved through the county political chairs and in 1913, after Governor Joe T. Robinson

resigned, he was elected governor in a special election.

Hays was inaugurated on August 6, 1913, on the steps of the Capitol. The legislature was not in session; therefore Hays could not be presented to a joint session of the General Assembly, as was customary. At first the plans were for Hays to take the Oath of Office in the Governor's Reception Room, but at the last minute it was decided to hold the ceremony on the Capitol steps, even though it was the hottest day of the year with temperatures of 100°. Two trainloads of well-wishers and supporters from Camden and El Dorado arrived in Little Rock early that morning and were met at the station by the governor-elect. The crowd went to the Gleason Hotel, where much celebration took place before time for the ceremony that afternoon. A military band from Magnolia opened the proceedings by playing "Dixie," and as the cheers subsided, the governor-elect elbowed his way through the crowd, Mrs. Hays and a few of her friends following closely behind. Supreme Court Justice Edgar McCulloch stood on one side of a small table and George Hays on the other. Without further ado the oath was given and answered. Murmurs could be heard from over the crowd, "Is it over?" An inspired reprise of "Dixie" did indeed end the proceedings, and the new governor walked back to his office, where he stood for hours receiving congratulations from his friends.

In June 1914 Governor and Mrs. Hays traveled to San Francisco, California, on official business to select a site for the Arkansas Building at the Panama-Pacific International Exposition. The trip was made in the private car of General Superintendent J.W. Dean of the Iron Mountain Railroad. He and Mrs. Dean were members of the party of about

Ida Virginia Yarborough Hays (here shown as No. 10) and her husband, Governor Hays (No. 1), on a trip to San Francisco, June 1914. (Photo courtesy of the Arkansas History Commission)

twenty other guests who made up this distinguished and privileged group. They were entertained royally in California.

During Hays's term in office, a reform movement grew in this country. Woodrow Wilson had been elected president. As president of Princeton University his educational reforms had won him high praise and the attention of the national press. As president of the United States he brought bold imagination and high ideals to the task of reform within this country, effecting changes in several important areas. In Arkansas this mood for change was evidenced by legislation that was favorable to women. Work days for women were restricted to nine hours a day for a maximum of six days a week. Another bill that advanced women's rights gave married women the right to own property and to manage their property personally. Women were also granted the right to enter into contracts. A woman's suffrage amendment was submitted to a vote. There

is no record that Ida Hays joined in the crusade for voting privileges for women, or that she influenced her husband in any of these matters. It is easy to believe that she did, for she was a progressive and caring person.

Ida Hays involved herself in social welfare work in her community. Of special interest to her were the inmates and conditions in the state prison, which she made her own special project. She visited often and did what she could to bring some cheer into the lives of these poor souls doomed to live their lives behind walls. They loved her.

Governor Hays's second inaugural address, given on January 5, 1915, was crowded off the front page of the papers by war news. In August 1914, Americans were stunned with the invasion of France by Germany and of Germany by Russia. World War I had begun. This country remained neutral as long as possible, but with the threat of war coming closer every day, Ida Hays joined with other women in war aid activities. When President

Wilson's daughter came to Little Rock on behalf of the war effort, Ida Hays was her hostess.

Ida was a devoted wife and mother. Her husband's career and their home and children came first with her. When the family moved to Little Rock, they rented the house at 1900 Marshall for the duration of his term in office. Deciding to stay in Little Rock and practice law, Hays bought a house on Battery Street, where the family lived for two years before moving to a newly built house at 2001 West Seventeenth Street. They lived there the rest of their lives.

Governor Hays died at home of pneumonia on September 15, 1927. Mrs. Hays lived for almost thirty more years. She died at her home on May 20, 1959. She was eighty-five. She was a member of Second Baptist Church, the Rose Garden Club, and Pioneers of Arkansas. Survivors were a son, Reverend William F. Hays of Melbourne, Florida, and two nephews, G.L. Church of Arlington, Virginia, and Maury Church of Alexandria, Virginia.

Anne Wade Roark as the bride of Charles Hillman Brough in 1908. (Photo courtesy of the Brough family)

ANNE WADE ROARK BROUGH
1917-1921

OUR TWENTY-FIFTH FIRST Lady met her husband in Fayetteville, Arkansas, when she went there to visit her cousins, Mr. and Mrs. H. King Wade. They introduced Anne to Dr. Charles Hillman Brough, a very eligible bachelor who was chairman of the Political Economy and Sociology Department at the University of Arkansas. Their courtship was interrupted by a serious lovers' quarrel. When something he said left the wrong impression with Anne, she fired off a letter expressing her keen displeasure and informing him she was returning the ring and bracelet he had given her. He was so upset when he read the letter that he didn't want to answer, but nevertheless he stopped in at the Washington Hotel in downtown Fayetteville and hastily wrote her, declaring his undying love, begging for forgiveness for inadvertently wounding the girl he loved more than life itself, and asking her to set a date for the wedding. He told her he would send the ring and bracelet right back to her and that if his letter did not convey to her how genuinely sorry he was, he was coming to see her at once "for you are more to me than ambition, the University and all the rest of the world." This letter was dated October 11, 1907. The two worked out this misunderstanding and were married at the Baptist church in Franklin, Kentucky, on June 17, 1908.

This wedding was the social event of the season in Franklin; the *Franklin Favorite* devoted three columns to the report of the wedding, which began, "Society, which for the past six months has been anticipating the brilliant wedding of Miss Anne Wade Roark . . . was amply repaid, it proving to be one of the most brilliant nuptial events in the history of Franklin, not only from an artistic standpoint, but from a personal and social one as well." After a description of the beautiful weather of that day and evening, the elaborate church decorations, the bride, and the bridal party were described. The "brilliant assemblage, taxing the capacity of the edifice," were treated to a lengthy program of wedding music. At the appointed time the matron of honor entered wearing "pearl grey silk over an underdress of pink silk taffeta, Princess, entrain, richly trimmed; hair adornments of pink roses, and carrying a shower bouquet of Killarney roses and maiden hair fern, from which hung pink satin ribbon streamers." The four bridesmaids and two flower girls were equally elegant in their dress and carried similar bouquets. The groom and groomsmen all wore full dress suits of black. The bride advanced unescorted to the altar.

Her slender, girlish figure draped in a costly bridal gown of ivory Marquisette, built on a foundation of ivory satin messaline. The outer robe paneled full front length with costly princess lace, the Princess style exquisitely suited to her style and figure, the train measuring two and one-half yards in length. She wore the regulation bridal gown veil of silk tulle, fastened with a wreath of orange blossoms, her only jewel being the costly diamond broach, a wedding gift from the groom. She carried a massive shower bouquet of bride's roses, lilies of the valley and maiden hair fern, adorned with myriads of white satin ribbon streamers. Her manner was the perfection of grace and womanly charm.

Immediately after the ceremony, a lavish reception was held at the home of the bride. After a three-month honeymoon in Cali-

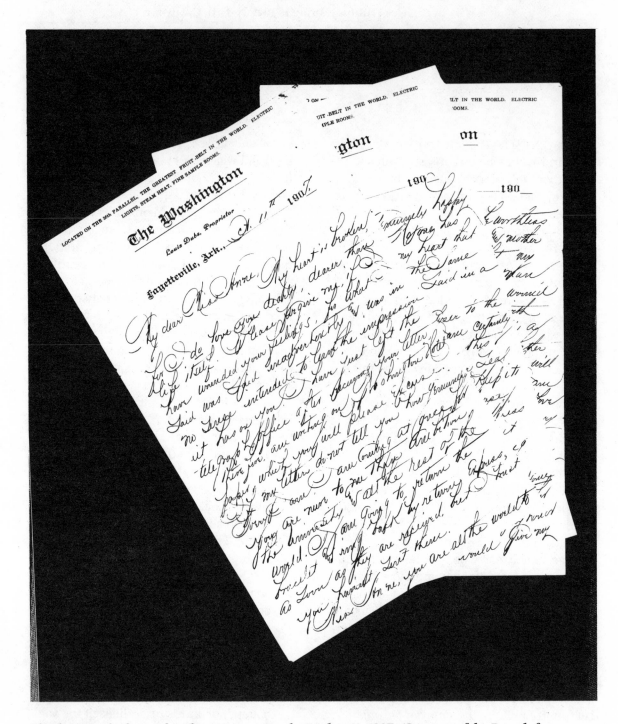

Charles Brough's letter of apology to Anne Roark, October 11, 1907. (Courtesy of the Brough family)

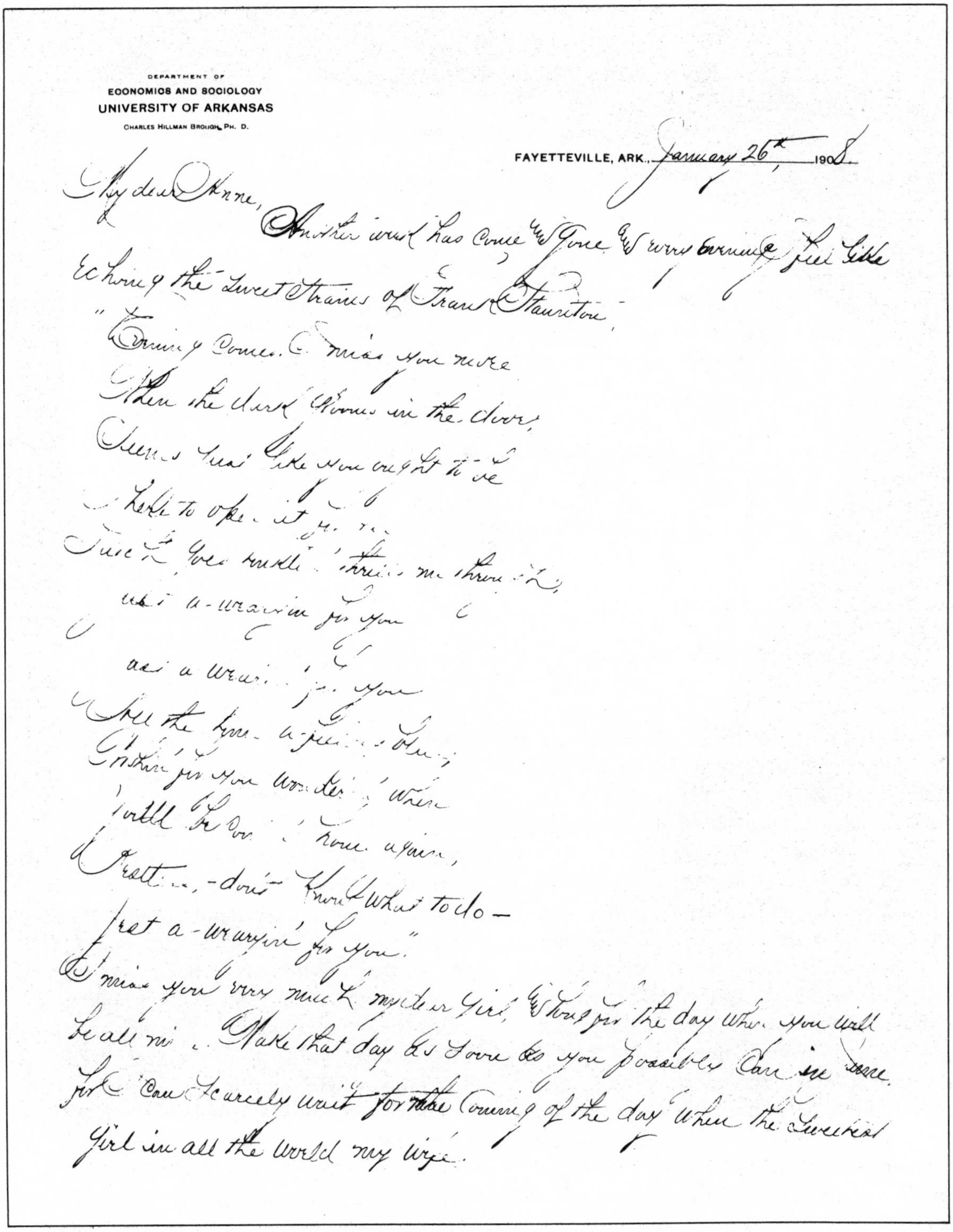

DEPARTMENT OF
ECONOMICS AND SOCIOLOGY
UNIVERSITY OF ARKANSAS
CHARLES HILLMAN BROUGH, PH. D.

FAYETTEVILLE, ARK., January 26th, 1908.

My dear Anne,

Another week has come and gone and every evening I feel like echoing the sweet strains of Frank Stanton:

"Evening comes. I miss you more
When the dark gloom's in the door;
Seems just like you ought to be
There to open it for me!
Latch goes tinklin'; thrills me through,
Sets me worryin' for you!

Jest a-worryin' for you!
All the time a-feelin' blue;
Wishin' for you, wonderin' when
You'll be comin' home again;
Restless,—don't know what to do—
Jest a-worryin' for you."

I miss you very much my dear girl, and long for the day when you will be all mine. Make that day as soon as you possibly can, sweet one, for I can scarcely wait for the coming of the day when the sweetest girl in all the world my wife.

A love letter from Charles to Anne, January 26, 1908. (Courtesy of the Brough family)

Mr. and Mrs. Granville Wade Roark

invite you to be present

at the marriage of their daughter

Anne

to

Mr. Charles Hillman Brough

on the evening of Wednesday, the seventeenth of June

Nineteen hundred and eight

at half-after seven o'clock

Baptist Church

Franklin, Kentucky

The wedding invitation of the future Governor Brough and his First Lady-to-be.

fornia with the groom's parents, the young couple returned to Fayetteville, and Dr. Brough resumed his teaching duties. The Broughs assumed a position of leadership in academic, social, and religious circles of Fayetteville. They entertained often, and their home was a haven for students either seeking help or out for a social evening. Games of rook and charades were a popular form of entertainment at the Broughs'. They had no children of their own, and in their eight years at the university they opened their home to several deserving students, some who boarded or lived with the Broughs and some who received financial help or needed encouragement. Anne Brough never knew in the morning just how many would sit down at her dinner table in the evening, but this didn't bother her—in fact she loved it!

Governor Brough was the son of Charles Milton and Flora M. Thompson Brough. His father, a prominent mine-owner and banker in the Utah Territory, was also active in local politics. His mother spent most of her childhood in Mississippi, where her family were educators of note. When C. Hillman Brough was six, he was sent to Mississippi to live with his mother's sister and her husband, Dr. and Mrs. Walter Hillman, co-founders of the Central Female Institute in Clinton, Mississippi. Governor Brough's mother had served on the staff of this college before she married and moved to Utah. She sent her child back there because of her own ill health and the fine educational facilities she knew were available. C. Hillman Brough proved to be an excellent student. He entered Mississippi College at the age of fourteen and had almost perfect grades for his four years there. He earned a bachelor's and a master's degree and then enrolled in John Hopkins University for his doctorate. In 1898 he returned to Mississippi College, where he taught a variety of subjects. After three years he resigned and entered the University of Mississippi to study law. He finished a two-year course in

Anne Wade Roark's childhood home in Kentucky. (Photo courtesy of the Brough family)

one year and was graduated with honors. (He never practiced law, although he was licensed to do so in both Arkansas and Mississippi.) He resumed his teaching career, this time at Hillman College in Clinton, and in 1903 he accepted a chair at the University of Arkansas. Four years later he met Anne Roark.

Anne Roark was of distinguished Virginia ancestry. She descends from Colonel Hugh Bulloch, who was a member of the Council in 1631 and a Trustee of Williamsburg. She was born on April 17, 1880, in Franklin, Kentucky, one of three children of Granville Wade Roark and Sarah Norvell Roark. Her father was a longtime successful lawyer in Kentucky, the president of Simpson County Bank and of Franklin Woolen Mills, and could afford a proper home and fine education for his children. Anne graduated from

Franklin Female College in 1896 and took further study at Hollins Institute near Roanoke, Virginia. She was described in her hometown newspaper as a real southern belle—"Accomplished and cultured—a universal favorite (who) is loved and admired by all classes." She was an excellent student and an accomplished musician. She continued her musical education in New York, where she spent a winter attending opera and symphonies. Back in Franklin she had served as organist for her church, and when she and Dr. Brough were to be married there was a piece in the paper commending her for this service to her church and lamenting her leaving.

C. Hillman Brough was always interested in politics and was famous for organizing the first "Woodrow Wilson for President Club." He seriously considered running for gover-

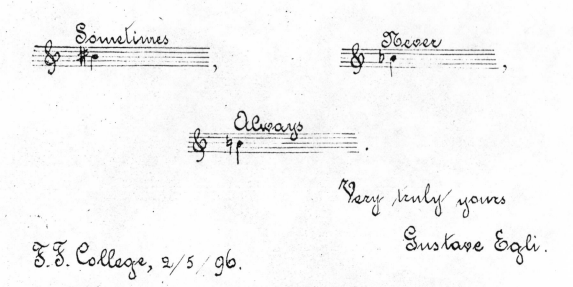

Sometimes , *Never* ,

Always .

Very truly yours
Gustave Egli.

F. F. College, 2/5/96.

"Sometimes sharp, never flat, always natural"—a compliment, appropriately written in musical form, that the talented Anne Wade Roark received from a teacher at Franklin Female College in Kentucky.

The Arkansas Women's Committee of the State Council of Defense, with Anne Brough seated on the second row, third from the left. (Photo courtesy of the Arkansas History Commission)

Anne Roark Brough (in dark jumper at center) attending Suffragette Rally on the Capitol steps, summer 1919. (Photo courtesy of Peg Smith)

nor in 1913 but decided against the race at that time. In the summer of 1916 he made a successful campaign for the office. When they left Fayetteville to come to Little Rock for the inauguration, five hundred people came to the train station to see them off. This popular couple had been very active members of the First Baptist Church of Fayetteville, and at a farewell dedicatory service at the church the congregation presented them with a handsome loving cup.

On Inauguration Day the new First Lady's picture and a short biography of her were featured in the society section of the *Arkansas Gazette*. Governor and Mrs. Brough had as their guests at the Hotel Marion his stepmother, Mrs. Cora Brough of Los Angeles; his aunt, Mrs. Mary Rice of Nashville, Tennessee; his brother, Knight M. Brough, and his wife and son; and cousins of Mrs. Brough, Mrs. Mena Montague of Franklin, Kentucky, and H. King Wade of Fayetteville. The inauguration took place as usual in the House Chamber, and Governor Brough's address was reported as being the longest ever presented.

Hillman and Anne Brough were an unusually close couple. Everyone who knew them remembers the compelling devotion between them. She was his campaign manager during his candidacy for governor and often his chauffeur, for he never learned to drive. He was subject to illness and more than once his recovery was credited to her

Anne Roark Brough being honored upon her retirement as Chairman of Hospital Donations at the Arkansas Baptist Hospital. (Photo courtesy of the Brough family)

devoted and determined nursing care.

Governor Brough's term coincided with World War I. Both he and Anne supported the war effort in every way possible. Anne Brough was a faithful and constant participant at Red Cross classes and supply-making sessions. She served as active chairman of women in the second, third, and fourth Liberty Loans and the Victory Loan. She was honorary chairman of the Women's Auxiliary to the State Council of Defense.

While in office they leased the Garland-Mitchell House at 1404 Scott Street, the same house where Governor and Mrs. Garland had lived. This spacious house was a proper setting for the official entertaining carried on by the Broughs while in office. After leaving

office, they bought a home at 1863 Arch Street where they continued to entertain their wide circle of friends and acquaintances. They both enjoyed the game of bridge and often attended bridge parties.

Hillman and Anne Brough loved to travel. During his time in office, they attended two national Democratic Conventions, one in San Francisco and another in New York. She accompanied her husband on the "Arkansas on Wheels" train, whose mission it was to advertise Arkansas and its products. After leaving office they traveled extensively in Europe and in the United States, covering over four thousand miles in eighteen states in their Buick sedan.

In 1934, Dr. Brough received an appointment from President Franklin D. Roosevelt as chairman of the Columbia-Virginia Boundary Commission. They lived in Washington while Brough and his commission arbitrated the 143-year-old dispute between the national government and the Commonwealth of Virginia. Charles Brough died suddenly on December 26, 1935. His body was returned to Arkansas to lie in state at the Capitol and at Second Baptist Church. He was buried in Roselawn Memorial Park Cemetery.

Mrs. Brough returned to her home in Little Rock and busied herself with worthwhile activities. She served two terms as president of the Little Rock branch of the Needlework Guild, an international organization devoted to charity. She was an active member and office-holder of the YWCA and of the Aesthetic Club. She was a member of the Arkansas Democratic Club, Daughters of the American Revolution, United Daughters of the Confederacy, and Colonial Dames. She continued as an active member of the Sec-

ond Baptist Church and devoted many hours of volunteer work to the Arkansas Baptist Hospital. In 1945 she was prevailed upon to take a full-time job on behalf of the hospital. Her title was Chairman of Hospital Donations. One co-worker was quoted in the *Gazette* as saying, "Whenever the hospital has needed anything, from a new wheelchair to a whole new building, we just went to Mrs. Brough and she made a phone call or wrote a few letters—or set a whole campaign in motion. We always got what we had to have."

Anne Brough was totally dedicated and devoted to her husband as long as he lived. After his death she set about making a new life for herself through which she rendered great service. Of her work for the Arkansas Baptist Hospital she said, "It is an inspiring task because I am continually renewing my faith in humanity."

Mrs. Brough died in October 1958 at the age of seventy-eight. She is buried beside her husband at Roselawn Memorial Park Cemetery in Little Rock.

Governor and Mrs. Tom McRae, 1925. (Photo by Shrader of Little Rock)

AMELIA ANN WHITE McRAE
1921-1925

AMELIA ANN WHITE became a resident of Arkansas when she was three years old. She was born in Decatur, Alabama, on October 6, 1855, the daughter of William Richard White and Mary Jane Clarke White. The family was living in Pine Bluff, Arkansas, when the Civil War broke out. Her father joined the Confederacy and served the entire four years, spending eight months as a prisoner of the Yankees.

When the Union Army marched on Pine Bluff, the family moved to Bradley County to escape the horrors of war. They did not move far enough, for there as a little girl, Amelia was an eyewitness to the battle at Mack's Mill—the second of our First Ladies to have the frightening experience of seeing an actual battle.

When Amelia Ann's father was released from prison he came home, and again tried to move the family to Texas. Illness forced them to stop at Falcon in Columbia County. The war ended and the family decided to remain in Falcon. This is where Amelia grew up. She attended the Masonic Male and Female Institute there, and met Tom McRae, a boarding pupil at the institute. Their courtship lasted for six years before they were married December 17, 1874.

Tom was faced with the responsibility of providing for the family, and not until his mother remarried could he devote time to his education. After attending the institute at Falcon, he spent one year clerking in a store in Shreveport, Louisiana, and another in a business school in New Orleans. He entered Washington and Lee University in Lexington, Virginia, in the fall of 1871, graduating with a degree in law, and was admitted to the Arkansas bar in 1873. He began the practice of law in Rosston, then the county seat of Nevada County, and married Amelia Ann,

the daughter of the county clerk. When the county seat was moved from Rosston to Prescott in 1877, the McRaes moved to Prescott and built a large home which they named The Oaks. The seven-bedroom house remained the center of this family for the fifty-five years of Amelia and Tom's marriage.

Tom McRae entered politics and held several city and county offices. In 1884 he was successful in his bid for representative of the Third Congressional District. They moved to Washington, D.C., where they lived at the old National Hotel. In those days the Senate and House Office Buildings did not exist, and many senators and congressmen lived at this hotel and had their offices there. Amelia McRae attracted a lot of attention with her brood of six small children. She was a real curiosity to the wife of a certain congressman from New Hampshire, who had never before seen a real Southerner! The two women formed a close friendship that lasted many years.

Tom McRae remained in Congress for eighteen years, with the family dividing its time between Washington, D.C., and Prescott, Arkansas. In those days Congress adjourned for the summer months. The McRae children had the advantage of life and school in the big city and also in a small town in Arkansas.

Amelia McRae remembered when horse-drawn cars were replaced on the streets of Washington by cable cars, and cable cars replaced by the wonderful electric trolleys. The Washington Monument had just been completed but not landscaped, and the Congressional Library wasn't even built when she first went to Washington.

McRae decided to retire from Congress, came home to Prescott, resumed his practice of law, and entered the banking business,

Tea service given to the McRaes when they left office. (Photo by Bob Dunn)

The McRae family home in Prescott. (Photo courtesy of the McRae family)

The McRae family, celebrating Governor and Mrs. McRae's 50th wedding anniversary in Prescott, December 17, 1924. (Photo courtesy of the McRae family)

where he was eminently successful.

In 1913 his friends began pleading with him to run for governor. He resisted, but in 1920 with great reservation he allowed his name to be entered as a candidate. He was sixty-eight years old, retired from politics, and had a good life and successful businesses that demanded his attention. Amelia, at sixty-five, suffered from painful and crippling arthritis. She spent her days in her favorite rocking chair or a wheelchair, and had to be helped into and out of bed. They had reared their family and were looking forward to a leisurely retirement together. It is easy to understand his hesitancy.

However, he made the race and won by a comfortable margin over eight other candidates. There was a record turnout due in part to a heated senatorial race, but more importantly to the fact that this was the first election in which women were permitted to vote. The Nineteenth Amendment to the Constitution, granting women suffrage, was proposed in 1919. Arkansas was the twelfth state to ratify this amendment. By the time the Arkansas primary election was held on August 10, sixteen days before the amendment was declared ratified, more than three-fourths of the states had joined Arkansas in her vote for ratification, and for all intents and purposes it was the law of the land. Women were no longer disenfranchised. McRae must have been their candidate, for he recommended to the legislature that women be appointed to state offices.

The inauguration of Tom McRae as governor took place on the afternoon of January 12, 1921, before a joint session of the General

Assembly in a crowded House Chamber. It was his wish that the ceremony be kept very simple. He had arrived in Little Rock the day before, accompanied by his family and friends and associates from Prescott. There was a reception at the Marion Hotel preceding the inauguration. A committee of distinguished citizens had been appointed to escort him and his family from the hotel to the Capitol. Escorting Mrs. McRae were Mrs. W.P. McDermott, Mrs. S.V. Bracy, Mrs. George R. Wyman, Mrs. Wallace Jackson, Mrs. C.S. McCain, Mrs. John Van Lear, Mrs. P.C. Fletcher, Mrs. Clio Harper, and Mrs. F.V. Holmes. Governor Brough had given his farewell address that morning; he and McRae treated the legislators to two speeches in one day offering diametrically opposing views! The band from the Arkansas School for the Blind gave a short concert before the start of the ceremonies.

The press never mentioned Mrs. McRae's infirmity. It was simply reported that "immediately following the inaugural ceremony, Governor McRae hastened to the reception room where, with Mrs. McRae and Mrs.

Thomas C. McRae Jr., he greeted many hundred men and women who offered congratulations."

A member of the family says Mrs. Thomas C. McRae Jr. (Clio) always stood beside the governor in any receiving line and Mrs. McRae sat nearby in her wheelchair. It is not known whether Clio volunteered as stand-in hostess or was selected, but she was perfect for the part and loved every minute of her public life.

Governor and Mrs. McRae celebrated their fiftieth wedding anniversary while in office. The lavish party was held at their family home in Prescott. Photographers and an orchestra came from Little Rock. Friends from all over the state came to call that afternoon, including many who had attended the wedding fifty years before.

Governor and Mrs. McRae retired from public life at the ages of seventy-three and sixty-nine, respectively, closing a long life in service to Arkansas. Their descendants are active in public life today, carrying on the traditions of a proud family.

EULA TERRELL TERRAL
1925-1927

AFTER LEAVING THE governor's office, Governor Terral returned to the practice of law in Little Rock. He died on March 6, 1946, after a long illness. When Mrs. Terral remarried she became Mrs. John W. Julian and moved to Pine Bluff.

I was privileged to sit next to Mrs. Julian at a luncheon held at the Old State House Museum on April 12, 1984. The occasion was the reopening of the exhibit of First Ladies' gowns. As I remember it, all the surviving First Ladies were in attendance except Mrs. Adkins, who was then living in a nursing home and was too feeble to attend. She was ninety-five.

Eula Terral was known for her social grace and charm. I was captivated by her as scores of others have been through the years. I regret that I had not yet begun this study of these women, or I would have had a better understanding of the things she was telling me. I certainly would have plied her with more questions! She was so interesting to talk to that I'm afraid I neglected the other five or six ladies at our table.

She began by telling me about being her husband's campaign manager when he ran for secretary of state; she worked in his headquarters in all of his campaigns. She talked about the lack of money in their early days, and I was startled when she said, "You know, Mrs. McMath, when I was First Lady I had neither silver nor pearls!" Things certainly had changed for her, for as she spoke she looked quite the grand dame—sitting in regal splendor in a beautiful dress of original design made in New York especially for her for that occasion, wearing a three-strand choker plus several ropes of pearls. She had felt she must do something special for the occasion—so she had ordered a new dress. She explained that the designer erred in

thinking it was for a tea and said she knew she was overdressed as a result, but it was too late to change.

At the end of our discussion she leaned back in her chair and dramatically announced, "You know, I'm eighty-five years old!" This statement produced the desired effect on me and evoked the compliment she was coyly inviting! She certainly didn't look her years.

More than once I have had people say to me they had seen "the state silver at Mrs. Terral's house." They were under the impression she had taken state property. That could not be. No silver was furnished by the state to any governor until the mansion was built. The schoolchildren collected money to buy silver for the battleship *Arkansas,* but none was ever furnished to a governor. When the battleship was decommissioned, that silver was returned to Arkansas. Some of it is on display at the Old State House Museum, but most of it is being used at the Governor's Mansion.

Many governors have received gifts of silver while in office. Governor and Mrs. McRae were presented with a silver service as a parting gift when he left office. Governor and Mrs. Faubus celebrated their twenty-fifth (silver) anniversary while in office and were presented gifts of silver. Our friends in Phillips County presented us with a beautiful silver tea service and friends from Magnolia and Columbia County gave us a handsome antique silver coffee urn. It is possible that the silver Mrs. Terral so proudly displayed in her home was just such a gift and was used in her home when she was First Lady.

The Governor's Mansion that is provided by the state was not completed until 1950. Until then the First Family lived in houses they rented or bought. Some were truly mansions and some were unpretentious family homes. Each of them, regardless of size, has been referred to as the "Governor's Mansion" simply because it was the house where the governor lived. It would not be out of line for Mrs. Terral to refer to her personal tea service as the one used in the Governor's Mansion, but the silver was always hers.

More than once during the luncheon, Mrs. Terral expressed her pleasure at being honored as a former First Lady. She felt that since she had remarried and changed her name, she had been overlooked on other occasions. I hastened to assure her that all former First Ladies receive little attention. To my knowledge the luncheon that day was the first time we had ever gathered as a group.

In researching this book I have found the descendants or survivors of these former governors to be very pleased to be recognized. They have been most helpful in providing pictures and information. They are proud of their relatives, and justly so.

Eula Terrell barely changed her name when she married Thomas Jefferson Terral. She was one of four daughters and two sons born to Mr. and Mrs. Nathaniel G. Terrell. The Terrells trace their lineage to the year 1066 to Sir Walter Tyrrell. In time the spelling of the name became Terrell. James, William, and John Terrell came to America in 1687 and settled in Virginia, where they received land grants of 1,500 acres from King James of England. Generations later Nathaniel G. Terrell came to Arkansas and settled in Lincoln County. He married Isabelle Caroline Johnson. She descends from Thomas Woodward, who came to America from England in the renowned company of Lord Baltimore. Thomas Woodward's son, Thomas, a large landholder in South Carolina and a personal friend of George Washington, served as regulator in the American Revolution.

Eula Terrell was born July 24, 1899, at Garnett, Arkansas. Her childhood was the secure, carefree life typical of a child of upper-middle-class southern planters. She grew up in a large colonial house surrounded by spacious lawns and magnolia and pine trees. She loved to read, enjoyed music, was an adept tennis player, and spent hours in the saddle riding the trails of her father's plantation.

She attended the public schools of Garnett High School in Monticello and Crescent Junior College in Eureka Springs, and graduated from the University of Chicago. She spent four years in Chicago in voice study.

She returned to Little Rock to pursue a career. While attending a winter holiday reception at the Marion Hotel, she was introduced to Tom Terral by his sister and her friend, Leila Terral King. Eula did not see Tom again until the following summer. He proposed on the second date. They were married February 25, 1914, in a private residence in Pine Bluff. Their best man was Governor George W. Hays.

Like many young couples, they rented a small apartment for their first home. Tom was engaged in the practice of law but soon decided to enter politics. Eula, who had no interest in politics, found herself in charge of a makeshift campaign headquarters in their apartment. He was elected secretary of state and served two terms. He was a candidate for governor in 1920, but ran third. He spent the next four years practicing law and building support over the state. He ran again in 1924 and was elected to the office of governor.

A motorcade of over fifty cars of friends and admirers escorted Governor-elect Terral from the Marion Hotel to the Capitol for his inauguration on January 13, 1925, before a joint session of the General Assembly in the House Chamber. As he entered the chamber, escorted by outgoing Governor McRae and a committee of legislators, the band from the Arkansas School for the Blind played "Dixie." The crowd rose to its feet, and amid thunderous applause Governor-elect Tom Terral and Governor Tom McRae made their way to the speaker's desk. After the oath was administered by Chief Justice Edgar McCulloch, Governor Terral gave his inaugural address, which was supposed to last thirty minutes. He was so often interrupted by applause that he did not finish his talk until one hour and twenty minutes later. Again there was prolonged applause, and dozens of boxes of flowers were brought to the speaker's stand and presented to the new governor. Mrs. Fannie Dunaway Hogan then unveiled an oil painting of Governor Terral, which was to be hung in his office.

Immediately after the ceremony the new governor and his family retired to the Governor's Reception Room for a public reception. In the receiving line with Governor and Mrs. Terral were Governor and Mrs. McRae, President of the Senate Robert A. and Mrs. Bailey, Speaker of the House Thomas A. and Mrs. Hill, Mr. and Mrs. Tom Campbell, Mr. and Mrs. Harvey G. Combs, and others who were not identified in the newspaper report in the *Arkansas Gazette.*

In answer to a questionnaire submitted to Eula Terral by the Old State House Museum, Mrs. Terral says of her gown:

As I looked forward to the inaugural, I had ordered my gown to be made in Paris, through the services of Saks Fifth Avenue, New York. It was a cream colored satin with panné velvet medallions embroidered with rhinestones and seed pearl appliqués on chiffon and inserted at the neckline and the scalloped hemline. I remember just before the ball that I stood before a mirror and pinched myself to see if it was really me in this beautiful creation. The whole effect was enhanced by a bouquet of American Beauty roses presented to me that night.

Although the cost seemed exorbitant at the time, the gown served its purpose on many occasions and Tom was very proud of me that night as I stood by his side, as well as on many other official occasions. Years later there was an exhibition in New York of gowns of some First Ladies

of each state, only one gown being chosen from each state. The lady who modeled my gown at that affair was Faye Emerson, wife of Elliott Roosevelt. The night of the Inaugural Ball I suddenly realized the implications of my position. After all, I was the youngest First Lady in Arkansas history—and I was scared to death!

(She was twenty-six and a half years old. This research has found that Mrs. Clayton was twenty-five years old when she became First Lady, and Mrs. Rector was twenty-one.)

Governor and Mrs. Terral were quite social. They entertained and were entertained by many prominent people, once attending a private dinner party at the White House with President and Mrs. Coolidge. Among the distinguished guests who visited the Terrals during Tom's term in office were the United States Secretary of State, Mr. Biddle; Mary Lewis, the Metropolitan Opera star, a frequent visitor and dear friend; the Cabot Lodges; and Senator Alvin Barkley of Kentucky (who later became Vice President and was affectionately called "The Veep").

Eula Terral says she was often called upon to endorse fundraising appeals for different charities. She belonged to the Presbyterian Church, Musical Coterie, Community Concert Association, Daughters of the American Revolution, Sesame Study Club, and a garden club.

In addition to her great interest in music, she was an expert bridge player and enjoyed needlework and church work. The volunteer work that was the most satisfactory to her was that of volunteer nursing at Arkansas Crippled Children's Hospital. She says,

Some of these children have been victimized by poor family environment and parental neglect. I did volunteer nursing there on a daily basis for several years.

When I saw little children mutilated by parental brutality, or seriously scarred by burns, or suffering from malnutrition, I was deeply touched. Some were there because they had been abandoned or orphaned. One such tragedy was five children whose father had deserted them. Their mother had left them to find work and the house had burned. The children were badly burned. As a result the mother lost her mind. But this was only one of hundreds of cases I saw. They were on my mind day and night.

For my years of service at Arkansas Crippled Children's Hospital, the federal government awarded me a gold nurse's pin as an honorarium. Of all the activities that occupied those days when I was First Lady of Arkansas, this daily nursing at the hospital is the project for which I would most like to be remembered—hopefully as one who may have made some impact in the lives of those dear children.

Eula Terral had liberal views in both the personal and political sense. She was tolerant, intelligent, tactful, and well-mannered. She was a tall dark beauty with excellent taste.

The historian Dallas Herndon says of her:

The story of her life could not be told without saying that the state of Arkansas never had a more charming First Lady than Mrs. Tom J. Terral, the wife of former Governor Terral. Besides the beauty of face and form, which she possessed, she had a very charming personality that completely won the hearts of all who had the good fortune to come in contact with her. She was, and is, a person without a semblance of ostentatious pretense, and her simple graciousness and modesty, which are of the heart, lent a tone of dignity to the position of the First Lady which has never been surpassed.

After leaving office the Terrals bought a house at 5241 Edgewood, an attractive house and a place where Mrs. Terral could indulge in her love of gardening. There were no children.

MABEL CLAIRE ERWIN PITTMAN THOMAS MARTINEAU
1927-1928

MABEL MARTINEAU CAN be described as the "glamour girl" of all the First Ladies. Her flamboyant style and a vivacious personality attracted people like a magnet. She gave the impression of being feminine and fragile, but underneath she was a very determined and strong lady.

Not everyone stood in awe of her. In her own circle of friends some were jealous, especially of her skill in entertaining. Mabel was aware that a secret rivalry existed between her and certain of her contemporaries, each trying to outdo her. Try as they might, as hostess Mabel Martineau had no peer.

People who knew Mrs. Martineau closely describe her in glowing terms. A niece, Mrs. Mamie Treadway, says she was a fascinating woman, truly a daughter of the Old South. A step-granddaughter, Powell Berryman, describes her as being beautiful and sweet. A grand-niece, Carrie Remmel Dickinson, says of her, "She was the most exciting, interesting person I've ever known. She was my ideal." Carrie Dickinson says that although she was just a little girl, she will never forget one dinner party Mrs. Martineau gave for the XV Club. Before the party Mrs. Martineau called members of her family to come to her home to see the table decorations. Wonder of wonders, there in the center of the table was a fish pond with real fish swimming in it. Porcelain figures had been placed along the edge of the pond to simulate fishermen, and the whole was landscaped with small plants and greenery. Not surprisingly, the main course of the dinner that evening was lobster ordered from Maine. Altogether, it was an unforgettable dinner party.

Mabel Martineau was the kind of person to whom exciting things happened and who, if nothing was happening, created her own excitement. She would give a party, or get in her big, blue LaSalle automobile, pick up a relative or a friend, and go where things were happening. Carrie Dickinson remembers many long Sunday afternoon drives with her grandmother and Aunt Mabel. The two women were sisters and very close—they talked on the phone every day. They became fascinated with the building of the lakes and the large concrete ornaments at Lakewood in North Little Rock. They would drive over, park, and watch the workmen in action. Even though little Carrie didn't want to, they made her go along. The women considered it something of a triumph that they were there when the water was turned on to fill the lakes. Everyone recognized Mrs. Martineau's car and gave way to her, for she thought it was safer to drive down the middle of the street than on one side or the other. And so she did! No one ever convinced her she should drive on only one side of the street, not even the city police.

Carrie Dickinson says that being related to Uncle John and Aunt Mabel brought much excitement into her life as a little girl. She remembers sitting on the Joe T. Robinsons' front porch with her mother (who was then Republican National Committeewoman), the Martineaus, and other dignitaries, visiting with Herbert Hoover and Will Rogers. When Colonel Charles Lindbergh came to Little Rock, Uncle John insisted that the children of the family be taken to meet this famous man.

Mrs. Martineau's ancestors came to this country during colonial days. In her background there are both a United States senator and a congressman, and three soldiers of the American Revolution, one being General

Bethel of North Carolina. Her grandfather settled in Austin, Arkansas, in early territorial days and became a large landholder and leader in political affairs. Her father, who served four years in the Confederate Army, was a state senator and a merchant in Des Arc. Mabel was born at Des Arc in Prairie County, Arkansas, the daughter of Ambrose Sevier Erwin and Lucy Ann Williamson Bethel Erwin. The family of five daughters and one son grew up in a large Dutch Colonial–style plantation house. This house had a wide veranda across the front and down one side, and a fireplace in every room. It was richly furnished with canopied beds for little girls to sleep in and fine wardrobes to hold their dresses. It was shaded by large trees, and the wide lawns were landscaped with many flowering shrubs. A vegetable garden in the back completed the setting.

After finishing the Des Arc public schools, Mabel attended school at Anchorage, Kentucky, and Arkansas Female College at Little Rock. She had special talent and training in music and voice.

She married early. Her first husband was Charles Pittman. They began their life together in true storybook fashion with a big wedding and the blessings of both families and many friends, but they did not live happily ever after. In two years Charles became ill and died. Later Mabel said that Charles Pittman and her first marriage were like a lovely dream.

Mabel Erwin Pittman went into mourning but was not left to pine away alone for long. Gradually suitors began to appear. Judge James S. Thomas was particularly attentive, and when he began urging Mabel to marry him, her father insisted that she go to Kentucky to visit relatives. Still in her widow's weeds, Mabel boarded the train. There are two versions of what happened next. One is that Judge Thomas just happened to be on the same train, and taking advantage of having her alone, persuaded her to marry him. They got off the train at Pine Bluff, she removed her black veil and pinned a red rose

to her black hat, and they were married! The other account is that the judge knew she was going to Kentucky and followed her. This version says Mabel sewed white lace to the brim of her black hat for her second wedding. However it happened, they were married. When Mabel returned home and told her father what she had done, he went into a rage. He never did quite forgive Judge Thomas and remained cool to him through the years. Judge Thomas was several years older than Mabel, a widower with five grown children.

As the wife of Judge Thomas, Mabel lived in Clarendon, Arkansas, in a large house. She had money, position, servants—even peacocks to stroll the sweeping lawns. After twenty happy years together, Judge Thomas became ill and died, leaving Mabel a widow again.

She moved to Little Rock to live near her two sisters, Carrie (Mrs. F. Pratt Cates) and Minnie (Mrs. Ernest Pettus). Once again suitors flocked to her side. She chose to marry John E. Martineau, a widower and successful lawyer who was then chancellor of the First Chancery Court.

John Martineau and Mabel Erwin Pittman Thomas were married on May 1, 1919. They lived in an imposing house on Wright Avenue at Battery Street. This majestic brick home, with its marble entrances and wide verandas, surrounded by spacious well-landscaped grounds, was a proper setting for Mabel Martineau's heavy schedule of official and personal entertaining. The house was beautifully decorated and richly furnished, typical of well-to-do Arkansans' homes of that period.

To say Mrs. Martineau was a perfectionist is an understatement. She was never seen unless she was impeccably groomed. She had a flair for clothes and a distinct style of her own. She loved color, wore lots of printed silks, and was given to laces, feather boas, and lots of jewelry. Even though bobbed hair was not in vogue then, she wore her naturally curly hair short, cutting and styling it herself. She assumed the responsibility of her husband's wardrobe and saw to it that he too wore only the finest and always looked his best.

She ran her house in the same manner as she dressed—always with her best foot forward. Every meal was served in courses and the table was set with the finest china, silver, crystal, and linen. She trained her staff of servants herself and always "asked" and never "ordered."

There was always music in her home. Once she had a man-servant who had an unusually beautiful singing voice. He was encouraged to put Mrs. Martineau's classical records on the machine and sing along while he worked.

Mrs. Martineau was a very genteel woman of high ideals. She never indulged in gossip nor said an unkind word about anyone. Without fail, all who were interviewed described her as being not only beautiful, but sweet. When Judge Martineau's younger brother, Ernest, married, he and his bride, Thelma Cook, lived several months with Judge and Mrs. Martineau. Thelma says, "She was so good to me. She was one of the sweetest people it's ever been my privilege to meet."

Mabel Martineau did not believe in discussing or even mentioning anyone's age, especially hers. She was born on Christmas Day, but there will be no birthdate given in this chapter. This writer will honor her wish and not tell. Thelma remembers that one day the maid answered the phone, came into the living room, and announced that the call was for the "Little Mrs. Martineau." Mabel said, "Thelma, the call is for you," and turning to the maid added, "And, Emma, we will discuss later how to call people to the phone." Thelma says, "Thank God, Emma didn't say 'the younger Mrs. Martineau' or I would have been banished before dawn!"

When John decided to enter statewide politics, the Martineaus' large circle of friends rallied around. He made an unsuccessful race for governor in 1924, but ran again in 1926 and was elected.

Mabel went on the campaign trail either with her husband or making speeches on her own. She spent many hours in headquarters meeting people and supervising the distribution of literature. She further aided the campaign by entertaining supporters and staff in her home.

Governor Martineau's inauguration took place on Tuesday, January 11, 1927, in a joint meeting of the Arkansas General Assembly and was the first ever to be broadcast by radio. The proceedings and speech were carried by station KTHS in Hot Springs. The public was invited to attend an informal reception held that evening in the Governor's Reception Room. Music was furnished by "The Arkansas Razorbacks" under the direction of Ted Dugan. A bank of smilax and palms formed a background for the receiving line of Governor and Mrs. Martineau and all the elected state officials and their wives. The rooms of the governor's suite were decorated with Premier roses, American Beauty roses, chrysanthemums, and other flowers. The serving table was covered with a Venetian lace, filet, and Italian cut-work cloth, an heirloom in the family of Mrs. Martineau. Punch was served from a large silver bowl surrounded by silver candelabra holding blue tapers and silver vases of Premier roses.

Mrs. Martineau was elegant in a gown ordered from Paris, France. The apricot silk and velvet gown was cut on long straight lines with an uneven hemline and was decorated with iridescent beads, sequins, and pearls. She carried a huge shower bouquet of Premier roses. During the evening, officials of the courthouse presented the new governor with a Consistory watch fob, set with a diamond.

The new First Lady began her duties the very next day. She attended a tea and stood in the receiving line all afternoon to greet the three hundred guests, loving her new role and fitting it perfectly.

Governor Martineau was an able and progressive governor. He resigned after fourteen months in office to accept an appointment as federal judge, a position he held until his death on March 6, 1937.

Mabel Martineau had three happy marriages, but John Martineau was the love of her life. For a time she continued to live in the family home, spending time caring for her flowers and the governor's favorite mint bed that surrounded the fountain. She involved herself with family and friends and was active in her church and clubs. She belonged to the First Methodist Church South, the United Daughters of the Confederacy, the Daughters of the American Revolution, the Fine Arts Club, the Woman's City Club, and the Country Club of Little Rock. Eventually she gave up her big house and moved to 809 North Jackson, where she lived until her death on November 27, 1952. It is interesting that this lady who so loved a celebration was born on Christmas Day, married on May Day, and died on Thanksgiving Day.

MABEL WINSTON PARNELL
1928-1933

ON APRIL 12, 1926, the Arkansas Supreme Court ruled that the office of lieutenant governor did indeed exist, and that it was vacant! State Senator Harvey Parnell decided to run for the office, was elected, and took office on January 11, 1927, along with Governor Martineau and the other constitutional officers. Fourteen months later when Martineau resigned to become federal judge, Lieutenant Governor Parnell became governor and served the balance of Martineau's term. Thus Mabel Parnell knew what would be expected of her as First Lady. Her husband's five years as governor came during the height of the Great Depression.

Harvey Parnell was inaugurated on January 17, 1929, before a joint session of the General Assembly. While the visitors were gathering, a concert was given by the bands from the Arkansas School for the Blind and the Arkansas National Guard. The governor entered the hall accompanied by Mrs. Parnell, Mrs. Noel Martin and Miss Alice Martin of Warren, Miss Evelyn Daroux of Pine Bluff, Mrs. Martha Anderson and Mrs. C.M. Measel of Little Rock, and the governor's daughters, Misses Martha Adele and Mary Frances Parnell.

A public reception was given that evening in the Governor's Reception Room at the Capitol. The hall was elaborately decorated with pink roses, ferns, and ivy. Music was furnished throughout the evening by an orchestra hidden from view by a screen of palms. Many friends came from all over the state. In the receiving line with Governor and Mrs. Parnell were their two daughters, the constitutional officers and their wives, and Judge and Mrs. Martineau. Mrs. Parnell was beautifully gowned in black satin with rhinestone trim, and carried a bouquet of roses. Daughter Martha wore a dress of yel-

low satin and Mary Frances wore pink georgette. They both carried bouquets of roses. The serving table was covered in lace and the punch bowl was surrounded by pink candles in silver holders and vases of pink roses.

Governor Parnell proposed and got through the legislature the first income tax law in Arkansas. With these new-found funds he built a new hospital at Benton for the mentally ill; enlarged the Tuberculosis Sanitorium at Booneville; built a school for the deaf at Little Rock; built Henderson State Teachers College at Arkadelphia; consolidated seventy-two school districts, spelling doom to the six-month, one-room schools in Arkansas; lengthened all school terms to eight months; added many more buses to transport children, thus greatly increasing attendance; and had an ambitious road-building program. Parnell's spending left no money in the treasury for emergencies. The depression, coupled with a drought, left many farmers in dire straits. Three hundred farmers marched to England, Arkansas, and demanded food. There was some yelling and broken windows—but the crowd dispersed when they were given bread. The national press picked up the story and blazed it across the nation that everyone in Arkansas was starving! This publicity helped Arkansas's two senators get five million dollars in relief money for the state. The legislature met, but showed no inclination to address the issue of relief for the people. Wages were cut, cotton acreage was reduced. Banks closed. Schools closed. Arkansas received more Reconstruction Finance Corporation farm loans than any other state. A commission disbursed this money to public works projects in every county. It was all spent in eight months. These were the times in which Mabel

Parnell was wife of the governor—hard times.

Mabel was born at Arkansas City in 1885, the daughter of Jack C. and Martha Crenshaw Winston. She descends from Isaac Winston, who immigrated to Virginia before 1700. The Winston progeny were prominent in the annals of early colonial history. Governor Patrick Henry, President Zachary Taylor, Dolley Madison, and the first Mrs. John Tyler were all related to this man. So was another First Lady of Arkansas, Ann Christian Pope, wife of Territorial Governor John Pope. Thus Arkansas added two First Ladies to this illustrious list. Isaac Winston's relatives contributed widely to the history of this country in times of both peace and war.

Mabel Winston grew up and attended school at Dermott in Chicot County. Her father owned a 3,000-acre plantation in this rich farming region. Mabel's college education was limited to one year at the University of Arkansas when on June 2, 1902, she married Harvey Parnell, a prosperous merchant in Dermott. They lived in Dermott until Parnell became governor.

The Parnells bought a spacious home at 1801 North Spruce, a house well-suited to the official and personal needs of the family. The grounds of this property supplied ample space for Mrs. Parnell to garden. It was a showplace and she planned it all. Her goldfish pond was a novelty; her patio was one of the first in Little Rock. People came from all over town to see her yard when it was in bloom. At her large tea parties it was a real treat for her guests to overflow onto the patio and to enjoy the beauty of her garden.

Mrs. Parnell was an active and caring citizen, serving in many different areas. She was a member of the Board of Directors of the Florence Crittendon Home and belonged to the state Federation of Women's Clubs, the Women's Democratic Club, and the Daughters of the American Revolution, and her ancestry entitled her to membership in the prestigious First Families of Virginia. She was a member of the Methodist Episcopal

Church and the Southeast Arkansas District Garden Club.

The Parnells traveled often on official business. At the National Governor's Conference at French Lick, Indiana, they became good friends with Governor and Mrs. Franklin D. Roosevelt of New York. Because of this friendship Governor Parnell was selected as a member of the Platform Committee of the National Democratic Convention the year Roosevelt was first nominated as the party's choice for president.

Mrs. Parnell was a real asset to her husband in his political career. She met people well, she entertained, and she could hold her own in a discussion of current topics. An attractive woman, she had excellent taste in selecting her wardrobe and was always well dressed. She enjoyed people and it showed. Both Governor and Mrs. Parnell were aware of civic and social obligations and were diligent in meeting these demands.

They were a devoted family and were very close to their two daughters, Martha Adele (Mrs. Eugene Warren of Little Rock) and Mary Frances (Mrs. J.P. Perry).

For years Harvey Parnell had been buying farmland that had been a part of Mabel's family plantation, and he had finally acquired the entire acreage. He named it the Winston Planting Company. After leaving office, the Parnells returned to this farm, where they had time to enjoy their hobbies of fishing and horseback riding. He built a lovely home for Mabel on the land of her birth. In December 1935 they moved into their new home. He died in January 1936.

Mabel Parnell took over the management of her 3,000 acres and 100 families of farm hands and successfully ran this big operation until two years before her death on June 7, 1964.

As a widow she remained the same interested and interesting person she always was. She never lost her love of gardening or entertaining. Her friends still speak in glowing terms of visits to her plantation.

She was a talented artist and her works are

treasured by her family. Daughter Mary Frances lives in Monroe, Louisiana. Daughter Martha died in the prime of her life. Martha's only child, Dawn Dockins, lives in Hot Springs. There are four grandchildren, seventeen great-grandchildren, and one great-great-grandchild. It is hoped all of them have inherited a goodly share of their grandmother's wonderful traits, for she was a very special lady.

TERRA ANN SMITH FUTRELL
1933-1937

ONCE AGAIN THIS state went through the uneasy experience of having two men claim the governor's office. When Governor Joe T. Robinson resigned, the president of the senate, W.K. Oldham, became acting governor. In a very short time J. Marion Futrell was elected the new president pro tempore of the senate, and he claimed to be the governor. The issue was resolved by the Arkansas Supreme Court in favor of Futrell. On March 27, 1913, Futrell became acting governor and served until George Hays was elected in a special election in July of that year. Twenty years later when Marion Futrell was elected to his own term as governor, the role of First Lady was not new to Terra Ann Futrell.

Ann Smith was one of five children born to William Richard Smith and Catherine Owen Smith. The Smiths moved from Tennessee to Arkansas and settled in Independence County before Ann was born in 1875. She attended school at Pleasant Plains Academy, where she excelled in Latin and mathematics and was president of her class. She did not attend college. Instead, on September 14, 1893, she married J.M. Futrell. She was eighteen and he was twenty-four years of age. At the time Marion Futrell was teaching school. He taught in Independence, Greene, and Craighead counties before going into the timber business and starting to farm in 1896. He took up the study of law and was admitted to the bar in 1913.

Like most young couples, the Futrells did not have a great deal of money. Ann Futrell had to learn to make do and to be thrifty in running her household. Six children were born into this family. The four daughters were Nye, Prentiss, Ernie, and Janice. The two sons were Byron and Dan.

Ann Futrell was a great help to her husband in his public life. He held various offices in Greene County and resigned as chancellor of the Twelfth District to run for governor. Ann maintained an interest in politics and served as a political weathervane for her husband. She was a level-headed lady with great common sense and got along well with people. It is said that she never lost a vote for her husband, but in fact many people voted for him simply because they loved her. In times of crises she was the "take charge" sort. Her husband often said, "Without her I could not get along. She is well nigh the perfect type."

Marion Futrell was inaugurated as governor on January 10, 1933, in the usual joint session, before the largest crowd ever assembled in the House Chamber. A special train brought three hundred families from Paragould alone. Hundreds were packed into the galleries and the aisles of the chamber, making it very difficult for Mrs. Futrell and members of the family to make their way down front to their seats. It is interesting that Mrs. Parnell was a member of Mrs. Futrell's party—the only time on record when the wife of an outgoing governor attended an inauguration of the newly elected governor. (Governor Parnell had made his farewell address the day before.) There was a large delegation of former governors in the audience.

A reception sponsored by the Futrell-for-Governor Clubs was held in the Governor's Reception Room. Governor and Mrs. Futrell headed the receiving line. Standing with them were their children and spouses, five former governors and their wives, Mrs. Tom McRae, the constitutional officers and their wives, and five judges and their wives! Little wonder there was a mad crush getting into and out of the room.

To entertain the crowd waiting to enter the

Reception Room, a band played lively tunes such as "Pink Elephant" and "You're Just About Right for Me!" The reception room was decorated with palm, smilax, and rose-colored torchière lamps. The central chandelier was decorated with maidenhair fern and the mantel was banked with pink Radiance roses. The serving table was covered with an Italian lace cloth over a pink underskirt. The centerpiece was an immense loop of white chrysanthemums on a base of fern and was flanked by silver candelabra holding pink tapers.

Mrs. Futrell wore a smart afternoon gown of black velvet and a shoulder corsage of orchids. Three of the young Futrell women also wore black, another wore beige, and the other wore gray.

The inauguration had interesting coverage in the *Arkansas Gazette:*

All the able-bodied readers of the *Gazette,* which means practically all the intelligent people of the state, who scamper over the frosty lawn in house slippers this morning to retrieve their papers, will read that Arkansas has a new governor, the Hon. J. Marion Futrell, in fact a Plain Man of the People. But it will not be news to them for most of them were at the state capitol yesterday to see the new governor inaugurated and to step on one another's corns.

And Governor Futrell with his arm sling, probably will be in no shape to sign bills for several days.

No powdered and painted movie star could have drawn a more enthusiastic crowd than the one which squeezed into the governor's reception hall and made the rounds of the state officials to shake hands, winding up at the refreshment table for a prolonged stay. The receiving line was headed by a short, stocky man, his light grey hair carefully combed and parted on the side, his smile radiating in

a hundred wrinkles, his dark suit set off by a white collar—in short, by the governor himself.

The day was auspicious for it marked the coming of the Reign of Terror for extravagance and waste in public service. The motto of this new administration should be "Waste Not, want not," and this economic policy runs all the way from the paper clips to $100 bills—if any such bills are left.

Austerity was the key word in Futrell's administration. It comes as no surprise that the legislation requiring a three-fourths vote of the house and senate to levy or increase a tax other than the sales tax, which is still in effect today, was passed during Futrell's term in office. Futrell was governor during the Depression. When he took office Arkansas was on the verge of bankruptcy. When he left, the state was on a cash basis with a surplus in the treasury.

When the Futrells first moved to Little Rock, they rented a house at Seventeenth and Center streets. They later bought a home at 4121 Woodlawn, where they continued to live after he left office. He resumed the practice of law. In July 1948, while en route to the funeral of a brother, Governor Futrell suffered a stroke and remained in poor health the rest of his life. He died on June 20, 1955.

Ann Futrell enjoyed going to football and baseball games with her husband. They both liked to fish. She had her own rod and tackle. The biggest fish she ever caught was a five-and-a-half-pound bass. She hooked an even bigger one, but failed to land it because her husband had neglected to bring the landing net. When she tried to get the fish into the boat without a net, the line broke and the big one got away. And of course it was all the governor's fault! She delighted in telling the story and the fish got bigger, as did Governor Futrell's negligence, with each telling.

MARGARET LENORA BRISTOL BAILEY
1937-1941

MRS. CARL BAILEY liked campaigning, maybe even more than the governor did. She traveled the state with Mr. Bailey during the campaign and later on official visits. She enjoyed people but cared not one whit for the social whirl. As far as can be determined, she and the governor gave only one dinner party in their home while he was in office, one for the department heads of state government. The closest she came to being a socialite was membership in the Eastern Star and the Woman's City Club.

Margaret was a tall, attractive woman with brown hair and eyes. She was an intellectual whose interests lay in areas other than frivolous society and the latest styles. She was always neatly dressed, made a pleasing appearance, and maintained a happy, even disposition. Even though her husband and children were the center of her life, she was by no means a homebody. She did not let her husband's election as governor cause great change in her life or that of her children. She kept right on with her Parent-Teacher Association work, her activities as band mother, her interest in gardening, and her bridge games with old friends.

Elizabeth Bailey, the youngest of the Bailey children, says she was hardly aware of her father's position. She was sixteen at the time and interested in the same things as most other sixteen-year-old girls. She does remember her mother's insisting that she meet Mrs. Franklin D. Roosevelt when she came to Little Rock as part of a multistate lecture tour in March 1937. Mrs. Roosevelt spoke at Little Rock High School on "The Responsibility of the Individual to His Community." Elizabeth rode with her mother and the chauffeur to pick up Mrs. Roosevelt at her hotel, but on the way to the speaking engagement Elizabeth was dropped off at home, since she was

not allowed to skip homework.

The Bailey children were taught to be unassuming. They always signed their father's occupation as "attorney" and not as "governor." Bobby, the youngest son, started to school while his father was governor. When Bobby's teacher asked all the children to tell what their father did, Bobby stood up and said, "My daddy works for the government." The next child answered, "My daddy works for the WPA too." The family never explained the difference to Bobby.

In bringing up her children, Margaret Bailey stressed punctuality and responsibility. She inspired her children to try for good attendance at school. Carl Jr. and Frank each had a perfect record for six years. Eugene and Elizabeth achieved the almost impossible goal of never being absent or tardy throughout the entire twelve grades. To earn this record Elizabeth elected to have a needed tonsillectomy during the Christmas holidays, and Eugene once had to recover from a weekend illness by Monday morning! However, it was to Elizabeth's credit that she finished her twelve grades in ten and one-half years.

The family consisted of five boys and one daughter, four of whom are still living. Bristol Bailey died in 1984 and R. Eugene Bailey died in 1985. The surviving children are Carl E. Bailey, Jr., Major General Frank A. Bailey, R. Robert Bailey, and daughter Elizabeth Bailey Benton. These family members, along with their uncle, Ted Bailey, have provided much of the information included in this chapter.

Margaret Bailey was very tolerant and loving with her children. The boys were crazy about pets of all sizes and were allowed to keep them all. In addition to the usual dogs, cats, and canaries, at one time there was a

Inaugural Banquet

Menu

Cocktail of Hempstead Fruits

Crisp Celery   Assorted Olives

Select Tenderloin Steak—Boone   Fresh Mushrooms—Pulaski

June Peas in Butter, a la Drew

Candied Yams, a la Union

Stuffed Tomatoes—Washington

Arkansas Brick Ice Cream

Petit Fours

Cigars   Coffee   Cigarettes

Addresses

Robert Bailey   John M. Bransford   H. T. Harrison

JOHN E. COATES, JR., *Master of Ceremonies*

Invitation and menu card from the Bailey inauguration in 1937. They were bound in a silver-colored jacket in the shape of Arkansas.

The Inaugural Reception and Ball

Honoring

Governor and Mrs. Carl Edward Bailey

and

Arkansas's Elected Public Officials

at

The Hotel Marion

on

Tuesday evening at nine o'clock

January twelfth

Nineteen hundred and thirty-seven

pet goat. Another time Carl Jr. came home leading a donkey and saying, "Look what followed me home!" Mrs. Bailey did not demand that her son return the donkey, but she did make him go back and pay the owner the price of five dollars! A vacant lot next door to the Bailey home at 1000 North Tyler provided a good place for the boys to keep their animals and was a neighborhood playground for all the children for blocks around. Margaret Bailey liked to cook—and it's just as well she did, as any mother of six knows. She did it all herself, with no house-hold help.

The family customarily vacationed together every summer. There were trips to the Chicago World's Fair, the New York World's Fair, and Mexico, and many trips to neighboring states in connection with the children's school activities.

Mrs. Bailey was an ardent worker in the Parent-Teacher Association and was responsible for the establishment of "The Campus Inn" at Little Rock Central High School. Her project as First Lady was a campaign for free textbooks for all schoolchildren in the lower grades. During World War II she was very active on behalf of the USO and was one of the first women to join the National Organization of Army Mothers. Margaret's great interest, other than her family and public schools, was gardening. She belonged to the Madonna Lily Club and the Hemoracallis Society. She didn't care for the usual flower-arranging studies, but instead her interest was in horticulture and the propagation of new plants.

She was a good Christian woman and got her brood of six up and off to Sunday school and church every Sunday morning. The Baileys belonged to First Christian Church in Little Rock.

Margaret Bristol was born February 21, 1892, in Campbell, Missouri, the daughter of a railroad telegrapher and farmer, Frank Allen Bristol and Sarah Ann Bridges Bristol. She and Governor Bailey were classmates in the Campbell public schools. The two were in love, but there was no money for marriage when they graduated, so they went their separate ways. She went to college for two years at Southeast Missouri Normal in Cape Girardeau, Missouri. He went from one job to another until he and Margaret eloped to Paragould, Arkansas, and were married on October 10, 1915. Neither mother of the young couple was too happy about the marriage, but Margaret's father rallied round and got Carl a job as bookkeeper of a lumber company at Trumann, Arkansas. To help support the young family, Margaret taught school during the early years of the marriage. Carl took up the study of law and continued his studies through several job changes. He said, "Day after day I rubbed shoulders with men without interest, without curiosity, without hope, knowing no more year after year than when they first began." Carl Bailey was an aggressive man with a lively curiosity and a great ambition. He said, "I can't idle on the tracks." He passed the bar in 1922 and moved the family to Little Rock where he worked for two years before opening a law office. In 1926, he

worked on the campaign of Boyd Cypert, who was running for the position of prosecuting attorney. This little taste of politics was Bailey's undoing. He loved it from the beginning. He became Cypert's deputy, was elected to succeed Cypert, and served for two terms as prosecuting attorney before becoming attorney general, then governor.

The celebration of Governor Bailey's inauguration began with services at the First Christian Church, which were attended by a large crowd, including Governor-elect Bailey, his family, and other constitutional officers. The inauguration took place on the morning of January 12, 1937, before a joint session of the house and senate in the House Chamber. Margaret Bailey, the six children, and the governor's mother (also Margaret Bailey) occupied places of honor at the left side of the rostrum. The seven justices of the State Supreme Court sat on the right. The administration of the Oath of Office by Chief Justice Griffin Smith was performed a second time on the Capitol steps for the benefit of the crowd of over five thousand who had gathered in the afternoon to hear the governor's inaugural address. As a part of these ceremonies, the governor's mother took the microphone, expressed pride in her son, and asked the support of the people of Arkansas. By the time the governor started his speech the Capitol was surrounded by floats, bands, and military personnel waiting to form up in the most elaborate and colorful inaugural parade ever held in Arkansas. The governor and other state officials led the parade in open cars to a reviewing stand on West Markham Street. There were sixty-seven floats, thirty-four bands, and a military section that covered three blocks. It took ninety minutes for the parade to pass in review. The threat of rain did not dampen the spirits of the thousands of people lining the parade route.

The night before the inauguration, Governor and Mrs. Bailey were guests of honor at the Marion Hotel, where 650 persons attended. On the front page of the paper the next morning there was a picture of the governor with his wife and mother. Both women wore large corsages of orchids and Margaret was gowned in black lace. The dress was unusual in that it was sleeveless but had separate, wide cuffs of matching lace at the wrist. Her hair was stylishly coiffed in a marcel.

Following the inauguration there was a ball and reception in the Marion Hotel Ballroom. For this occasion, Mrs. Bailey chose an original gown of gray metallic by Kalmour.

Governor Bailey was born in Bernie, Missouri, on October 8, 1894, the son of William Edward and Margaret Elmyra McCorkle Bailey. Although Governor and Mrs. Bailey were born and brought up in Missouri, they both were loyal Arkansans and devoted Razorback fans who attended games whenever possible.

When Governor Bailey's term was over he resumed his law practice. About two years later he and Margaret were divorced and he married Marjorie Compton. Margaret Bailey was devastated. She lived alone the rest of her life. She died on March 9, 1975. He died October 23, 1948.

ESTELLE ELISE SMITH ADKINS
1941-1945

THE PATHS OF Estelle Smith and Homer Adkins crossed over a period of two years on two continents. They first met at Camp Beauregard, Louisiana, in 1917 where she was stationed as a Red Cross nurse and he was in the Army Medical Corps. Their initial meeting took place when she and a friend were out for a walk. The two young women paused for a rest, and two privates on a motorcycle stopped to chat with them. One of these men was Homer Adkins. Since nurses were not allowed to date enlisted men, very little came of this first chance meeting, but a strong friendship developed between Estelle and Homer when the two were again stationed at the same base in France. When the war was over they arrived back in New York on the same day but on different ships. Fate, that ever fickle lady, seemed to be saying they belonged together but at the same time to be toying with this pair.

Estelle Smith, the daughter of William Edward Smith and Blanche A. Perkins Smith, was born on July 31, 1889, near Hermanville in Claiborne County, Mississippi. Her father, who tried farming and butchering before he became a railroad man, was determined his children would get an education. When Estelle finished the local grade school, she was sent away to high school. One day coming home on the train she happened to sit next to a lady whom she knew and who told Estelle about the big, new hospital that had just been built in Jackson, Mississippi. She suggested that Estelle study nursing. Estelle says she wasn't hospital-minded but went into nursing school anyway. She thought she would die, she was so lonely; but she didn't die; she became a nurse. When World War I broke out she went into the Red Cross and was stationed at Camp Beauregard. She was

one of five from her base who volunteered for overseas duty, and she was sent to France.

Estelle had a fine time in France. She was too young to be frightened and too far from the front to be in any danger. She and her roommate, Dodie, who became her best friend for life, would slip off and go to the enlisted men's dances even though it was against the rules. They eventually paired off with a couple of soldiers who were drivers for two colonels. When the soldiers went off duty, they requisitioned the car for their own pleasure. One spoke French fairly well, and often arranged for the foursome to have dinner in the homes of local residents. Thus they ate well, met lots of people, and had a different adventure every night. The greatest danger they faced was getting caught.

Estelle's romantic adventures ended with her return to the states, when she went to work at a small hospital in Louisiana. Homer Adkins was a pharmacist at Snodgrass and Bracey Drug Store in Little Rock. He often went to Louisiana to see Estelle and after each visit would ask her, "Are you ready to go back with me?" For a long time the answer was always "No," until one day he told her he wasn't going to ask her anymore. She knew he meant it and she must finally make a decision. She decided the answer would be "Yes" and they were married on December 18, 1921, in a Presbyterian church in Shreveport, Louisiana.

As Mrs. Homer Adkins, Estelle did not work except as a volunteer. She spent many hours in Red Cross work, and during emergencies such as floods or tornadoes she gave direct nursing care. Her interests were always in the field of health. There was a great need in this area, for the public health program was inadequate. She often drove her own car to transport children and adults for needed medical services.

Estelle Adkins was not at all politically minded. Neither was she shy or reserved. She simply busied herself with things that were important to her—her home, her husband, her church, and the Red Cross. She and Governor Adkins were very close and shared many interests. They liked to hunt, fish, and ride horseback. She was almost as avid a hunter as he, and once killed her seasonal deer in her own back yard at their place in the country. Estelle and Homer Adkins both enjoyed genealogy and together researched their families. They had a close relationship with both the Smith and Adkins families and attended many family reunions. They taught Sunday school and worked in their church together.

In Little Rock they lived at 1601 Dennison Street. Mrs. Vernon Plunkett and Mrs. Cecil Parkerson, who as little girls lived in the same block of Dennison, remember Mrs. Adkins as a charming lady, very pretty in her white nurses' uniform, who always had a smile and a kind word for the neighbor children. When the children reached their teens, she recruited them for Red Cross volunteer work and also took them in groups for a weekend at their country home.

Prior to her ninetieth birthday, Mrs. Adkins in an interview with an *Arkansas Gazette* reporter told about buying their place in the country in 1935. Mr. Adkins saw an ad in the Sunday paper offering for sale an old house and some acreage. They drove down that very afternoon to see it, and while walking over the land with the real estate agent, a covey of quail was flushed up. That cinched the sale! They bought the place called Sleepy Hollow at Social Hill near Malvern, Arkansas. The land had been homesteaded in 1848 and a large one-room cabin was built on it. The house had been enlarged and improved through the years, but was in deplorable condition when the Adkinses bought it. They had a great time making the place liveable, doing much of the work them-

selves. When they finished their remodeling job, the house had electricity, indoor plumbing, and porches back and front on which to sit and enjoy the beauty of the countryside. Mr. and Mrs. Adkins thoroughly enjoyed this retreat. They kept pleasure horses there, and they and their friends took many long rides in the area. They built a house and hired a couple to live there to look after the horses and cattle and to work in the house when the Adkinses were in residence.

Homer Adkins was elected governor in 1940 and was sworn in on January 14, 1941. This inauguration was very simple, with only an afternoon reception at the Capitol to mark the occasion. For this occasion Mrs. Adkins wore a dress of pink silk and lace.

Governor and Mrs. Adkins were at Sleepy Hollow when they heard the news of the attack on Pearl Harbor. They both immediately busied themselves with the war effort. He was instrumental in recruiting millions of dollars' worth of defense business to Arkansas, thus causing a complete turnaround in the state's economy. Mrs. Adkins recruited for the Army Nurse Corps, took a refresher course in nursing, gave full-time help at the Red Cross, was in charge of her own group of volunteers, and somehow still found time for volunteer work in the American Legion.

In 1944 Governor Adkins ran for the United States Senate but was defeated by Rep. J. William Fulbright. Returning to private business, he spent the next four years behind the scenes of politics. In 1948 Governor Sidney S. McMath appointed Mr. Adkins as administrator of the Arkansas Employment Security Division, where he served four years.

Eventually Governor and Mrs. Adkins moved to their home in the country, where they lived the rest of their lives. Here she exchanged her Red Cross work for 4H Club work with both boys and girls. She organized and was active in the Home Demonstration Club in the area. She and Governor Adkins both served on the board of the local

Methodist church, where they both taught Sunday school classes and he was church superintendent. Every Sunday, in the wintertime, he would get up early, go to the church, and build a big wood fire so the building would be warm when the worshippers arrived. It is no accident that this church is named the Adkins Memorial United Methodist Church, for Estelle and Homer Adkins devoted many hours and a great deal of money to it.

When asked what she would most like to be remembered for, Estelle Adkins said, "Supporting all World War II efforts and supporting and actively participating in efforts intended to enhance the welfare and well-being of the state's children."

Governor and Mrs. Adkins had no children.

In addition to the organizations already named, Estelle Adkins was an active member of the Ouachita Chapter of the Daughters of the American Revolution, the United Daughters of the Confederacy in Malvern, and Colonial Dames. She was a longtime member of both state and national nurses' associations.

Governor Adkins died in 1964 and is buried at Roselawn Memorial Cemetery in Little Rock. Estelle continued to live in their home but after two years decided it was too much responsibility for her. She sold it and built a small house for herself next door to the Adkins Memorial Methodist Church. She finally had to give this up and move to a nursing home, where she died on November 13, 1985, at the age of ninety-six.

LUCILLE KIRTLEY LANEY
1945-1949

BEN LANEY RAN for governor in 1944 and became the Democratic nominee when his opponent suddenly withdrew from the race between the primary and the runoff in August. Laney won the November general election with 85 percent of the vote. He served two terms. The star piece of his legislative program was the Revenue Stabilization Act, which is still in effect and which, in simplest terms, prohibits deficit spending by the State of Arkansas. Another piece of legislation passed during the Laney administration—and of great interest to this book—was the bill authorizing the building of the Governor's Mansion.

Governor Laney was sworn into office in January 1945 in a simple ceremony at the Capitol. Because the country was still at war, there was no governor's ball. Instead a reception was held. Mrs. Laney, always fashionably and neatly dressed, wore a black lace dress trimmed with aqua grosgrain ribbon.

In Little Rock, the Laneys first lived in an apartment in the Hillcrest area, living quarters not conducive to official entertaining. Later they moved to a house at 10 Ozark Point, where she held a reception for the wives of the members of the legislature. She attended the many required public functions with her husband and was always pleasant and very much a lady. Historian Dallas T. Herndon said of her, "Mrs. Laney . . . has been a great factor in the amazing popularity and swift growth to power of her eminent and distinguished husband . . . ." Of her relationship with her politician husband, she said, "He always wanted to know what I thought about things, but the ideas were his. He was definitely his own man." She was always supportive of him, and always by his side up to and during his walkout during the 1948 Democratic National Convention when

he led dissidents in forming a new political party called the Dixiecrat Party.

The Laneys had three sons: Benjamin Travis III, who obtained B.A. and M.A. degrees from Arkansas State Teachers College; William David, who attended Southern State College in Magnolia; and Phillip, who attended Georgia Tech University.

Business interests caused the Laneys to live for a time in Helena and Pine Bluff, but they eventually settled in Magnolia. Governor Laney died of a heart attack in January, 1977. Mrs. Laney is still living in her home in Magnolia.

Lucille Kirtley was born on March 10, 1906, the daughter of Ethel Lucille Bright and Henry A. Kirtley. She grew up in the small town of Lewisville, Arkansas, and upon graduation from the local schools entered Arkansas State Teachers College at Conway, where she studied speech and voice. There she met Benjamin Travis Laney, Jr., who was attending Hendrix College across town. Ben Laney was born in Ouachita County, one of eleven children in the family of Martha Ella Saxon Laney and Benjamin Travis Laney, Sr. By turns, Ben Laney taught school, served in the Navy during World War I, and obtained his A.B. degree in 1924. He and Lucille were married on January 19, 1926, in Lewisville. Their first home was in Conway, where he and his brother owned a drugstore and Ben worked in a bank. Oil was discovered on the Laney farm in Ouachita County, and Ben and Lucille moved to Camden to oversee their oil, farming, and banking interests. Ben Laney began to acquire all sorts of businesses—cotton gins, mills, grocery, feed and hardware stores, thus earning his political nickname, "Business Ben."

Their various business and political interests caused the Laneys to live in different cities around the state. While living at Conway, Mrs. Laney busied herself with membership in a music club, the Methodist Church, and bridge clubs. When they lived in Camden, she was very active in a music club, the Parent-Teacher Association, Boy Scouts, and the Red Cross.

When asked what she would most like to be remembered for, she said, "I would like to be remembered for performing the duties of First Lady of Arkansas in a manner that brought credit and respect to our state. At that time, Arkansas had no Governor's Mansion, no formal facilities for entertaining the many visitors to Little Rock and the state." In addition, she said, "I truly enjoyed our years in Little Rock. It was such a pleasure to be asked to be a part of the historical, literary, and musical groups which contributed so much to the quality of the life there."

SARAH ANNE PHILLIPS McMATH
1949-1953

IN THE SPRING of 1944 Lt. Colonel Sidney S. McMath was stationed at Camp Pendleton, California, after having spent two years on combat duty in the South Pacific. I met him in May 1944 when he was called to U.S. Marine Headquarters in Washington, D.C., for two weeks' temporary duty to sit in on the Marine Corps planning and training sessions for the invasion of Japan. We met at the end of his first week of duty in D.C., and it was actually love at first sight. We had a date every night the following week. When he returned to the West Coast, the courtship continued by long-distance telephone and mail. He never remembered the time differences between the West Coast and Washington and couldn't understand why I wasn't sitting by the phone at 2:00 a.m. eagerly awaiting his call!

In September he was reassigned to Marine Corps Headquarters Plans and Policy Section as Infantry Training Officer. He proposed on the third date, and we were married two weeks later in the small chapel at the Mount Vernon Place Methodist Church in Washington, D.C., on October 6, 1944.

In February 1945 we visited our families in Mississippi and Arkansas and took Sid's son, Sandy, back to Washington with us. Sid had been married to his high school sweetheart, Elaine Braughton. She died on their fifth wedding anniversary, leaving a nine-month-old son. Sandy was three and a half years old when he, Sid, and I became a family.

The war ended, our son Phillip was born in December 1945, and we established a home in Hot Springs, Arkansas, in January 1946. Sid opened a law office and began to make plans to run for prosecuting attorney of that district—no surprise to me, for he had clearly stated his political ambitions and plans during our courtship. I had worked for four years as a congressional secretary on Capitol Hill and had become absorbed in the world of politics. I was as eager as Sid to start the campaign. Leo P. McLaughlin was the leader of an entrenched political machine that had complete control of the city of Hot Springs and Garland County. Sid was elected prosecuting attorney, narrowly defeating the incumbent in the primary. After this breakthrough an entire slate filed as independent candidates for every office in the county, and all were elected in the November general election.

Life in Hot Springs the next two years was both good and pretty terrible. The political opposition saw to it that I was followed, that when Sid went out of town I received obscene and threatening phone calls, and that Sid's dad, an alcoholic, was supplied with enough whiskey to drive him out of his mind. Our home in the country two miles from the nearest neighbor made it easy for the opposition to play its harassing game of terror. This is a very simple description of a long and hideous nightmare. Somehow we survived it all, and Sid ran for and was elected governor.

He was inaugurated January 10, 1949, before a joint session of the General Assembly. Sid's arrival in the House Chamber was announced by a fanfare from the American Legion Drum and Bugle Corps, stationed in the Capitol rotunda. U.S. Secretary of the Treasury John W. Snyder preceded Sid down the aisle to the speaker's platform. A Marine Corps color guard, wearing dress blues and carrying the national and state flags, entered the chamber and took up stations flanking the rostrum. Sid proudly marched down the aisle in the glare of floodlights, winked at me as he passed by, mounted the platform, and was given the Oath of Office by Chief Justice

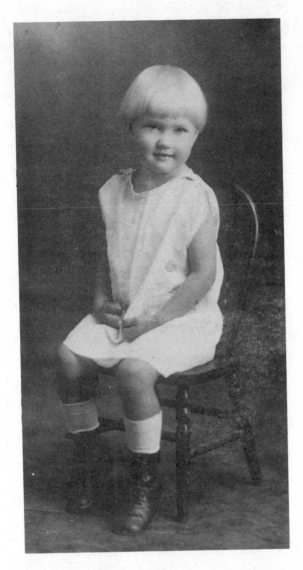

Sarah Anne Phillips at age four. (Photo courtesy of Mr. and Mrs. Sid McMath)

Griffin Smith.

After the ceremony, another fanfare by the Drum and Bugle Corps and the Marine Hymn played by Tommy Scott provided background music while the color guard escorted the new governor out of the hall and across the building to the Capitol steps. As he was preparing to leave the House Chamber, a moment of panic occurred—no one seemed to know where Secretary Snyder's and the governor's speeches were! Sid borrowed an advance copy from a newspaperman, stuffed it in his coat pocket, and marched to the podium, only to find both speeches on the lectern where they were supposed to be. Secretary Snyder read a personal message from President Truman and in his speech Sid outlined an ambitious program for the state. A huge flag, forty feet by sixty feet, had been stretched across the front of the Capitol to form a background for the ceremony. Wives of the constitutional officers and other dignitaries sat in an honor section on the steps. Baskets of flowers from well-wishers were placed on the steps both inside and outside the building. It was cold and windy and I shivered in my black wool suit. Eight-year-old Sandy was cold and totally bored with the whole thing and slumped down up to his ears in his coat! It was estimated that 2,500 people attended the ceremony.

There was a reception that evening in the Governor's Reception Room at the Capitol. Sid's mother, Nettie McMath, and sister, Edyth Crane of Chicago, Secretary Snyder and his daughter Drucie, Senator and Mrs. J.W. Fulbright, and the constitutional officers and their wives joined Sid and me in the receiving line.

Flowers decorated the hall and refreshments were served in another part of the building. A committee planned the reception, and I never saw the serving table so I am unable to describe it. For this special occasion, I wore a black velvet dress and cape ensemble. The dress was cut on slim lines with a modified off-the-shoulder neckline and was embroidered in silver Venetian beading. The long cape with stand-up collar, embroidered across the shoulders with the same beading, was very full and graceful. I wore black velvet pumps with jeweled silver buckles and carried a black velvet purse on which was pinned an orchid corsage.

A sculpture of the flag-raising on Iwo Jima was the center of attention on a table in the reception room. Felix de Weldon, the artist and our personal friend, attended the inauguration and presented this statue to Sid. It is an exact replica of Mr. de Weldon's magnifi-

Anne Phillips McMath, November 1948. (Photo by Campbell Studios; courtesy of Mr. and Mrs. Sid McMath)

Phillip and Anne riding Nell, and Sandy and Sid riding Colonel, during the 1948 campaign for governor. (Photo courtesy of Mr. and Mrs. Sid McMath)

cent Marine Corps War Memorial in Arlington, Virginia. Sid donated this model to Catholic High School in Little Rock, where it is on permanent display and serves as an inspiration to the members of the Marine Corps ROTC unit.

It was necessary that we buy or rent a house to live in until the new mansion was completed. Since we planned to have a series of dinner parties for the members of the legislature, the house had to be large enough to handle official entertaining. I found an older home at 220 Ridgeway that suited our needs. We bought the house in November after the general election and hurriedly remodeled and redecorated, moving in

before Christmas. We left our home in Hot Springs partially furnished, planning to go back there for relaxing weekends that never materialized! I was so busy overseeing the work on the house, buying some new furniture, moving, celebrating Christmas, and preparing for a house full of guests for the inauguration that the whole time just ran together in one big blur.

One entire chapter could be written about those legislative dinner parties. Sid's sister Edyth talked me into hiring her house-keeper, Mimi, to come help during those weeks of heavy entertaining. That was a mistake—a big mistake. Mimi made fancy hors d'oeuvres and, in her sedate gray uni-

Governor and Mrs. McMath in a receiving line at his first inauguration, January 1949. To Anne's left are her mother-in-law, Nettie McMath, and sister-in-law, Edyth Crane of Chicago. (Photo by J.R. "Scotty" Scott; courtesy of Mr. and Mrs. Sid McMath)

form and starched apron and cap, served them as though she were offering up something precious. And she was! She had spent hours with the pastry tube, cream cheese, handcut flowers, and so on. The dinner hour came and went, and the guests had enjoyed a precious tidbit and admired our little boys that Mimi had somehow managed to corral, dress up, and parade through the living room, but the roast hadn't even been put in the oven! When I checked the kitchen I found my regular help in such a state they were about to mutiny. While Mimi was distracted we turned on the stove and belatedly started dinner. When this episode was

repeated at the second party, Mimi was sent back to Chicago.

My two maids, Marie Clayton and Queen Esther Bohlar, and our houseman, Charlie Clemmons, came with us from Hot Springs and lived in quarters on the lower floor of our house. All three of them were excellent cooks and knew exactly how I wanted meals prepared and served. We gave three legislative dinner parties a week with twenty to twenty-six people at each. Sid felt these visits gave him a much stronger working relationship with the members of the General Assembly, and I made lasting friendships with some of their wives.

Anne and Sid McMath at the opening of the Old State House after its renovation. Guests wore clothing of 1836 vintage. (Photo by Arkansas Resources and Development Commission; courtesy of Mr. and Mrs. Sid McMath)

Anne and Sid McMath entering the Governor's Mansion for the first time. (Photo by J.R. "Scotty" Scott; courtesy of Mr. and Mrs. Sid McMath)

The McMaths with baby Bruce, 1949. (Photo by Arkansas Resources and Development Commission; courtesy of Mr. and Mrs. Sid McMath)

One of the first groups to call on Sid after the general election was the mansion commission. They asked for an interview with both of us, and brought with them a copy of the plans for the house and a plea for an appropriation with which to complete the building that was only half-finished. The first appropriation had been spent. I knew immediately that the house was too small and it was too late to make any real changes. After studying the plans, I met with the commission and requested certain alterations. Since the second-floor bedrooms were needed by our large family, I asked that the east wing

Sandy, the First Lady, Governor McMath, and Phillip enjoying a rodeo in Fort Smith, June 1950. (Photo by Doc Miller's Photo Service; courtesy of Mr. and Mrs. Sid McMath)

be made into a guest house instead of an at-home office for the governor. The west wing was planned as a servants' quarters. This one-bedroom sitting-room cottage was inadequate for the staff, so it was agreed that both wings would be finished as guest houses. However, the west wing eventually became housing for the state troopers who lived on the grounds. The original house plan showed a large screened-in porch adjoining the drawing room on the east side. Since there were terraces across the back that would serve the same purpose as the porch, I asked that this porch be enclosed and made into a much-needed living room. The commission agreed, but there was no money for this

additional expense. The maintenance appropriation for the mansion began with the new fiscal year in July. This money was offered to me to pay the cost of running our own house. I refused it and let it accrue. I used this money to buy china, silver, and table linens for the mansion and furnishings for one guest house, and to pay the seven hundred dollars needed to enclose the porch.

There is no way to describe my astonishment when I learned that only a few dollars of the appropriation had been set aside for furnishings. I discovered this only after a decorator had been chosen. He had precious little money to work with, and as I remember it, he donated his commission and

Actress June Alyson holding Bruce McMath, with Dick Powell and the governor on the sofa, during the 1950 Rose Festival. (Photo by Bob Beerman Photo; courtesy of Mr. and Mrs. Sid McMath)

worked only for his expenses. Bill Heerwagen was the decorator selected by the commission—a fitting choice, for it was his grandfather who had been the decorator for the new state Capitol building. When Bill asked my ideas on furnishings, I told him to buy only quality pieces in keeping with the style of the house. I didn't think then, and still do not think, that the First Lady should be allowed to decorate the public rooms according to her taste. It isn't her house. It is also my opinion that the state has no responsibility to furnish anything upstairs for the family's personal use. Most people would rather use their own things.

Bill Heerwagen decorated the downstairs with seafoam green paint, carpet, wallcoverings, and draperies. The draperies in the drawing room and dining room were of a pale green nylon damask and the dining room walls were upholstered with the same material. This damask was specially woven in that color for that house. Since I had nothing to do with the decorating, I feel free to express the opinion that the house has never been prettier than in its original state. The huge chandelier that now hangs in the entrance hall was originally in the dining room and caused a lot of conversation. Many people thought it a bit overpowering, hang-

Anne McMath with sons (l-r) Phillip, Bruce, and Sandy, in the drawing room of the Governor's Mansion, 1950. (Photo by John Blundell; courtesy of Mr. and Mrs. Sid McMath)

Sandy and Phillip McMath displaying coonskin caps as their mother, Anne, looks on. (Photo by J.R. "Scotty" Scott; courtesy of Mr. and Mrs. Sid McMath)

ing from the low ceiling as it did. Whatever one thought of it, it was designed to hang low and was indisputably the focal point of the room. The family dining room and the east living room were decorated in Williamsburg style and colors.

All family meals were served at the pine lazy-susan table in the family dining room. The children's nurse and the two state troopers were a part of the family and had their meals with us. On looking back, that was probably a mistake—there was possibly too much grown-up talk at the table and not enough attention paid to the children. We used an upstairs sitting room for family gatherings, but the formal rooms were not off

limits to the children. We used them when needed for the family, but made a real effort for the children to feel that certain areas were really theirs.

Our personal furniture, china, silver, and linens were used to supplement the state furnishings. The kitchen was completely furnished with my utensils, except for one set of chef's cutlery. By not installing hardwood floors under the carpet in the public rooms of the first floor, we saved enough money out of construction costs to buy a commercial range, refrigerator, and freezer.

There was a wonderful little Colonial cottage on the west side of the grounds that solved the problem of servants' quarters.

The McMaths, with sons Sandy, Phillip, and Bruce, watching home movies at Christmastime. (Photo courtesy of Mr. and Mrs. Sid McMath)

Landscaping underway at the new Governor's Mansion. (Photo by John Blundell; courtesy of Mr. and Mrs. Sid McMath)

Phillip McMath and Roy Rogers. (Photo by Arkansas Resources and Development Commission; courtesy of Mr. and Mrs. Sid McMath)

Originally there were two of these houses, but one had been torn down before I became aware of its historical significance. I grieve that neither exists today—they had been used as hospitals during the Civil War. The one that remained was quite adequate for the staff.

We moved into the mansion on February 3, 1950, a year and a month after taking office. When we attended meetings with other governors during that year, I took advantage of the opportunity to quiz their First Ladies on how they ran their mansions. Most used prison help. I did not want to do this. I tried hiring waiters to come in and serve the parties but that didn't work. There was no one in the kitchen to show them where things were or where to put things away after a party. Paying them was a problem. In the first place there wasn't enough money, and secondly, they did not want to wait for a check from the comptroller's office.

The operating fund provided by the state was just enough money to pay the utilities, hire a chef and two maids, and pay part of the grocery bill. I had no housekeeper, bookkeeper, or secretary. There were over seven acres of lawn and no lawn-mower. I finally realized I had to call on the prison farm for help.

Over the three years, there were several men who came from the farm for temporary duty, but two remained with us until the end of the term—Phil Newman and J.L. Walker. They came straight out of the cotton field with nothing but the clothes they were wearing. I managed to buy work uniforms for them with money from the maintenance fund, but Sid and I furnished them with everything else—shoes, socks, underwear, shirts, a warm coat and raincoat, toilet articles, and a small weekly allowance. Phil had a little experience in housework, but for the most part neither of them knew about cleaning and serving. I trained them to be household servants. For weeks we had a practice session every morning until they learned how to set the table and serve different kinds of parties. They became quite good at serving, answering the phone, cleaning and polishing—in fact they did anything that needed to be done, including taking groups on tours of the house. They worked long hard hours without complaint and earned their freedom. My husband pardoned them at the end of his term in office. They both became good citizens and were never again afoul of the law.

My chef was a godsend. I could not have run the mansion with anyone less talented, even-tempered, capable, and willing than Johnnie Wright. He was a railroad chef who wanted to take a leave of absence in order to be home during his children's teenage years.

If the truth were known, he probably would have had more time at home if he had stayed on the railroad. He was at the mansion six days a week from breakfast until after the dinner hour, no matter how late that was. He never complained nor sought help and often turned down offers of assistance.

Together he and I planned menus around different meat courses of roast beef, chicken, fish, or wild duck. Johnnie was given a free hand to serve any of these menus according to the supplies on hand or seasonal availability. This saved hours for both him and me.

I learned the hard way that security is an absolute necessity for the entire family. Two state troopers lived on the mansion grounds, and one was there at all times, seven days a week. They divided the work and planned their free time between themselves. In the three and one-half years we lived at the mansion, there were several men who had this duty, but Fred McKinley, Ben Kent, Carl Chambers, and Jack Murphy were the four who were with us the longest. They were like members of the family and were very helpful to John and me. When they realized that John and I had more than we could do, one volunteered to take John's daily grocery list to the store to be filled and the other volunteered to post my books and turn in the monthly statements to the comptroller's office. They took turns answering the phone in the butler's pantry. Usually Sandy chose to walk or ride his bike the few blocks to Rightsell Elementary School. Four-year-old Phillip was driven across town to kindergarten, often riding with his dad when he went to the office. One officer served as my chauffeur, and the other drove Sid to the office and on his trips around the state. No security officer ever accompanied Sid on out-of-state trips. On at least two occasions one of them drove us on a family vacation; we paid their expenses.

When there were not sufficient funds to cover the grocery bill, we paid it. No flowers nor alcoholic beverages were bought with state money. Any group could tour the man-

Governor McMath as storyteller to his children, August 1950. (Photo by Arkansas Resources and Development Commission; courtesy of Mr. and Mrs. Sid McMath)

sion by appointment, but I set a policy of allowing only statewide organizations to use the house for parties. These groups furnished their own refreshments and flowers and were responsible for hiring extra help and renting any dishes when needed. We had linen tea napkins and china to accommodate up to 144 guests for tea, but no punch cups.

The largest party we ever had was the first one ever held at the mansion. It was for a statewide teachers' meeting, and I'm sure all three thousand came. One lady fainted and there wasn't room for her to fall to the floor! She had to be lifted and carried out above the heads of the crowd. The cases of beverages ordered for punch were soon consumed, additional supplies were quickly used up, and finally the company sent over a truckload. The truck parked beside the back porch, the bottles were taken from the truck, and the punch was mixed there on the porch. The first order of business the next day was the purchase of a first-aid kit complete with smelling salts. From then on, the size of the expected crowd for a party was carefully checked and none that large was ever again scheduled.

I was twenty-eight years old and having my family at the same time I was having teas, luncheons, and dinner parties and attending official functions with my hus-

Sandy and Phillip McMath attending their father's second inauguration with their mother, 1951. (Photo courtesy of Mr. and Mrs. Sid McMath)

band. Sandy was eight years old and Phillip was four when Sid went into office. Bruce was born the following October—and according to my research he was the first baby born to a gubernatorial family since the birth of Ernestine Flora Rector in March 1861. Bruce was a severe asthmatic and it took all hands and the cook to keep him going.

The day we moved into the mansion, Phillip got into a fight with the little boy next door, Billy Koch, before the moving van was unloaded, but they settled their differences and became close friends. They both were creative and intelligent little boys and the mischief they got into was sometimes very imaginative. Once they had a great business going for themselves by charging a ten-cent admission at the gate of the mansion

grounds! It worked fine until they made the mistake of stopping the governor's car. He promptly put an end to this enterprise.

Sandy made lifelong friends in the neighborhood. The children were young, and as far as I know only Sandy felt the pressure of having a father in public office. He had a terrible time at school the first year. During lunch and recess a gang of children would back him up against the wall of the building and chant, "Your dad's the governor! Your dad's the governor!" He would come home crying and wanting to know what was wrong with his dad. He and I had lots of long conversations that year and made plans for him to go to summer camp and learn to fight. He went to Billy Kramer's Boys Camp and became quite good at boxing. The next fall

L-R: Mesdames Robinson, Hays, Brough, Parnell, Laney, McMath, Faubus, and Mrs. R.S. Warnock, Jr., of Magnolia. Mrs. Warnock underwrote the expense of the original First Ladies' Gowns exhibit. (Photo courtesy of the Arkansas History Commission)

he was sent to school with the admonition from me not to pick a fight, but not to let himself be mistreated—he was told if he had to defend himself to make sure his first lick was hard enough that the fellow wouldn't come back for a second one. This took care of the matter. In later years the other children had to learn to cope with having a prominent father. Some children have real problems with this, but ours have adjusted very well. I am proud of all of them.

Sandy, Phillip, and Bruce all have law degrees from the University of Arkansas, and all practice law together with their father. Patricia and Melissa, our twin daughters, were born the year after we went out of

office. They also live in Little Rock. Patricia has a degree in design from Stephens College, Columbia, Missouri. She has her own design and construction business. Melissa graduated with a B.A. from William Woods College in Columbia, Missouri, and a Masters in Science from the University of Central Arkansas at Conway. She has her own business as a trial consultant. There are eight grandchildren.

I was born December 20, 1920, in Slate Spring, Mississippi, the daughter of Jimmie Belle Vance and James F. Phillips. My mother was a teacher and my father a farmer. I have one sister, Dorris (Mrs. J.B. Spencer), of Grenada, Mississippi.

My ancestors came to America in colonial days and settled in Virginia and North Carolina. One relative, Zebulon Baird Vance, was both governor and senator in North Carolina and one of two representatives of that state in Statuary Hall of the United States Capitol. My people settled in Mississippi in territorial days and homesteaded great tracts of land. Because of the family custom of parcelling off a farm for a newly married son, the land has gradually been divided up and ownership has passed from the family. When the last parcel was sold, my sister and I kept a little acreage for sentimental reasons. I descend from a long line of proud and dignified people who did their share in helping build this nation.

I graduated from the local high school and at sixteen I was a freshman at Mississippi State College for Women. My mother was a graduate of this college and a former math professor there. At the time I was a student, many department heads were old classmates of hers. This made it difficult for me because they expected me to be the excellent student that my mother was. During my orientation week all freshmen were shown a glass case containing an annual opened to her picture with a citation stating that no student had ever equalled or surpassed her scholarship in higher mathematics! She held degrees in mathematics and in Latin from the University of Chicago and was offered a scholarship in medicine by Johns Hopkins.

Severe asthma forced me to drop out of college my second year. Later I went to Washington, D.C., for what was meant to be a two weeks' visit but stayed four years. It was tremendously exciting to be in "the capital of the world" during World War II.

As the first resident of the new mansion, I had the privilege and responsibility to set precedents in the use of the mansion, to staff it, and to establish operational procedures. There was no time for me to become involved in outside civic endeavors. I belonged to several organizations but was not active in any of them. Since leaving public office I have served as president of the Twentieth Century Club and Regent of the Gilbert Marshall Chapter of the Daughters of the American Revolution, held office in the Churchwomen of Trinity Cathedral, worked for a time as a regular volunteer for the State Hospital Auxiliary, and served on the Board of Directors of Twentieth Century Hope Lodge.

Being married to Sid McMath is something like having one foot on and one foot off a spinning merry-go-round and hanging on for dear life. Together we have been through three careers—politics, the military, and the law. I've loved it all. Being a lawyer's wife is the easiest!

A Note from Sid McMath

To compensate for the many TV dinners she served me during the writing of her book, my wife promised me a brief footnote to her chapter.

I was introduced to Anne by a mutual friend in Washington, D.C. She was intelligent, beautiful (Miss Capitol Hill), and—the clincher—keenly interested in politics. We were engaged, married, and came home to Arkansas, motivated by my fervent ambition to be governor of my state.

She served as a consultant and a friend and never hesitated to tell me when she thought I was making a wrong decision.

I was never, while governor, out of communication with the mansion—my command post—for any length of time.

Once I was in Clinton, Arkansas, making a

speech when a tornado hit nearby at Judsonia and Searcy. I proceeded to Searcy, checked at Truman Baker's Chevrolet agency where a temporary aid station had been set up in Truman's garage. I had radio messages from the Director of the State Police and the Director of Prisons, and the Commanding General of the Arkansas National Guard was there waiting for orders. They had contacted the mansion. Anne informed them where I would be and said that their help would be needed without delay. She had made a correct evaluation of the situation, acted on it, and saved valuable time in the state's efforts to give emergency help to those citizens in distress.

Earlier in my first political effort, Anne's help was critical. I was running for prosecuting attorney in Hot Springs. We were endeavoring to throw out illegal poll taxes which the Hot Springs machine had used to stay in power. We had petitioned the United States District Court, Judge John Miller presiding,

to declare several thousand poll taxes null and void. This was the key to victory or defeat.

We had alleged in our complaint that the poll taxes were fraudulently obtained, but we had to prove it. This we had not been able to do. We could not get witnesses to testify, and although we had subpoenaed the records, it was a mystery how these poll taxes had been issued and concealed from an inspection of the poll tax books.

Judge Miller recessed court and gave us until the next day at 9:00 a.m. to solve the mystery. After an all-night session, when no one could break the code, and when the nine o'clock court session was about to convene, Anne, an excellent bridge player and an avid worker of crossword puzzles, solved the enigma. We marched into the court with the proof. The illegal poll taxes were thrown out, and the GI forces won the day. This made it possible for me to realize my ambition to be governor of Arkansas.

MARGARET FRIERSON CHERRY
1953-1955

PETITE MARGARET FRIERSON was a popular co-ed, a member of Chi Omega sorority, and a beauty queen at the University of Arkansas, as was her mother before her. Charlotte Galloway, Margaret's mother, was elected "Most Beautiful Young Lady" in the first such election ever held on the campus. The Chi Omega sorority was organized at the University of Arkansas, and Charlotte Galloway was a charter member, serving also as the first treasurer of the national sorority. Margaret Frierson was a Beauty Queen in 1933, Campus Queen in 1934, and held the offices of secretary, treasurer, and vice-president of Chi Omega. She was secretary of the senior class, president of the Women's League, chairman of the Women's Vigilance Committee, vice-president of Rootin' Rubes, and a member of Sigma Alpha Iota and Lambda Tau. She was listed in *Who's Who* in 1934 and graduated magna cum laude with a major in English and a minor in music.

At the time Margaret Frierson attended the university, an important part of campus social life was a Saturday night dance at the student union. This is where she met her future husband. She says: "He was introduced to me at a student dance at the university when I was a senior and he was a first year law student. He was a wonderful dancer and his wavy dark hair was already sprinkled with silver. I was impressed when I met him!" She says further, "Oh, what a pleasure today's students have missed in not knowing the Saturday night ballroom dancing with lots of 'breaking in'!" "Breaking in" was a way of changing partners on the dance floor. A young man wishing to dance with a certain young lady would tap her partner on the shoulder and ask, "May I?" and the young lady changed partners.

Margaret and Francis Cherry waited to marry until after he graduated from law school and was established in a legal practice in Jonesboro. They were married on November 10, 1937, at the First Presbyterian Church in Jonesboro, Arkansas. Ten years later they had their family of three children: Haskille Scott, Charlotte Frierson, and Francis A. Cherry, Jr. Scott Cherry graduated from Duke University in North Carolina. He married Dianne Draper, and they have two grown children, Martha Jeanne and Patrick Scott. They live in Williamsburg, Virginia, where Dianne is a physical therapist and Scott is at the printing office of the College of William and Mary.

Daughter Charlotte did not change her name when she married Ted A. Cherry, a young man whom she met in Washington, D.C. They both had careers in the Central Intelligence Agency, but after several years they resigned and moved to Arkansas. They now live at Cotter, Arkansas, where they own a bookstore and, as Charlotte says, "enjoy the Ozarks and the beautiful White River."

Francis, Jr., married Paula Burns of Nashville, Tennessee, graduated from Vanderbilt Law School, settled in Richmond, Virginia, served as assistant attorney general for the Commonwealth of Virginia for three years, and is now in private practice there. They have three children: Elizabeth Burns, Francis A. Cherry III, and Emily Katherine.

Margaret Cherry says of her children at the mansion,

The children settled into life at the mansion very well, with visits from their hometown friends to help. Margie and John Johnson, the children of my secretary, were wonderful companions. The servants were good to them. In our early days in the mansion I arrived home one

The Francis Cherry family in a happy moment. (Photo courtesy of the Arkansas Gazette)

Governor and Mrs. Francis Cherry. (Photo by Gene Prescott; courtesy of the Arkansas Gazette)

day to find Willie Walton, the houseboy, playing with Francis, Jr., in the front hall. A fierce battle was going on with Willie firing an imaginary gun from the stairway and our son firing from a crouching position below!

The children were involved in Boy Scouts, Girl Scouts, Sunday school at First Presbyterian Church and Junior Cotillion. Scott even had a paper route.

Of her life at the mansion Margaret says,

How fortunate I was that the Legislative Council asked if I'd like to have a housekeeper-secretary to head a staff of about seven. I was very glad to agree to that and was delighted that Mrs. Robert

Margaret and Francis Cherry and their younger children, Francis Jr. and Charlotte, celebrating Scott's birthday in the family dining room at the mansion. (Photo by Gene Prescott; courtesy of the Arkansas Gazette)

Johnson would accept that job. She brought great warmth as well as efficiency to that position. We hired, as quickly as possible, a cook, a maid and houseboy and never did fill all the positions, finally employing Liza Ashley, who is still at the mansion, and a yardman. Perhaps we could have assembled a more efficient staff but not a more loyal and warm-hearted one.

Our youngest son was five years old and he told his aunt that I was always having a tea, which sort of sums up most of the entertaining we did. Many organizations requested a tea or reception at the mansion during state or national conventions with the organization bearing the expense of food and drink. I was happy to open the house to groups and let them experience pride in their mansion.

I was usually asked to be in the receiving line with the officers of the host group and I found it amusing and perhaps a bit frustrating when, after going down the line one of the guests would say, "Where is Mrs. Cherry?" How insignificant must have been my bearing!

When asked what she accomplished as First Lady, Mrs. Cherry responded:

The Francis Cherry family on Inauguration Day, January 13, 1953. (Photo courtesy of the Arkansas Gazette)

Margaret Frierson Cherry braids her daughter Charlotte's hair. (Photo courtesy of the Arkansas Gazette)

I hope I gave some warmth and a measure of dignity (in spite of not being recognized sometimes) to the position and was a support to my husband and family, which included my mother who spent the time with us. She had been quite ill just before our move to Little Rock so I insisted she come to stay with us. I think she enjoyed the stay in the mansion. I had no particular "project" but tried to respond to church, civic, and charitable requests.

Francis A. Cherry was inaugurated in January 1953 in the customary ceremony on the steps of the Capitol. His minister from Jonesboro gave the invocation and benediction.

Music was furnished by the Jonesboro High School band, and the governor's junior-high–aged son, Scott, was allowed to play with the band on that important occasion in the life of the Cherry family. Chief Justice Griffin Smith administered the Oath of Office.

There was an open reception at the mansion in the afternoon. The congressional delegation and the constitutional officers along with their wives were on hand. Mrs. Cherry describes the party:

Because we thought the ladies would grace the occasion in long party dresses (including a dozen or so lovely young girls who had campaigned over the state and whom we'd invited to help serve), we requested long dresses be worn, but did not ask the gentlemen to change from business suits since this was an afternoon reception. Punch and cake were served. The money for the caterers came out of our own pockets. We were grateful to good and dear friends for flowers and music, some of my old friends from Jonesboro taking turns at the organ during the reception. My inaugural gown was rather dressy perhaps for an afternoon reception, but it did grace that lovely drawing room at the mansion, I

Ed Sullivan chatting with the Cherrys and Jack Pickens before his show, **Toast of the Town***, in December 1953. (Photo courtesy of the Arkansas Gazette)*

felt. By the way, my mother had been ill and my children needed my time when I was not campaigning so I had little time for shopping. Therefore, I simply ordered by mail (from a rather smart shop) two evening dresses and a suit. So my inaugural gown was a "mail order gown"!

In Little Rock Margaret belonged to the Woman's City Club and was an honorary member of the Florence Crittenden Home board, Girl Scout board, Parent-Teacher Association groups, and the Arkansas Association for the Crippled.

Margaret Cherry has always been civic-minded. In Jonesboro she kept busy with

PTA, scouts, and volunteer work through her membership in Junior Auxiliary— particularly a class for exceptional children that later became a part of the public school system. Music has always been important to her. She sang in choral groups and at weddings and funerals, and kept active in her two music clubs. She did not resign her Jonesboro affiliations when she moved to Little Rock.

She lists offices held in church and clubs as follows:

> I have served as president of the Women of the Church both in Washington and Williamsburg and have been circle chair-

man several times. I have been president of two Music Clubs, three PTAs, Chi Omega Alumnae Association of Washington, D.C., the Independent Agency Women in Washington, and Regent of Williamsburg DAR and of Williamsburg United Daughters of the Confederacy. Also, I've been the director of Colonial Capitol Branch of the Association for the Preservation of Antiquities and president of the Garden Club Council of Williamsburg, as well as my own Garden Club.

The Cherry family lived in Washington, D.C., on two separate occasions. During World War II Francis Cherry took a leave of absence from the bench, volunteered for military duty, and was accepted into the United States Navy. Margaret and the children went with him and lived in Washington the two years he was in the service.

After leaving the governor's office, Cherry was appointed by President Eisenhower to serve on the Subversive Activities Control Board. He was reappointed to that position by Presidents Kennedy and Johnson and served until his death in 1965.

Margaret remained in Washington, D.C., until her children all went off to college. While she was packing to move back to Arkansas, she took time out to attend a meeting of the Chevy Chase Women's Club. The speaker was a Colonial Williamsburg hostess trainer, dressed in costume. Margaret was intrigued by what she heard, made inquiries about becoming a Colonial Williamsburg hostess herself, and was interviewed and accepted. She moved to

Williamsburg, Virginia, and went to work on her very first job at the age of fifty-seven! She enjoyed this work immensely but has now retired. Once a week she does volunteer work in the local hospital gift shop and for Meals on Wheels, and she enjoys her grandchildren who live next door.

Margaret Frierson Cherry was the daughter, granddaughter, and wife of judges. In 1942 her husband was elected chancellor of the Twelfth Chancery District.

Living in a mansion was nothing new to Margaret Cherry. In 1924, when she was twelve, her parents moved across the lawn to the beautiful mansion that her grandparents had built some time after the Civil War. After the death of Margaret's father in 1947, the Cherry family moved in to take care of her mother. Thus this gracious old house became permanent home to the fourth generation of Margaret's family. The house has been on the National Register of Historic Places for several years. It is a two-story, columned, white frame mansion with ornate banisters edging the upper and lower galleries that extend across the front. It bespeaks old money, old family, inherited furniture, and a family retainer or two!

In 1976 Mrs. Cherry and her children presented to the Arkansas Governor's Mansion a beautiful antique tall case clock as a memorial to Governor Cherry. The clock was made about 1770 at Waterford, Ireland, by William Maddock. Mrs. Cherry purchased the clock at an antique shop in Yorktown, Virginia. Her choice of this beautiful clock reflects her interests and cultural background, and is a handsome addition to our mansion.

CELIA ALTA HASKINS FAUBUS
1955-1967

IN RESEARCHING THESE ladies I have often thought that the title of this book should be *What Price Glory!* Many of these women have paid a high personal price for their years as "Wife of the Governor." The cost of a position of power is high and often it is the wife and/or children who pay it. Flora Rector, Adeline Clayton, this writer, Barbara Pryor, Harriet Baxter, Cinderella Drew, and probably Margaret Bailey and Jeannette Rockefeller should be included in the list of those whose husbands' political success cost them dearly. Certainly Alta Faubus belongs on the list.

She was near collapse at the end of her husband's twelve years in office. Governor Faubus was such a controversial figure that the time had been extremely stressful for Alta and their son, Farrell. In their early years she, Orval, and Farrell had enjoyed a normal family closeness. The security and support of this closeness disappeared for the child when the father entered state politics. When Orval Faubus was elected governor and the family moved into the mansion, Farrell was taken away from family and friends and the comparatively small rural school he had attended all his life. At the impressionable age of fifteen he was transferred into a large city school where he knew no one. His father was the subject of most breakfast-table conversations in Arkansas every morning. Farrell's classmates were merciless in taunting him with the many accusations heaped on Orval, and the boy ended up in so many fights in defense of his father that it was decided he should return to his hometown of Huntsville, live with his maternal grandmother, and attend his old school. This solved the problem of school fights, but did nothing for Farrell's ego. He felt he had not measured up—that he had been banished.

When Orval began to talk about running for governor in 1954, Alta asked him not to make the race. She had no desire to enter politics. Orval told her that Cherry could be beaten and that "it might as well be me."

Alta was a reluctant First Lady in the beginning, and worrying about her child back in Huntsville added to her unhappiness. Gradually she began to feel comfortable in and enthusiastic about her role. She was always interested in her husband's career and he often asked her opinions. She did not hesitate to speak up. They had discussed the issue of his having attended Commonwealth College. He had warned her that it would come up in the campaign, and being warned, she was able to cope. Her opinion was not sought on the Little Rock Central High School crisis in 1957. There was no way she could avoid being drawn into the turmoil and strain of those times.

The school desegregation crisis, a sad chapter in our history, has been well chronicled and will not be rehashed in these pages. Governor and Mrs. Faubus were attending a Governor's Conference in Sea Island, Georgia, when the Federal troops landed in Little Rock. They immediately flew home. When they arrived at the Little Rock Airport, they found it crowded with members of the press from all over the world. (In 1978 when Alta was traveling in Jerusalem she met a reporter who told her he was there at the airport on that day!) They were rushed from the airport to the mansion by police car and were greeted by a group of children carrying hastily made signs that said, "Welcome Home, Governor Faubus"—a gratifying gesture of friendship on that day.

As one might well imagine, life at the mansion during those days was hectic, unpleasant, and sometimes frightening. People from

Orval and Alta Faubus on August 10, 1954. (Photo by Larry Obsitnik; courtesy of the Arkansas Gazette)

all over the nation sent flowers; mail came by the sackful. Phone lines had to be added and staff hired to answer them. So many crank calls were received that Alta had to stop answering the phone. The state police decided she should carry a small gun in her purse even though she was never without police protection. A planned shopping trip was cancelled on advice of the state police.

Alta's schedule loaded up with people both for and against the governor's stand who were trying to reach him through her. On one occasion the national news broadcast originated at the mansion with many famous reporters on hand. Chet Huntley and David Brinkley called, and while they were waiting for the governor to come on the line, Alta overheard David saying to Chet, "I think the

Alta Faubus relaxing at the Governor's Mansion, August 10, 1954. (Photo by Gene Prescott, courtesy of the Arkansas Gazette)

Eleanor Roosevelt addressing a Little Rock crowd, with (l-r) Mrs. Merlin Moore, Mayor A.C. Perry, Mayor Pratt Remmell, Governor-elect Faubus, and Mrs. Faubus behind her on the platform, January 6, 1955. (Photo by Larry Obsitnik; courtesy of the Arkansas Gazette)

Alta and Farrell Faubus on Inauguration Day, January 11, 1955. (Photo by Gene Prescott; courtesy of the Arkansas Gazette)

president is trying to humiliate that governor." In retrospect it all seems unreal—like a movie she might have seen. At the time, it was all very real and distressing.

When Governor Faubus fainted and fell to the floor, his aides decided he had to get away for a while. It was arranged for Orval and Alta to slip away and spend a few days in Newton County with Bill and Nina Fowler. Although the two couples had never met, the Fowlers welcomed the Faubuses into their home. The four of them became fast friends, and the Fowler home was a sanctuary for Alta and Orval on several occasions. Later Orval offered Bill Fowler a job with the Veterinarian's Department. He came and spent the night at the mansion. Alta went down to have coffee with him the next morning and Bill told her, "Mrs. Faubus, when he asked me if I would like the job it was like asking a duck if he would like a twenty-acre lake!"

There were many visitors who came to the mansion during the twelve years the Faubuses lived there—rich and poor, famous and infamous. One of the happiest events for

Alta was the reception they gave for the Marching Razorback Band, when the band in return entertained Governor and Mrs. Faubus and their guests. The most interesting guest was former President Harry Truman. The Faubuses held a large reception for him at the mansion and invited the press and prominent Democrats. Truman rose early the next morning for his customary walk. He played the Missouri Waltz for Alta but would not let her take his picture while doing so. He sent two dozen yellow roses. She amused Mr. Truman with a story of how on his last election day she had hauled voters to the polls in support of him. She was the postmistress of Huntsville and was not supposed to be active in politics. When the postal inspector came and found that $37.50 was missing on election day, Alta confessed that she had been out helping elect Mr. Truman. The inspector, a close friend and supporter of Truman's, told his assistant to charge the clerk on duty with the shortage and to write up a good report for the postmistress!

Orval and Alta Faubus on July 31, 1956. (Photo by Gene Prescott; courtesy of the Arkansas Gazette)

Alta Faubus greeting Mrs. Gary H. Jones and her son, Casey, February 1, 1955. (Photo by Gene Prescott; courtesy of the Arkansas Gazette)

The Christmas parties that Alta arranged for the children of the neighborhood and for her employees were a special joy to her. A friend trucked in reindeer from Texas, harnessed them, and drove them onto the mansion grounds, where, complete with a red-nosed Rudolph in front, they brought Santa with his pack of candy and fruit.

In November 1956 Governor and Mrs. Faubus celebrated their twenty-fifth anniversary with a large reception at the mansion. Friends from all over the state came bringing traditional gifts of silver.

In their twelve years in office there were plenty of unexpected happenings—such as the governor's forgetting that the cook was on vacation and inviting guests to a dinner; a mouse who came to a tea party; and Alta's causing a traffic jam in front of the mansion when she decided to show the gardener the proper way to plant tulips!

While First Lady, Alta did volunteer work at the Arkansas Training School for girls. She bought a piano for this home, and the new recreation building was named "The Alta

Faubus Hall." She served in an advisory position on the Board of Mental Health for the construction of community health centers and was honorary chairman for the state beautification program and honorary fund-raising chairman for the Cystic Fibrosis Foundation.

During President Johnson's administration, Alta was selected to head the Head Start program. She devoted herself to this cause, traveling to nearby states to observe and learn about their programs. Due to her interest the Arkansas Head Start Program was the number one program in the United States. She was honored at the White House for her efforts, and *Reader's Digest* and *Time* credited her with the program's success in Arkansas.

When Lady Bird Johnson came to Arkansas on a campaign swing across the

Orval and Alta Faubus celebrating their twenty-fifth wedding anniversary on November 21, 1956. (Photo courtesy of the Arkansas Gazette)

nation, Alta joined her in Fort Smith and flew with her on her stops in Arkansas. These two women shared an interest in the Head Start Program, their names were Claudia Alta Johnson and Celia Alta Faubus, they were almost the same age and size, and their husbands were prominent Democratic politicians. Little wonder they were on a first-name basis! Governor and Mrs. Faubus attended the Johnson inauguration.

It was often necessary for Alta to fly, which she hated and feared. Her first flight was on election day the year Orval was first elected governor. They had ended their campaign in Jonesboro, the hometown of Governor Cherry, and had to fly in a private plane to Huntsville in order to vote. Winthrop Rockefeller often made his plane available to Gov-

ernor and Mrs. Faubus. On one harrowing trip bad weather closed in and caused a rough ride on a long trip home from Atlantic City, New Jersey. There had been business stops in Illinois and Kansas City, and at each stop Alta had to force herself to stay on the plane for the next takeoff. When they finally reached Little Rock they landed on a flat tire. During the trip she noticed Orval taking notes, and she later learned he was writing instructions in case they didn't survive. She said of this trip, "I was so tired. I had held the plane up all day, and my back was killing me!" She has somehow overcome her fear of flying, for today she is a world traveler, having visited all fifty states and many foreign countries.

As the years went by, Alta became more at

The Faubuses opening a silver tray. (Photo courtesy of the Arkansas Gazette)

ease as First Lady and as a politician. She had begun to feel at home in the mansion and by the 1964 campaign was a seasoned campaigner. She was assigned a car and driver and took on a full schedule. Many voters assured her it was she for whom they were voting.

In November 1964 Governor Faubus was ill and unable to accept his nomination at the Democratic State Convention. He called her in, handed her a few notes, and told her she had to go before the convention and make his acceptance speech. She was a smash hit with the delegates, and when it was all over she decided that she had really rather enjoyed it. In 1970 there was a bona fide movement for her to run in her own right. She toyed with the idea for a while, but decided against a race of her own. She returned all campaign contributions and has since devoted herself to her business interests, her travels, and her two granddaughters.

During his father's term in office, Farrell

had finished high school in Huntsville, entered Arkansas Technical University for one semester, and then transferred to the University of Arkansas at Fayetteville. He married his high school sweetheart, Martha Jo Culwell, finished law school, served one term in the legislature, and did graduate studies in law at the University of Texas at Austin. He practiced law in Little Rock and Huntsville. He and Martha Jo had two daughters, Fara Elizabeth and Frances Ellen.

At this writing, Fara has a degree in accounting from the University of Arkansas and is an outstanding student in the law school of Georgetown University in Washington, D.C. A top student, she was selected for Law Review and graduates as a tax lawyer in 1989. Frances Ellen is studying journalism and broadcasting at the University of Alabama. She will work for CNN Cable television in Washington, D.C., during the summer of 1989 and will graduate in 1990. These two young women are the joy of Alta's life. She has provided for most of their educa-

Alta Faubus and her granddaughter Fara, age three, admiring roses sent by the American Mothers Committee in honor of Mother's Day. (Photo courtesy of the Arkansas Gazette)

tion, spends lots of time with them, and often takes one or both of them with her when she travels abroad.

Fara was with her on a fairy-tale trip to England when they were privileged to meet Prince Charles and Lady Diana at a dinner-dance at the home of Lord Mountbatten. They were guests at a polo match in which Prince Charles and his team played in Windsor Great Park, and attended a cocktail party in London hosted by Gucci, the renowned designer.

Another year Alta took Fara with her to Egypt, and through her good friend Helen Boehm they were privileged to meet and visit with Mrs. Anwar Sadat, widow of the prime minister. Frances Ellen did not want to go to Egypt, and chose instead a trip on the "Love Boat" of television fame. She and Alta took an Alaskan Inland Waterways Cruise on the *Sun Princess,* the original Love Boat—Alta's fourth trip to Alaska.

Alta Faubus is a strong person. She has great will power and strength of character. She is made of stuff as stern as the hills from whence she comes. She was born in Madison, Arkansas, on August 31, 1912, the daughter of Rachel Shipp and Jessie Clarence Haskins. She spent her early life and attended schools in this county. She met Orval at a teachers' meeting at the University of Arkansas in 1929, and they were married at Ball Creek Community Church on November 21, 1931.

After being certified to teach school, Alta taught for two terms in a one-room school in her area during the 1930s. Orval taught in these schools for ten years.

Alta always joined Orval in any undertaking and very often had to step in and finish things that he started. When World War II came along he enlisted in the army as a private, and Alta served out the balance of his

second term as circuit clerk and recorder. At the end of the term she and their son, Farrell, joined Orval and lived for a time at army bases in several states. When Orval was sent overseas, she and Farrell returned to California to live with relatives and friends while she worked in a defense plant.

Alta and Farrell returned to Huntsville in the fall of 1945, and Alta took a job with the employment security division as claims deputy. Orval returned in the fall of 1946. In 1947, he and Alta bought the *Madison County Record.* He arranged to have Alta named acting postmaster so he would have more time to spend publishing the *Record.* Alta paid for the newspaper with her postmaster's salary. When Orval became administrative assistant to Governor McMath, he moved to Little Rock and left Alta in Huntsville to run the paper and the post office.

During his tenure in the governor's office, Alta was his number one supporter. Twelve stressful years as the governor's wife left her physically and emotionally drained. Their divorce in 1969 and the death of her only child in 1976 were tragedies that tested her resources for survival. Like a true mountaineer, she fought back and by fighting began to regain her strength. Today she keeps busy as publisher of her newspaper and owner and sometimes manager of her motel, the Faubus Motel.

When she looks back over her years as First Lady, she always recalls her last night at the mansion. She says, "My granddaughter Fara and I stayed by ourselves. We were in my bedroom looking out the window watching my bed being loaded into a moving van. Three-year-old Fara said, 'Mema, this makes me real sad. Even your bed is gone. I could cry.' As we went down the winding stairs she said, 'I'll cry tomorrow'—spoken like a true daughter of Alta Faubus!"

Jeannette Edris Rockefeller. (Photo courtesy of the Arkansas Gazette)

JEANNETTE EDRIS ROCKEFELLER
1967-1971

JEANNETTE EDRIS WAS brought up to be aware of her civic and social responsibilities and began her career of volunteer work at the age of eighteen. She was born on July 13, 1918, in Seattle, the daughter of Mr. and Mrs. William Edris. Her father was a financier with interests in real estate, hotels, and theaters.

Jeannette descends from the first Edris who came to America and settled in Pennsylvania before 1700. Her great-grandfather left Pennsylvania and migrated to Oregon, coming west over the Oregon Trail by covered wagon. Her grandfather left Oregon and settled in Seattle.

When Jeannette was only four years old her mother died, leaving the little girl and her sister, Frances, under the watchful eye of Grandmother Skinner, who lived next door. They lived in almost identical large Georgian houses side by side.

Jeannette attended St. Nicholas School, a private school for girls in Seattle. At the age of eighteen she was a seasoned traveler, having been to Europe twice and around the world once on a four-month trip with her grandmother. She was graduated from Finch College in New York and attended the University of Washington.

She was living in New York in 1950 when she met Winthrop Rockefeller. She was separated from her third husband and he was separated from his first wife. She had two children from her second marriage, Bruce and Anne Bartley. He had one son who lived abroad with his mother, Barbara Sears Rockefeller.

Winthrop Rockefeller moved to Arkansas in 1953. Their long-distance courtship ended in marriage in a quiet ceremony at Hayden Lake, Idaho, on June 11, 1956. Jeannette and her children moved to Rockefeller's home on his farm at Petit Jean Mountain, Arkansas. The children became a part of the social and academic life of the area, attending schools in Morrilton. Rockefeller's son, Winthrop Paul, attended schools in Europe, but spent summer vacations on the farm with his father. He loved it on Petit Jean, and later chose to make it his home. All three of these children grew up to be productive and caring citizens of Arkansas.

Jeannette Rockefeller has always been interested in mental health programs. While living in New York, through the Junior League she became one of the first trained volunteers who actually worked with teen-aged drug addicts, at New York's Riverside Hospital. She did casework in the Social Service Department at New York Infirmary and volunteer work at the psychiatric clinic of the juvenile court.

When Winthrop Rockefeller moved to Arkansas, he immediately began to devote his time and money to various state projects. Jeannette joined him in his endeavors and pursued her own interests. She became a member of the Pulaski County Mental Health Association and the Urban League and served on the boards of the Florence Crittenden Home and Philander Smith College. She was women's state chairman for the United States savings bond drive from 1956 to 1959. She was named Woman of the Year by the readers of the *Arkansas Democrat* in 1962.

From 1961 to 1963 she was president of the Arkansas Mental Health Association and through this office worked for a change in attitudes regarding mental health and retardation. She campaigned for more and better mental health clinics and programs in this state. In 1964 she was elected president of the National Association for Mental Health.

Winthrop Rockefeller serving his wife, Jeannette; sister-in-law, Happy; and brother, Nelson, at a 1963 party celebrating the tenth anniversary of Winthrop's moving to Arkansas. (Photo courtesy of the Arkansas Gazette)

Jeannette Rockefeller presenting the key to the city of St. Louis to Maurice Chevalier, on behalf of the National Association for Mental Health, May 17, 1964. (Photo courtesy of the Arkansas Gazette)

The Rockefellers and family: Anne and Salvatore Papa and Sherry and Bruce Bartley, November 9, 1966. (Photo by Larry Obsitnik; courtesy of the Arkansas Gazette)

Through this organization she campaigned for federal funds for mental health centers, encouraged high school students to become interested in mental health careers, and sought to update the leadership of mental health groups.

In 1966, as the representative of the National Mental Health Association and nine other nationally recognized health organizations, she appeared before the House Banking and Currency Committee to protest legislation that would allow the American Health and Cancer Associations to purchase three million dollars' worth of silver dollars and resell them for profit. Mrs. Rockefeller believed this special aid to these two organizations would be at the expense of the ten other health groups.

Both Winthrop and Jeannette Rockefeller devoted a great deal of time and money toward the building of our very fine Arkansas Arts Center. In 1958 the Junior League joined with the Museum of Fine Arts and formed a Community Arts Center Board. This board sought permission to raise $250,000 in a capital funds drive. Permission was granted, and Larry Kelly and Winthrop Rockefeller became chairman and vice-chairman of the drive. By September 1959, $328,000 had been collected.

The second phase of the campaign was a statewide solicitation of funds. Both Mr. and Mrs. Rockefeller agreed to attend twenty-one meetings over the state, present the idea of a community arts center, and seek financial support.

*Jeannette and Winthrop Rockefeller leaving a
general store on Petit Jean Mountain after voting
in the November 8, 1966, election. (Photo by
Gene Prescott; courtesy of the Arkansas Gazette)*

*The new governor and his wife descending the
Capitol steps on Inauguration Day, January 11,
1967. (Photo by Gene Prescott; courtesy of the
Arkansas Gazette)*

*The Rockefellers greeting visitors at an inaugu-
ral reception, January 10, 1967. (Photo courtesy
of the Arkansas Gazette)*

Groundbreaking ceremonies took place on
August 20, 1961. The program lists Winthrop
Rockefeller as chairman of the state cam-
paign for the Arkansas Arts Center and Jean-
nette Rockefeller as president of the Board of
Trustees of the Arkansas Art Center.

A project that started out as a modest community center for the arts and sciences grew
into a full-fledged state art museum and
teaching facility consisting of five galleries, a
389-seat auditorium, five classrooms—and a
$1.5 million price tag.

Jeannette had the idea for an Artmobile to

Jeannette Rockefeller speaking at an NAACP meeting, September 8, 1968. (Photo by Pat Patterson; courtesy of the Arkansas Gazette)

take paintings and sculpture around the state for display. She, Winthrop, his brother David and his wife, and the Barton Foundation of El Dorado donated $65,000 for the purchase of this art gallery on wheels.

The Rockefellers aided the building of the arts center in every way possible. They gave money and time, raised money, moved trees, and elevated the artistic sights of the community. Jeannette presided over art shows, made speeches, and stuffed envelopes. On the day of the formal dedication of the arts center, the *Gazette* carried an article which said in part,

The Arkansas Arts Center, which is set for dedication at 11 a.m. today, might

appropriately have been designated Arkansas's Rockefeller Center in honor of the couple without whose guidance, financial support and on-the-spot direction it probably would never have come into existence.

Mr. and Mrs. Winthrop Rockefeller took the Arts Center project under their wing soon after the Junior League of Little Rock had proposed the construction of a state arts center. Aside from their personal fund-raising tour of the state that brought in about $800,000 toward the construction costs, the Rockefellers' contributions have been enormous and largely unheralded.

The Rockefellers and supporters, November 2, 1968. (Photo by Morris White; courtesy of the Arkansas Gazette)

After the arts center was opened the funds available for operation were inadequate. The Rockefellers personally subsidized the operating costs for several years.

Winthrop Rockefeller ran for governor in 1966, was elected, and took office in January 1967. He was inaugurated in a simple ceremony before a joint session of the house and senate. Jeannette chose a simple, short, three-piece aqua wool suit for the occasion. A reception was held afterward at the mansion. Though the day was bitterly cold, the crowd stood in long lines waiting to go through the receiving line. The Rockefellers were touched that so many came to wish them well.

After the election in November, Mrs.

Faubus graciously invited Mrs. Rockefeller to come to the mansion for a visit and a tour. Mrs. Rockefeller saw that much renovation was needed and learned that new wiring was necessary. The house was then seventeen years old, but in terms of usage it was many years beyond that figure.

During the Rockefeller renovation, the drawing room and state dining room finally got the hardwood floors that were originally planned for them. Mrs. Rockefeller managed to get this flooring donated and also marble for the floor in the entrance hall. The Rockefellers donated museum-quality oriental rugs for the drawing room and state dining room and had the furniture recovered. After leaving the mansion, in an interview with

Jeannette Rockefeller addressing a gathering, December 1, 1968. (Photo by Morris White; courtesy of Arkansas Gazette)

Betty Woods of the *Arkansas Democrat* Jeannette said, "You know as a family home I thought the mansion was beautiful, but it was too small for a public building." Every First Lady who has lived there agrees with her.

The Rockefellers worked together to promote better race relations in this state. About desegregation Jeannette said, "It is not discussed objectively; you're either for it or against it and there's no middle ground." During her husband's administration blacks were given responsible jobs, and civil rights groups found they had a governor with a sympathetic ear. Mrs. Rockefeller held an all-day picnic on the mansion grounds for Head Start groups, and hoped that it would become an annual affair.

She didn't care for campaigning and made only a few appearances with her husband, but she traveled over the state making speeches on mental health. She often called on Pat Britt, wife of Lt. Governor "Footsie" Britt, to fill in for her as hostess at the mansion. Jeannette says, "Pat was marvelous. She really worked awfully hard. I couldn't have done my work without her."

Jeannette has high praise for chief cook Liza Ashley and often asked Liza what had

Jeannette Rockefeller and William Bowen at the Arkansas Arts Center construction site, January 12, 1970. (Photo by Larry Obsitnik; courtesy of Arkansas Gazette)

The Rockefellers at the Arkansas-Stanford game, September 12, 1970. (Photo by Pat Patterson; courtesy of Arkansas Gazette)

been done before in a given situation. When needed, Ben Mitchell and Billy Sparks came down from the Rockefeller farm to help out at the mansion. Jeannette says she tried to keep her entertaining simple and inexpensive and not set a precedent that would be impossible to follow. It is her opinion that it would be nice for state organizations to have yearly teas at the mansion paid for by the state. She thinks it is part of the governor's job to provide entertainment at the mansion for statewide organizations.

Mrs. Rockefeller has always been dedicated to the idea of women's accepting community responsibility and has certainly been a living example of this concept. In addition to activities already mentioned, she served as a trustee of both Finch College in New York and Philander Smith College here in Little Rock. She was a member of the advisory board of the Hogg Foundation and a member of the Board of Directors for the Joint Commission on Mental Health for Children. She was the recipient of honorary degrees from both Finch and Arkansas College.

If the truth were known, as First Lady she probably accomplished more than any of us. This busy lady has spent her life in service to humanity. Certainly Arkansas is a better place because Jeannette and Winthrop Rockefeller came to live among us for a time.

BETTY FLANAGAN BUMPERS
1971-1975

BETTY BUMPERS SAYS that as wife of the governor she shamelessly used her position to promote causes in which she was interested. As wife of the senator she admits she is still using her position to further her interests.

While First Lady of Arkansas, she devoted her time and energy to areas not previously open to her. The Center for Disease Control came to Mrs. Bumpers to enlist her help in organizing an immunization program for all schoolchildren. Once she was made aware of this need, Betty's answer was, "If the children need to be immunized, then we will immunize them." She committed herself to an active role in accomplishing this goal. She called on many public and private organizations to help her inform the public of the need for an immunization program.

Betty says, "Perhaps Nell (Mrs. Alton) Balkman, who had been head of the Arkansas League for Nursing, is due more credit for the success of the program they called 'Every Child in '73' than anyone else. She was determined and never looked back once the project was begun." The "Every Child" program succeeded in immunizing ninety percent of the schoolchildren in Arkansas.

When Governor Bumpers was elected to the United States Senate, Betty Bumpers immediately tried to get President and Mrs. Gerald Ford interested in a nationwide immunization program. When the Fords showed no interest, Betty called all the governors' wives and urged them to start programs in their own states just as she had done in Arkansas. Many of them embraced the idea, and when the Carters moved to the White House and were receptive to the program, much of the ground work had already been done by the First Ladies. Through the Center for Disease Control, Betty and Secretary of

Health, Education, and Welfare Joe Califano designed a nationwide plan for immunizing all children in America. The plan was almost an exact copy of the Arkansas plan and was proclaimed a complete success.

As First Lady of Arkansas, Betty was also instrumental in bringing the public health nurse program under the State Health Department and generating statewide support for it.

Governor and Mrs. Dale Bumpers, September 11, 1970. (Photo by Larry Obsitnik; courtesy of the Arkansas Gazette)

The First Lady praising Nutritional Poster Award winners. (Photo courtesy of the Arkansas Gazette)

Art has been a lifelong interest of hers. She was very supportive of Mrs. Rockefeller's efforts to spread an appreciation of the arts among the schoolchildren of Arkansas, and made a special effort to continue this program. She worked closely with the State Department of Arts and Humanities, and through grants and legislation the entire program of state services for the arts was continued. This program included the Artmobile, Tell-a-Tale Troupe, Arkansas Ballet, and Children's Theater. As a result many Arkansas children were able to see fine paintings, and through exposure to live actors and dancers they gained a greater appreciation of theater and ballet.

Before moving into the mansion, Betty Bumpers interviewed all the former First Ladies who had lived there to get their views on how best to run this very public house. She says she benefited greatly from this and all the ladies were gracious and helpful. It was suggested to her by this writer that there was a real need for a Mansion Commission to assume the responsibility of this property and to oversee the expenditure of monies used for upkeep and repairs. Other states have spent a fortune allowing each new First Lady to redecorate and refurnish their mansions according to individual taste. We in Arkansas cannot afford this luxury. Betty Bumpers personally assumed the responsi-

Governor Bumpers speaks as the First Lady and son Bill listen, March 4, 1972. (Photo courtesy of the Arkansas Gazette)

bility for the passage of legislation that established this much-needed commission.

All the First Ladies with whom Betty talked emphasized the need to share the house with the people of the state. Acting on their advice, Betty set up tours of the house and grounds and encouraged schoolchildren to visit. Through her efforts scout troops could earn a merit badge by identifying the trees on the grounds. She had a rare variety of oak tree, an Arkansas oak, added to the grounds and a screen of pines planted across the south side where curiosity-seekers would park and train their binoculars on the First Family.

At some time in the past, the state had sold off two lots from what was original mansion property on the east side, and houses had been built on them. Betty thought this a

Betty and Dale Bumpers and their son Brent, January 12, 1971. (Photo by Gene Prescott; courtesy of the Arkansas Gazette)

Betty Bumpers with a beneficiary of her child immunization program, November 13, 1974. (Photo by Gene Prescott; courtesy of the Arkansas Gazette)

Governor and Mrs. Dale Bumpers accepting a flag, with daughter, Brooke, in background, January 3, 1975. (Photo by Larry Obsitnik; courtesy of the Arkansas Gazette)

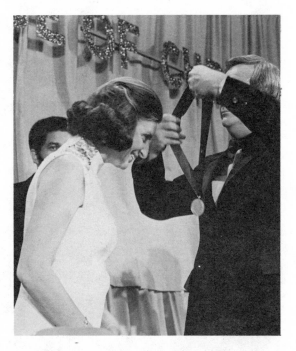

*Betty Bumpers receiving the National Confer-
ence of Christians and Jews annual award, July
25, 1974. (Photo by Pat Patterson; courtesy of the
Arkansas Gazette)*

*Betty Bumpers campaigning, October 29, 1970.
(Photo by Morris White, courtesy of the
Arkansas Gazette)*

rather awkward situation and asked the state
to buy this property back to square off the
grounds. The state agreed, and purchased
the lots. The two houses still stand and have
been put to good use either as housing for
employees or for storage.

Betty Bumpers developed a long-range
plan for adding or replacing furnishings, and
hired a landscape architect to devise a permanent planting plan for the grounds. She
had two fire escapes installed, a cabinet built
to display the state silver, a new chandelier
purchased for the dining room, and a rug

*Betty Bumpers with Miss Lily Peters at the
Arkansas Post Bicentennial celebration. (Photo
courtesy of the Arkansas History Commission)*

Betty Bumpers speaking for Peace Links, the nuclear awareness organization she founded, on October 9, 1982. (Photo by Jeff Mitchell; courtesy of the Arkansas Gazette)

The Bumperses receiving an award, November 6, 1982. (Photo by John D. Simmons; courtesy of the Arkansas Gazette)

made in the design of the State Seal for the foyer. She called on her friend Randall Byars, ASID, to help her with these important purchases. Even though the legislature had appropriated more money than she was spending, Governor Bumpers, who was involved in a campaign, asked her not to authorize payment from the state treasury until after the election. She didn't listen. The governor was on a campaign trip when he heard a news broadcast quoting his opponent saying Governor Bumpers was the most extravagant governor the state had ever had, citing the $15,000 Mrs. Bumpers had spent on furniture. The governor called home and chewed Betty out. She calmly told him that he could be intimidated by that "junk" if he wanted to be, but she thought the people of Arkansas wanted nice things in their mansion, and no one would mind if she spent money for things they could take pride in. She was right. Dale won the election and the three nice pieces are still there—although

the rug has had to be mended and moved to a lower floor where it gets less use.

Betty Bumpers ran the mansion with a skeleton force. Liza Ashley was the chief cook. "She did a fantastic amount of work," Betty says. "In addition to preparing the meals, Liza planned the menus, did all the grocery shopping, and hired the waiters to serve parties. Liza was the best friend I had." Liza had been at the mansion through the Faubus and Cherry terms and was well experienced in serving large parties. Betty relied heavily on Liza's expertise in this area, saying she was not accustomed to having large parties and that probably the biggest party she had ever had before becoming First Lady was when she hosted Dale's fellow choir members from the First Methodist Church following their annual Christmas cantata. In addition to Liza, there was only an upstairs maid, a downstairs maid, and one state trooper for security. The Bumperses chose to hire college students to patrol the grounds

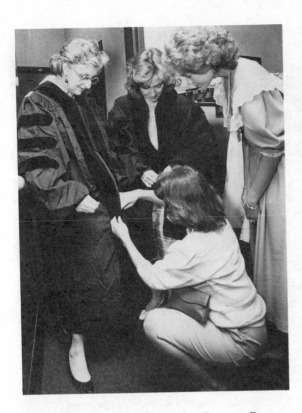

Betty Flanagan Bumpers and Hillary Rodham Clinton don academic robes before receiving honorary doctorates from the University of Arkansas at Little Rock, May 8, 1985. (Photo by Kelly Quinn; courtesy of the Arkansas Gazette)

Betty Bumpers at a reception honoring her as winner of the Wilton Peace Prize, April 7, 1986. (Photo by Kelly Quinn; courtesy of the Arkansas Gazette)

rather than have a number of police around. A part-time employee was a lady who came on a regular basis to arrange flowers. Betty says fresh flowers are a must in that house, and to cut down on this expense she resorted to bouquets of silk flowers combined with fresh greenery for permanent use, using fresh flowers only for special occasions.

When the Bumpers family moved to the mansion, their family friend, Henrietta Coleman, who had virtually lived with them from the time their first son was born, came with them to serve as a nurse-companion to eight-year-old Brooke. "Hennie" lived upstairs in the family quarters, but had difficulty adjusting to the frenetic pace of the mansion and moved back to Charleston after a year and a half. Linda Miesner, a family friend who had just graduated from the Uni-

versity of Central Arkansas, was hired as Mrs. Bumpers's personal secretary. In addition she served as a great companion for Brooke and conducted tours of the mansion.

Brooke thoroughly enjoyed being the "governor's daughter" and living at the mansion. She kept her dollhouse in the recessed space on the stair landing, which made a private and secret place to play. A neighbor who attended Cathedral School with Brooke, Gerry Sharpe, became her best friend and constant companion. A common sight during parties was two pairs of feet dangling over the edge of the stairway from the upstairs floor. The little girls would seat themselves with their feet and legs sticking through the stair railing and listen to and peek at the grown-up parties below. If there was a function on the back lawn, their perch

Community Service Award winners: (l-r) Robert E. Wheeler, Betty Bumpers (Distinguished Citizen Award winner), Bob Gannaway, and Georgia and Frank Hickingbotham, June 30, 1987. (Photo by Steve Keesee; courtesy of the Arkansas Gazette)

was the fire escape.

When Governor and Mrs. Bumpers attended the National Governor's Conference at Sea Island, Georgia, they were presented a golf cart which became Brooke's transportation around the mansion grounds. She and her neighborhood friend spent every afternoon after school "exploring" the seven acres of the grounds.

Son Bill, who was fourteen years old when his father was elected governor, never quite got over the embarrassment of being driven to school by a state trooper. He asked the trooper not to wear a uniform and would quite often ask for permission to get out of the car and walk the last block. Bill graduated from Hendrix in 1978 and earned a master's degree in economics from the University of Tubingen, Germany, and a law

degree from the University of Virginia. He now practices with a law firm in Washington, D.C., and is married to the former Heidi Hughes, also a lawyer. They are expecting their first child in 1989.

Son Brent entered Hendrix the year his father was elected governor and lived apart from the fish-bowl life of the mansion. He and his friends would stop in long enough to pick up a tin of Liza's chocolate chip cookies, but for the most part he studiously avoided mansion life. He graduated from Hendrix and later earned a law degree from the University of Arkansas Law School. He and his wife, the former Lea Ann Farmer, live in Little Rock, where Brent is an attorney with the United States Attorney's office.

Brooke graduated from Walt Whitman High School in Bethesda, Maryland, earned a

B.A. degree from Vassar College, and now works for the California Medical Association in San Francisco as a medical writer.

Betty Bumpers is one of four children born to Herman Edward Flanagan and Ola Dale Callan Flanagan. Betty Flanagan and Dale Bumpers both lived in the small community of Grand Prairie, near Charleston, Arkansas. When Betty was twelve years old the family moved to Fort Smith, returning to Charleston just before Betty's senior year in high school. To quote Betty, during their residence in Fort Smith her father "rose from abject poverty to become a well-to-do cattle trader, hauling Jersey cattle to states in the Midwest, principally Iowa and South Dakota, and then returning home with an equal number of Holsteins, at that time relatively unknown in Arkansas. He literally made money 'going and coming' and used the money to accumulate substantial land holdings around Charleston."

Betty and Dale began dating during their senior year in high school, but went separate ways for college. Dale entered the University of Arkansas; Betty's father moved his family to Ames, Iowa, and entered his three daughters in Iowa State University. When they moved back to Charleston and Betty entered the University of Arkansas, Dale went into the Marine Corps. In 1946 when his tour of duty was over, he came back to the University of Arkansas at the same time that Betty entered the Chicago Academy of Fine Arts. Betty returned to Charleston, taught fifth grade for a while, and went back to the University of Arkansas just as Dale was leaving to study law at Northwestern University in Chicago. Finally, tired of their paths crossing only periodically, they married on September 4, 1949.

After Dale graduated from law school, they returned to Charleston, where Dale ran family businesses and practiced law. Betty kept busy as wife, mother, elementary school-teacher, church worker, garden club member, and as she says, "as a participant in other local activities designed to make Charleston a better place in which to raise children."

When Dale ran for governor, Betty and her sister Maggie were aggressive campaigners, traveling over the state winning votes for Dale. He credits Betty's tireless efforts as a major and maybe a deciding factor in his election.

Dale Bumpers was inaugurated as governor on January 12, 1971. He took the Oath of Office before a joint session of the house and senate in the House Chamber. Betty and the children attended. There was a parade afterward. Betty wore a red dress that matched her car, and a mustard-colored coat. The inaugural address, attended by two thousand people, was given from the Capitol steps at 7:00 p.m. in a heavy fog. For the reception that followed in the Governor's Conference Room, Betty chose a pale blue satin gown with a wide band of crystal passementerie down the front and on the cuffs of the hip-length jacket.

Betty's hobbies of gardening, flower arranging, and sewing are things of the past. She is the founder and president of Peace Links, a grassroots women's organization designed to raise consciousness about the nuclear arms race, which is a full-time job and takes her to various parts of the world. Betty has traveled all over the United States and to China, the Middle East, and the Soviet Union. Some of these trips have been family vacations, some have been as the senator's wife, and some have been as "Betty Bumpers, president of Peace Links." As a result of her work she has received honorary doctorate and peace awards.

Betty Bumpers says she loved being First Lady. She made a career of the position, and because every cause became a crusade, she accomplished a great deal—and still does!

BARBARA JEAN LUNSFORD PRYOR
1975-1979

OUR THIRTY-NINTH FIRST Lady was one of five children and the only daughter of Bruce and Rosa Lee Lunsford, antique dealers in Fayetteville, Arkansas. Barbara lived all of her early life in Fayetteville, attended public schools there, and entered the University of Arkansas in 1956. In her freshman year she met upperclassman David Pryor from Camden, Arkansas. They were married a year later in Fayetteville on November 28, 1957.

They returned to Pryor's hometown of Camden and established a weekly newspaper, the *Ouachita Citizen*. Ten years later they had their family of three sons; Pryor had earned a law degree and was a practicing attorney; he had served three terms in the Arkansas legislature and had just been elected to the United States House of Representatives. During the six years he served in Congress the family commuted between Washington and Camden. In 1972 they moved to Little Rock, and Pryor ran unsuccessfully for the United States Senate. In 1974 he ran for and was elected to the office of governor.

The Pryors broke with the custom of having the inauguration on the steps of the Capitol. Instead, on a cold, clear day in January 1975, their inauguration ceremonies took place in front of the Old State House, the first to be held there in approximately sixty years. The choice of the handsome old building was a natural for David Pryor. He has a passionate interest in historic preservation and restoration of old buildings and houses. He has been influenced in this by his mother, Susie Pryor, who has spent a lifetime restoring and remodeling.

After the inaugural ceremony at the Old State House, there was a luncheon at the Governor's Mansion attended only by the families of David and Barbara. Relatives from all over Arkansas and some from out-of-state came to celebrate this great day.

For the inaugural ceremonies that morning Mrs. Pryor wore a black-and-white houndstooth checked suit. The suit was originally a dress that had been given to her two years before by Mrs. John McAllister of Fayetteville. Mrs. Pryor had the dress made into a suit and on Inauguration Day she wore it with a yellow turtleneck sweater and yellow orchids. For the public reception held in the Governor's Conference Room from five to seven that afternoon, she chose a floor-length gown of printed quiana made with a square neck, long sleeves, and banded waist. This dress was a gift from June and Henry Brown of Benton. The crowd of well-wishers at the reception was served hot mulled cider and gingerbread. Music was provided in turn by the Rackensacks, Jimmy Driftwood, the Philander Smith Choir, and the Pine Bluff Singers. This reception was followed by a large dinner party that filled two private clubs.

After the dinner party there was an inaugural ball at the Little Rock Convention Center. For this occasion Barbara Pryor wore a gown of green chiffon. She says, "My dress—which was the most beautiful I have ever worn, or ever seen, for that matter—was a gift from Roslyn and Merritt Fruhman of Pine Bluff. They had it designed in New York by the House of Richilene. It is now on display with other inaugural gowns at the Old State House." The gown was made of yards and yards of green chiffon with a matching green satin ribbon belt ending in a bow in front. The bodice was shirred to a deep V-neck in front and back. The long sleeves were full and fitted at the wrist.

As is customary, the second-term inauguration was a simple oath-taking and speech

Governor and Mrs. David Pryor address voters, May 30, 1972. (Photo by Larry Obsitnik; courtesy of the Arkansas Gazette)

The Pryors and supporters, May 31, 1972. (Photo by Larry Obsitnik; courtesy of the Arkansas Gazette)

before a joint meeting of the house and senate. Some governors do not have receptions following their second inaugurations. However, the Pryors did receive their friends in the Governor's Conference Room.

Barbara says:

We moved into the mansion a couple of days after the first inauguration. From the very beginning, we loved living in that house and wanted to make it a home as much as possible, while keeping it available to the people of Arkansas at the same time. The upstairs was not quite large enough for all of us, so we converted a study into a bedroom for one of our sons.

David, Jr., was then fifteen years old, Mark was twelve, and Scott was nine. David—we still call him Dee—went on to graduate from Central High and Mark

Barbara Lunsford Pryor, c. 1975. (Photo courtesy of the Arkansas Gazette)

Barbara Lunsford Pryor, February 2, 1975. (Photo courtesy of the Arkansas Gazette)

Barbara Pryor, First Lady-elect, modeling her inaugural ball gown in the yard of the family house on Ridgeway Street. (Photo courtesy of the Pryor family files)

David Pryor entertaining schoolboys. (Photo courtesy of the Arkansas Gazette)

The Pryor family in the living room of the Governor's Mansion: (l-r) Mark, Scott, Barbara, and David, Jr. (Photo by Lela Garlington; courtesy of the Pryor family files)

graduated from Walt Whitman in Bethesda, Maryland, after David was elected to the senate. Scott graduated from Catholic High in Little Rock.

We are very proud of our three sons and the lives they have made for themselves in the years since then. David is now an account executive at Hill and Knowlton public relations firm in Washington; this is one of the largest in the world, and David is finding a real place for himself there. Mark graduated last year from law school in Fayetteville and is an attorney at Wright, Lindsey, and Jennings in Little Rock. He loves living there and he loves the law. Scott lived for nearly a year in Alaska and now lives and works in Fayetteville. He has taken to Northwest Arkansas just like everyone else who has lived there.

Our children are remarkably normal when you consider they have always lived a political life. We're just grateful that they adjusted so well to it. I some-

The Pryors at their inaugural ball, January 15, 1975. (Photo by John Partipilo; courtesy of the Arkansas Gazette)

Barbara Pryor visiting Fort Chaffee, January 1975. (Photo courtesy of the Arkansas Gazette)

Barbara and David Pryor visiting neighbors. (Photo courtesy of the Pryor family files)

times think that Scott was more affected by politics and by life in the mansion then either of the older boys. He seemed more lonely than the others, more vulnerable when David and I were gone so often. But he seems to have adjusted and to have found himself.

Barbara always campaigned actively alongside her husband. In his first campaign they vowed to call at every house in Ouachita County and probably accomplished this goal. Together she and David often wrote their own radio and television spots and drew up their own newspaper ads.

In an interview with Betty Woods, women's editor of the *Arkansas Democrat,* Barbara talked about the strenuous senatorial campaign coming so soon after her major surgery. It was their first loss and very hard to accept. They sold their Washington home, moved back to Arkansas, bought and remodeled a house in Little Rock, and then it was

time to hit the campaign trail again. Only those who have been in a statewide campaign can understand the strain of it. Of this campaign for governor, Barbara said,

Politics and the people involved I love, but I never stopped. Our home was really a campaign headquarters. I was running a hotel. Campaign workers came in, and we asked them to stay the night. I prepared their breakfast. There was seldom a night I didn't have twenty to thirty people for dinner.

I had no household help. I cooked the food, served it, and then cleaned up afterward. During the day I was washing and ironing when I wasn't on the campaign trail.

The arduous campaign for the governor-

The Pryors watching election returns, June 13, 1978. (Photo by Steve Keesee; courtesy of the Arkansas Gazette)

ship, the flurry of planning and work needed to produce an elaborate inaugural, the rigor of dismantling her home and moving into the mansion, topped off by the heavy demands made on a new First Lady, was enough to exhaust anyone. After participating in a ribbon-cutting ceremony in March, Barbara finally had to admit she needed to rest. Her doctor hospitalized her several weeks for complete exhaustion. After leaving the hospital she went to her home on Lake Hamilton in Hot Springs for further recuperation. For a time she directed affairs at the mansion from her Lake Hamilton home, even planning her family's daily meals. She spent the summer with her family. She said, "I slowed down completely. I did nothing of a public nature during this time. I hardly left the grounds. I just enjoyed being with my family again." In the fall she resumed activity but on a limited basis. "I will never become that rushed again," she said.

She assumed the duty of redecorating the mansion and personally supervised every bit of the work, although for some changes she had to have approval by the mansion committee. "The members chose the fabrics for the living room, but they chose those I like."

While First Lady, Barbara Pryor served on the Board of Directors of Goodwill Industries and was one of the original members of the Committee of One Hundred. She also worked on behalf of the Arkansas Repertory Theater, Arkansas Children's Hospital, Little Rock public schools, and Arkansas Arts Center.

In 1976 she went to the University of Arkansas at Little Rock for a semester, taking courses in the arts and sciences department. That summer she became involved in the production of a movie being filmed at Texarkana. After that film was made she became secretary-treasurer for a newly formed company, Fair Winds Productions,

The Pryors celebrating re-election, November 6, 1984. (Photo by John W. Cary; courtesy of the Arkansas Gazette)

Inc., and co-produced her own movie, *Wishbone Cutter,* filmed entirely on the Arkansas River.

In response to a questionnaire for the Old State House file she said, "I have always thought of myself as a person in my own right as well as being the governor's wife, and I'm proud of the accomplishments I have made . . ." Presently she has her own interior decorating business in Washington and maintains an interest in her husband's project of displaying works of Arkansas artists and books published by the University of Arkansas Press in his senate office. She remains interested in the movie business, is a supporter of the American Film Institute, and attends many of the functions they sponsor in Washington. She and David continue their interest in antiques and enjoy visiting junk shops and antique stores together.

While her husband was governor, Barbara had three good secretaries. The first was Sissy McGuire, followed by Marilyn Brown. Marilyn was there most of the four years and became not only a secretary, but a babysitter, cook, confidante, and stand-in for the Pryor family. Peggy Simpson, who had worked in Pryor's Washington office, was there for the last few weeks of the second term.

Barbara credits Liza Ashley with holding things together at the mansion and says Liza was a mother both to her and to her three sons. The Pryors had a close relationship with the state troopers and civilian guards and Barbara says "their influence on our boys was formidable and always favorable."

During Governor Pryor's second term a

gardener was hired, but the first two years prison inmates tended the rose and vegetable gardens. The Pryors solved the problem of fresh flowers for the house and the many parties by growing their own.

Barbara liked to use her own china and silver for small parties, but groups of two or three hundred people were usually entertained less formally for picnics on the back lawn.

Barbara Pryor says, "I found living in the mansion very exciting and very overwhelming. It seemed that no matter how much I did there was always more." She learned that daily physical exercise works wonders in dealing with tensions and demands. She took up swimming and has kept it up through the years.

She says, "My time in the mansion and as the governor's wife was distinctly one of growth every day. It is something I'll always remember with fondness and affection."

Governor and Mrs. Frank White. (Photo courtesy of the Arkansas Gazette)

GAY DANIELS WHITE
1981-1983

WHEN GAY WHITE became First Lady she brought a glowing enthusiasm to the role. She had worked long and hard to help elect her husband and had a positive attitude of acceptance toward her new position. She had already come to terms with the demands that would be made on her and vigorously set about fulfilling her duties. She hired a staff, made out her schedule, and went to work. One of the first things she did was to involve herself with the redecorating of the mansion already underway. She insisted on changing the color of the walls to give the house a warmer, more inviting look. To further soften the rooms she added sofa pillows, candles, and many plants and fresh flowers. She filled the walls with many fine paintings borrowed from the Arkansas Arts Center.

In answer to a questionnaire submitted to her by the Old State House staff, Gay says:

My concerns as First Lady were no different from my concerns as a private citizen. The first priority in my life is to God and to glorify Him. I was privileged to speak to many groups about my personal faith in God and the significance He has in my life. My second most important concern was to my husband and children. I always tried to spend time with them and listen to, love, and encourage them. Having three teenagers in the Governor's Mansion is a challenge! I continued a longtime love for and interest in senior citizens. I visited senior citizens centers, spoke to many of their meetings around the state, and orchestrated their needs and concerns to my husband. I also spoke often about the benefits of and need for vocational/technical education.

Gay White held the usual teas, luncheons,

and dinner parties at the mansion and entertained many visiting dignitaries from the United States and abroad, as well as many Arkansas citizens. She and Frank were the first to host an Appreciation Day for the Retired Senior Volunteer Program and were prepared for the usual percentage of acceptances from the one thousand invitations sent out. Instead their guests arrived by the busload, and Gay and Frank stood in line greeting their guests for several hours! It was later determined that around one thousand people came to the party. This reception at the mansion has become an annual affair.

A very meaningful experience for Gay was the reception for the blind. She led them in a touch tour of the house. Through their fingers they "saw" the cool marble floor of the entrance hall, the furniture in the different rooms, the carving on the grandfather clock, and the patterns on the large silver pieces from the battleship *Arkansas*. They enjoyed the fragrances of the rose and herb gardens before being served Liza's tea and cookies in the formal dining room. Gay says the afternoon of witnessing these people enjoy the world through their senses of touch, taste, hearing, and smell heightened her own awareness and appreciation.

Another afternoon Gay and Frank held a reception for the handicapped. At the end of the party one of the guests was rolled in his wheelchair to the piano and in spite of his palsied hands gave a moving rendition of "America the Beautiful," reducing Gay to tears.

While First Lady, Gay served as honorary chairman of the Mother's March of Dimes. Whether in or out of public office, she worked for her community. She is a member of Fellowship Bible Church, the Republican Women's Club, the Scattered Seed Garden

The Whites eating banana cake to celebrate the governor's forty-eighth birthday, June 4, 1981. (Photo by Gene Prescott; courtesy of the Arkansas Gazette)

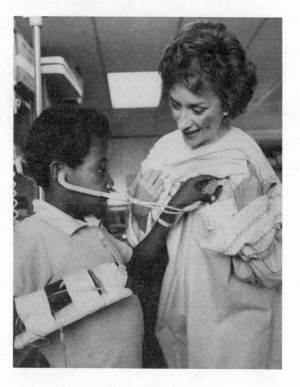

Gay White showing a patient, twelve-year-old Percy Holley, how to use a stethoscope. (Photo courtesy of the Arkansas Gazette)

The Whites at a Veterans' Day ceremony at the Capitol, November 11, 1981. (Photo by Steve Keesee; courtesy of the Arkansas Gazette)

Club, and Kappa Kappa Gamma Alumnae. As a member of the Twentieth Century Club, she lectures at public schools on the hazards of smoking; as a member of the Arkansas Children's Hospital Auxiliary, she was chairman of the major fundraising event in 1980; as a member of Volunteers in Public Schools she teaches English to Vietnamese students, and recently she served on the publicity campaign for the United Negro College Fund.

Gay Daniels was born March 7, 1947, in Oakland, California, one of three children born to Russell Perry Daniels and Nan Lee Henry Daniels. Her father was a career navy man and the family lived in several states as well as Trinidad and the British West Indies. Gay attended both Tulsa University and Marshall University in Huntington, West Virginia, but did not get a degree. She married and she and her husband worked as non-salaried members of the Campus Crusade

Gay White and helpers looking over the vegetable garden behind the Governor's Mansion, May 7, 1981. (Photo by Hank Wilson; courtesy of the Arkansas Gazette)

The Whites at a prayer breakfast, April 21, 1982. (Photo by Gene Prescott; courtesy of the Arkansas Gazette)

A reception for participants in Olympics of the Mind, August 24, 1982. (Photo by John D. Simmons; courtesy of the Arkansas Gazette)

Arkansas Day at the World's Fair in Knoxville, July 16, 1982: (l-r) Fair President S.H. Roberts, Jr., fiddler Kari Woods, Miss Arkansas Mary Stewart, and Governor and Mrs. White. (Photo courtesy of the Arkansas Gazette)

for Christ, traveling several states. By the time she was twenty-two, they were divorced. A few years later she moved to Little Rock and obtained a job as secretary to the director of the State Finance and Administration Department, a position she held from 1971 to 1977. It was there in August 1974 that she met Frank White. Of the meeting Gay says: "Frank, then vice-president of Commercial National Bank, made a business call on my boss, Richard Heath. Being a good secretary, I ushered Frank into Mr. Heath's office and fixed him a cup of coffee, and thirty minutes after the meeting was over, he called to ask me out! (Must have been the coffee.)" A courtship followed and they were married on March 22, 1975, in the First United Methodist Church of Little Rock. Gay continued to work for a while after their marriage, but resigned to be a full-time mother when Frank received custody of his three children by a former marriage. The children were thirteen-year-old Elizabeth, eleven-year-old Rebecca, and seven-year-old Kyle.

Frank White took office as governor on January 14, 1981. Inaugural Day festivities began with a prayer breakfast held at the Convention Center. Six hundred fifty persons attended.

Governor White and the other constitutional officers were given the Oath of Office in the House Chamber. The oath was administered by Chief Justice Richard B. Adkisson. An hour later the oath was administered a second time for the benefit of a large crowd that had gathered to hear the inaugural address. After the address state troopers formed a V at the top of the Capitol steps as

L-R: Gay White, Orval Faubus, Liza Ashley, and Frank White celebrating Mrs. Ashley's 65th birthday at the Governor's Mansion, October 11, 1982. (Photo courtesy of the Arkansas History Commission)

Governor White received a nineteen-gun salute fired by a Field Artillery Battalion of the Arkansas National Guard. The Little Rock Air Force Base saluted him with a fly-by of three C-130's (Governor White was formerly a C-130 pilot). After these ceremonies Governor and Mrs. White, along with the other constitutional officers and their wives, formed a receiving line and greeted their 1,500 well-wishers.

Governor and Mrs. White's three children attended all the day's functions. That evening there was an inaugural ball at the convention center. It was necessary to divide it into two parties—one in the Camelot Hotel and one in Robinson Auditorium. Mrs. White had a beautiful white gown designed for the occasion. The gown was a sheath with a diamond-shaped area of beading in the midriff, symbolic of Arkansas the Diamond State,

The Whites campaigning, November 2, 1982. (Photo by John D. Simmons; courtesy of the Arkansas Gazette)

Gay White rousing students' interest in the Reading for Fun program, November 14, 1983. (Photo by Steve Keesee; courtesy of the Arkansas Gazette)

and more beading on the shoulder. After she put the gown on it was discovered the shoulder beading had pulled loose. There wasn't time to take off the dress and make repairs. The problem was solved by the new governor, who had never before used a needle and thread, but nevertheless managed to attach the beading while en route to the ball!

The security for this inauguration was tighter than ever before. Two weeks before, an Oklahoma businessman had somehow been hooked into a telephone conversation between two men about killing the Arkansas governor. Since it was not known whether they meant Clinton or White, security was stepped up around both men. The day of the inauguration there were seventy-five state troopers at the Capitol—thirty-six inside, and

teams of three sharpshooters armed with rifles on the Capitol roof and atop a nearby office building. In addition there were numerous Little Rock police officers on inaugural duty. No untoward incidents occurred.

Of the children's reaction to life in the mansion, Gay says:

Our children at the time were nineteen, seventeen, and thirteen. They adjusted to life in the mansion as well as could be expected for three teenagers! Obviously, there were adjustments. Probably the most difficult thing they had to deal with was being singled out of other groups of teens as the "governor's son/daughter." This obviously put undue stress in their lives, but they handled it and grew and

The Clintons and the Whites at the Governor's Mansion Association ball, December 1, 1985. (Photo by Kelly Quinn; courtesy of the Arkansas Gazette)

learned from the experience. They also enjoyed the special privileges that came with living in the mansion—such as Liza Ashley's cooking(!), a lovely graduation party that we hosted for Rebecca when she graduated from Hall High School, and eleven wonderful, caring state police security guards to "pal" around with when Mother and Dad were gone. The security detail and the mansion staff were all so warm and thoughtful and caring. They seemed just like an extended family on the occasions when we were away.

Elizabeth graduated from Wheaton College in Illinois and at this writing is an administrative assistant for Heifer Project International. Rebecca, a graduate of the University

The Whites relaxing at home, November 3, 1986. (Photo by Pat Patterson; courtesy of the Arkansas Gazette)

The Whites at the end of the campaign, November 4, 1986. (Photo by Steve Keesee; courtesy of the Arkansas Gazette)

Barbara Bush wiping something from the eye of Gay White as Virginia Hammerschmidt looks on, July 22, 1987. (Photo by Jeff Bowen; courtesy of the Arkansas Gazette)

of Arkansas, is employed in communication sales, and Kyle is a midshipman at the United States Naval Academy.

Gay and Frank White share many interests other than politics and their devotion to the church. They both love gardening and in fact had a small vegetable plot on the mansion grounds. They are faithful to a physical fitness program and run or walk at least twenty miles each week. An amusing incident happened to First Lady Gay White during an early morning run through MacArthur Park. The plainclothes officer following her in an unmarked car thought he was being discreet, but a passing motorist spied him, came to a screeching halt beside Gay, and excitedly said, "Lady, lady, there's some guy following you, but don't worry, I've cut him off and I'll call the police if you want to hop in my car!"

Gay and Frank both have a great sense of humor and a wonderful ability to laugh at themselves. An amusing incident happened to Gay the first week they were in the mansion. In response to her cat's demands at 3:00 a.m., Gay sleepily followed the cat down the winding staircase in the dark. She opened the front door, let the cat out, closed the door, and was scared out of her wits when suddenly all the lights came on! By opening the door she had set off an alarm and the security man on duty had rushed in, only to find that the "intruder" was a greatly embarrassed First Lady in her nightgown.

Hillary Rodham Clinton. (Photo courtesy of the Arkansas Gazette)

HILLARY RODHAM CLINTON
1979-1981, 1983-1991

OUR PRESENT FIRST Lady is typical of her time. Like many young women of today she has a full-time job outside the home, even though home is the Governor's Mansion. Several First Ladies have made a career of volunteer work, but Hillary Clinton is a practicing attorney associated with the Rose Law Firm in Little Rock.

Since her career demands most of her daytime hours, she has totally institutionalized the running of the mansion. She has a mansion administrator who runs the house, keeps the books, interviews people who wish to use the mansion, and is hostess when Hillary cannot be on hand. At the time of this writing, Anne McCoy is the attractive and efficient person who fills this job. Hillary is on hand at the mansion during the day by appointment and on special occasions. She attends some civic meetings during the day, and often her evenings are spent attending meetings or banquets of an official nature.

Liza Ashley is still chief cook at the mansion, and there are an upstairs maid and a laundress who pinch-hit in the kitchen when needed—as does everyone on the staff when there is a large function in the works. Two trusties take care of the cleaning and serving. The seven acres of lawn is cared for by a permanent crew supervised by a regular gardener.

Mrs. Clinton hires a companion for her daughter, Chelsea. By carefully planning her time, this busy woman handles her career and her roles as wife, mother, and First Lady.

Hillary is the daughter of Dorothy Emma Howell and Hugh Ellworth Rodham. She was born in Chicago, Illinois, on October 26, 1947. In 1969 she graduated with honors from Wellesley College in Massachusetts, and in 1973 she graduated from Yale Law School. At Yale she was a director of the Bar-

rister's Union and a member of the board of editors of the *Yale Law Journal.* It was at Yale that she first became aware of Bill Clinton. Walking through the student lounge of the law school one day, she heard a voice say, ". . . and not only that, we grow the largest watermelons in the world." She asked her companion, "Who is that?" and was told, "That's Bill Clinton, and all he ever does is talk about Arkansas."

One of her main interests is children's programs, and after graduation Hillary worked as an attorney for the Children's Defense Fund in Cambridge, Massachusetts, and as a legal consultant for the Carnegie Council on Children in New Haven, Connecticut.

Following this she was employed in Washington, D.C., on the House Judiciary Committee's Special Staff during the inquiry of the possible impeachment of former President Nixon. This job ended in August 1974 when Nixon resigned.

She then accepted a position as assistant professor at the University of Arkansas Law School, where in addition to teaching she opened a private law practice in Fayetteville. She organized the state's first legal aid clinic which trained law students in indigent legal work, and joined in creating Northwest Arkansas Legal Services, a legal aid bureau serving six counties.

Bill Clinton, her classmate from Yale, was also a law school professor at the University of Arkansas. Hillary and Bill were married October 11, 1975, at his home in Fayetteville. Hillary's two brothers, Hugh and Tony Rodham, who were students at the university, were among the guests.

In 1977 when Clinton became attorney general, they moved to Little Rock, and Hillary secured a position with the prestigious

Hillary Rodham Clinton in her first inaugural ball gown, worn January 9, 1979. (Photo by Gene Prescott; courtesy of the Arkansas Gazette)

Rose Law Firm. She is now a partner in this firm.

In 1978 Bill Clinton was elected governor of the State of Arkansas and took office on January 9, 1979. At the age of thirty-two, he was the youngest governor in the United States and the second youngest in the history of this state. (John Seldon Roane was thirty-two in January prior to becoming governor in a special election on March 14, 1849). The inaugural festivities lasted three days, beginning on Sunday with a dedication service at Immanuel Baptist Church, followed by a reception at the Territorial Restoration. Monday night there was a "Diamonds and Denim" gala at Robinson Auditorium featuring all Arkansas talent.

The Oath of Office was given Tuesday morning by Chief Justice Carlton Harris. Bill Clinton was sworn in before a packed house, but only 250 people chose to leave the warm Capitol on the bitterly cold day to hear his outdoor inaugural address. Two former governors, two United States representatives, the state General Assembly, President Carter's son Chip, and the families of both Hillary and Bill Clinton were among those in the crowded House Chamber. Hillary held the Bible on which the governor-elect placed his left hand, and his mother, Virginia Dwire, and half-brother, Roger Clinton, stood beside him.

That afternoon there was a concert by the Arkansas Symphony Orchestra in the Capitol rotunda. Then there was a reception in the Governor's Conference Room at the Capitol, and that night an inaugural ball followed at Rick's Armory. Hillary commissioned Connie Fails, a Little Rock designer, to create a gown for this special occasion. The gown was made of dusty rose panné velvet, with a fitted bodice, tiered skirt, and set-in sash. It was trimmed in antique black lace, jet beads, rose and jet sequins, and silk embroidery. All the trim were antiques and were taken from gowns of the 1870s that had belonged to Mary B. Schrader's family and were donated for use on this special dress.

As First Lady Hillary was active in a number of volunteer efforts with special interest in public education, health care, children's needs, and the arts. She served on the Board of Directors of the Children's Defense Fund and as president of Arkansas Advocates for Children and Families.

She had quite a successful career as Hillary Rodham, attorney, and continued to use this name after marriage—a common practice with career women. However, it didn't go over too well with the electorate of Arkansas. President Carter didn't seem to mind, for he appointed Hillary Rodham to the Board of Directors of the Legal Services Corporation in Washington, D.C., and she was elected chairman of that board in 1979. She was also a member of the Concilium on International and Area Studies at Yale and on the board of Winrock International Livestock Research and Training Center.

Bill Clinton was not successful in his bid for a second term, losing to Republican Frank White. He ran again in 1982 and was reelected. On January 11, 1983, after a prayer breakfast at Immanuel Baptist Church, Clinton was inaugurated in a traditional ceremony in the House Chamber. The oath was administered by Chief Justice Richard B. Adkisson. Governor Clinton gave his inaugural address from the Capitol steps. Music was provided by the Arkansas National Guard Band and choirs from the University of Arkansas and Philander Smith College. Governor and Mrs. Clinton hosted a reception that afternoon in the Governor's Reception Room. The Arkansas Symphony String quartet played during the reception, and Jimmy Driftwood and other groups performed at different times throughout the Capitol.

The inaugural ball took place in the Excelsior Ball Room and the Statehouse Convention Center ballroom adjoining the Excelsior Hotel. Betty Fowler's orchestra performed in the Statehouse Center and Art Porter in the Excelsior Ball Room. It was estimated the crowd at this black tie affair numbered around six thousand. Following the ball the

Oklahoma Governor George Nigh and his wife, Donna, joining the Clintons at an outdoor reception, September 27, 1984. (Photo by Art Meripol; courtesy of the Arkansas Gazette)

Democratic party hosted a champagne breakfast in the Great Hall of the Camelot Hotel.

For the ball Hillary chose an elegant gown designed by Rina di Montell, of jeweled taupe silk chantilly lace over champagne silk charmeuse. She was privileged to wear the 4.25-carat canary yellow Kahn diamond, a rare gem mined from the Arkansas Crater of Diamonds State Park. The stone is valued at $20,000 and was loaned to Mrs. Clinton by the Mid-America Museum. It was made into a ring in a contemporary setting for this occasion. When Hillary wore it for the inauguration in 1979 it was set as a Victorian necklace to complement her antique-style gown.

Governor Clinton's third inaugural ball was

The First Lady showing a report on progress made in lowering infant mortality, March 13, 1985. (Photo by Art Meripol; courtesy of the Arkansas Gazette)

The governor opening headquarters for the 1986 campaign, March 22, 1986. (Photo by Art Meripol; courtesy of the Arkansas Gazette)

One of the varied duties of the governor's wife—making the opening pitch at a TCS Orthopedic Clinic softball game, May 19, 1986. (Photo by Kelly Quinn; courtesy of the Arkansas Gazette)

The Clintons and Donald Duck, 1984. (Photo by Walt Disney Productions, courtesy of the Arkansas Gazette)

held on January 14, 1985, at the Statehouse Convention Center. About two thousand people came to dine, dance, and celebrate. The Clintons entered the ballroom around 10:05 and walked the length of the hall on a red carpet to the platform which held a blue lighted ice sculpture of the Capitol. For this occasion Hillary chose a three-piece gold lamé ankle length ensemble that shimmered in the spotlights. Whispers of "gorgeous," "beautiful," and "stunning" came from over the audience. After a few brief remarks, the Clintons walked to the dance floor and opened the dancing to Jim Johnson's band from Memphis. The Jazz Ensemble from the University of Arkansas at Pine Bluff and the

Jimmy Church Revue had entertained earlier.

Hillary's parents, Mr. and Mrs. Hugh Rodham, the governor's mother and her husband, Dick Kelley, daughter Chelsea, and brother Roger Clinton attended the inauguration in the House Chamber. There had been a dedication service earlier at Immanuel Baptist Church. A reception for the public was held in the Governor's Reception Room that afternoon.

Governor Clinton was inaugurated on January 13, 1987, for his fourth term as governor and the first four-year term for an Arkansas governor since Reconstruction days.

For the daytime activities Hillary Clinton chose a smart robin's egg-blue cashmere suit, and for the ball she wore a turquoise blue cracked-ice-on-jersey gown designed and

At a "roast" for Hillary Rodham Clinton—Mary Steenburgen, Mary Ann Campbell, and Father George Tribou burning the First Lady's ears, May 5, 1987. (Photo by Art Meripol; courtesy of the Arkansas Gazette)

made for her by Martha Dixon of Arkadelphia. She shared the spotlight with six-year-old Chelsea, who was allowed to stay up late and attend the ball. Chelsea wore a long gown of blue taffeta made especially for her by Pat Qualls of the Public Service Commission. The daytime festivities followed the usual pattern of a dedication service at Immanuel Baptist Church, the midmorning swearing-in ceremony in the House Chamber, the noontime inaugural address on the Capitol steps, and an afternoon reception in the Governor's Reception Room. The ball was held at the Statehouse Convention Center, which was decorated with green, gold, and white balloons and twinkle lights in live trees. Music was provided by the Little Rock Jazz Machine.

Hillary Clinton has taken an active part in her husband's campaigns, making speeches on his behalf and attending political rallies. He named her head of a 44-member state Rural Health Advisory Committee and honorary chairman for the International Year of

Hillary Rodham Clinton in the cashmere suit she wore to the daytime inaugural events on January 13, 1987. (Photo by Art Meripol; courtesy of the Arkansas Gazette)

the Child activities in Arkansas, which had children's health as its main focus. Probably her appointment by him as chairman of the Educational Standards Committee has been her most influential role.

Each year the Clintons hold a reception at the mansion honoring all the high school valedictorians and salutatorians and their parents. In September 1986 there was a

The First Family at the inaugural ball, January 13, 1987. (Photo by Art Meripol; courtesy of the Arkansas Gazette)

Hillary Rodham Clinton speaking while the governor listens, July 15, 1987. (Photo by Jeff Mitchell; courtesy of the Arkansas Gazette)

The First Lady with Donna McLarty at a press conference, October 12, 1988. (Photo by W.L. [Pat] Patterson; courtesy of the Arkansas Gazette)

reception for the Older American Volunteer Program attended by two thousand people. They were served the largest cake in Arkansas, baked at Rogers, Arkansas. The Clintons have made the mansion available to the public for receptions and entertainment more often than any other governor.

In addition to her many other accomplishments Hillary has organized a Governor's Mansion Association for the purpose of raising funds to preserve and enhance the mansion and grounds. This was a much-needed action, as the mansion has never been completely furnished and the constant and

heavy use of the house makes repairs imperative.

This attractive and talented young woman is a tremendous asset to her husband and to this state. As the current resident of the Governor's Mansion, she lives on the former site of the home of Matilda Fulton, wife of the last territorial governor of Arkansas. These two women are as different as the times in which they have lived. As with their sister First Ladies, their lives reflect transitions in the activities of women in our society and in the contributions they make to the welfare of the state.

Index

Bruce McMath and Chelsea Clinton, the only babies born during a First Family's tenure in the Governor's Mansion since Ernestine Flora Rector was born in 1861. (Photo by Robert Dunn)

Pike, Albert, 43, 47
Pioneers and Makers of Arkansas, 50
Pittman, Charles, 156
Plunkett, Mrs. Vernon, 172
Polk, James, 95
Pope, Ann Christian, 32, 160
Pope, Elizabeth, 32
Pope, Florida, 32
Pope, Frances Watkins Walton, 31–33
Pope, John, 29, 30, 31, 32, 33, 57, 160
Pope, W.F., 36
Porter, Art, 251
Powell, Dick, *184*
Pryor, Barbara Jean Lunsford, 201,
    229–37, *230, 231, 232, 233, 234, 235, 236*
Pryor, David Hampton, 229, 230, *230, 232,*
    233, 233, 234, 234, 235, 236, 236
Pryor, David, Jr., 230, 233, *233*
Pryor, Mark, 230, 233, *233*
Pryor, Scott, 230, *233,* 234
Pryor, Susie, 229

Quaille, Catherine, 98
Quaille, Frederick, 98, 99
Quaille, George, 98
Qualls, Pat, 254
Questenberg, Henrich, 98
Quexon, Manuel, 131
Quisenberry, Frances, 98
Quisenberry, Thomas, 98

Reagan, Nancy, 14
Rector, Elias, 57
Rector, Elias, Jr., 57
Rector, Ernestine Flora, 15, 59, 60, 191
Rector, Ernestine Flora Linde, 57–60, 153,
    201
Rector, E.W., 60
Rector, Fannie Thurston, 57
Rector, Frances, 57
Rector, Frank, 57
Rector, Henry, 57
Rector, Henry Massie, 15, 16, 57, 58, 59, 60
Rector, John Jacob, 15
Rector, Julia, 57
Rector, William, 15, 16, 41, 57
Rector, William F., 59
Remmell, Pratt, *203*
Rice, Mary, 143
Roane, John Seldon, 50, 53, 250
Roane, Samuel Calhoun, 42
Roark, Granville Wade, 141
Roark, Sarah Norvell, 141
Roberts, S.H., Jr., *242*
Robinson, Ewilda Gertrude Miller, *130,*
    131–32, *132, 192*
Robinson, James Madison, 132
Robinson, Joseph Taylor, *130,* 131–32, 133,
    155, 163
Robinson, Matilda Jane Swaim, 132

Rockefeller, Barbara Sears, 211
Rockefeller, David, 215
Rockefeller, Happy, *212*
Rockefeller, Jeannette Edris, 201, *210,*
    211–18, *212, 213, 214, 215, 216, 217, 218,*
    220
Rockefeller, Nelson, *212*
Rockefeller, Winthrop, 206, 211, *212,* 213,
    213, 214, *214,* 215, 216, *216,* 217, 218, *218*
Rockefeller, Winthrop Paul, 211
Rodham, Hugh Ellworth, 249, 253
Rodham, Hugh (First Lady's brother),
    249
Rodham, Tony, 249
Rogers, Roy, *188*
Rogers, Will, 155
Roosevelt, Edith, 14
Roosevelt, Eleanor, 13, 165, *203*
Roosevelt, Franklin D., 132, 145
Roosevelt, Theodore, 14
Ross, Prudence Winfrey, 133

Sadat, Mrs. Anwar, 209
Sanders, Simon, 80
Sanders, Zenobia, 80
Savin, Elizabeth, 35
Savin, William, 35
School Improvement Association, 113
Schrader, Mary B., 250
Scott, Andrew, 25
Second Baptist Church, 120, 135, 145
Second Presbyterian Church, 89
Sevier, Ambrose H., 33, 36, 91, 95
Sevier, James S., 45
Sevier, John, 15, 95
Sevier, Martha Conway, 45
Sevier, Valentine, 45
Shinn, Josiah, 50, 66, 76
Shippen, Thomas Lee, 28
Shippen, William, 28
Simms, Zenobia, 80
Simpson, Ellen House, 115
Simpson, Peggy, 236
Sims, Clifford Stanly, 65
Smith, Al, 132
Smith, Blanche A. Perkins, 171
Smith, Catherine Owen, 163
Smith, Griffin, 168, 178, 198
Smith, William Edward, 171
Smith, William Richard, 163
Snyder, John W., 177
Southern Baptist Convention, 107
Sparks, Billy, 218
Spencer, Dorris, 192
Stanley, Blossom, 103
Stanley, J.H., 103
Statue of Washington from Life, 113
Steenburgen, Mary, 254
Stewart, Mary, *242*
Stratford Hall, 27, 28
Sullivan, Ed, *199*